SOCIAL DIFFERENCES in CONTEMPORARY AMERICA

SOCIAL DIFFERENCES in CONTEMPORARY AMERICA

James A. Davis
Harvard University

Under the general editorship of
Robert K. Merton
Columbia University

HARCOURT BRACE JOVANOVICH, PUBLISHERS

San Diego New York Chicago Austin Washington, D.C.
London Sydney Tokyo Toronto

Cover photo: Copyright © Harry Callahan, courtesy Pace/MacGill Gallery

Copyright © 1987 by Harcourt Brace Jovanovich, Inc.

All rights reserved. No part of this publication may be reproduced or transmitted in any form or by any means, electronic or mechanical, including photocopy, recording, or any information storage and retrieval system, without permission in writing from the publisher.

Requests for permission to make copies of any part of the work should be mailed to: Permissions, Harcourt Brace Jovanovich, Publishers, Orlando, Florida 32887.

ISBN: 0-15-581425-7

Library of Congress Catalog Card Number: 87-80630

Printed in the United States of America

Contents

Preface   ix

1   Introduction   1

     About *Social Differences*   2

     About Computers and Statistics   2

     Quantitative Sociology   4

     The Data   5

     The Sociological Framework   9

Part I   Social Structure   17

2   Ethnicity   19

     The Tribal Mosaic   20

     How Ethnic Variables Are Related   26

     Some Ethnic Differences   37

     Summary   39

3   Socioeconomic Status   41

     The Vertical Variables   42

     Gender, SES, and Poverty   68

     Summary   74

4   Culture, Class, and Behavior   75

     The Research Problem   76

     Ethnicity and SES   77

     Ethnicity, SES, and Fertility Norms   78

     Summary   87

Part II Social Process 89

5 The Big Change 91

On and Off the Farm 92

Growing Up in 1900 and 1950 94

Cohorts and Status Inflation 96

A Note on Income Trends 98

Summary 100

6 Intergenerational Mobilities 101

Mobility 102

Vertical Mobility (and Status Inheritance) 118

The Mobility System 130

Summary 131

7 Trends in Inequality 133

Introduction 134

Ethnicity and SES 135

Trends 136

Summary 140

8 Cohorts and Short-term Social Change: The Stouffer Hypothesis 143

Counting Your Change 144

How Race Gaps Change 156

The Stouffer Hypothesis 157

Summary 161

9 The Changing American Family 163

Some Background 164

Marital Status 165

Fertility 173

Women's Employment 175

CONTENTS

    Summary   178

Appendix A   Suggested Readings   181

Appendix B   The CHIPLIB Data Set Library   187

    CHIPLIB Data Sets   187

    GSS Mnemonics, Set Numbers, and Clusters   200

Appendix C   Other Data Sets   203

    Labels, Variables, and Categories   203

Appendix D   What Whatif Actually Does   223

    A Three-Variable Example   224

    Larger Systems   232

    Summary   233

Index   235

Preface

TO THE INSTRUCTOR

My professional life for the last two decades has centered on what might be called "Price's Paradox":

> The feature of contemporary sociology that is perhaps its greatest strength—its relatively solid factual base—is underrepresented in introductory sociology textbooks and anthologies, whereas the features of relative weakness—its concepts, propositions, and theory—are overrepresented.[1]

I came to sociology from journalism with the aim of mastering sociological theory. Instead, I was exposed to empirical "survey" research and it "took." To me the excitement of discovery combined with the discipline of method make sociological research an extraordinarily rewarding craft. And yet, as Price observed almost twenty years ago, very little of this excitement, much less the empirical knowledge, comes across in our undergraduate courses.

There have been some changes since 1969, especially in terms of technical developments—the explosive growth in good sociological data and the information revolution brought about by affordable personal computers. But not all the developments have been positive. Our profession seems to be bifurcating into two mandarinates—theoreticians who juggle cloudy, politicized concepts and methodologists who juggle abstruse mathematical formulas. Although the two camps believe they are enemies, they share a disdain for empirical knowledge and a total lack of curiosity about people—the academic parvenu's fear that if you say something definite, somebody might show you are wrong.[2] Meanwhile, on the teaching side, the battle for enrollment survival has led us to the craven belief that nothing "hard" can be included in a college sociology course

---

[1] James L. Price, *Social Facts*, New York: Macmillan, 1969, p. iii.

[2] Howard S. Becker, *Writing for Social Scientists*, Chicago: University of Chicago Press, 1968, pp. 1–10.

(for which, of course, we earn the routine contempt of our students).

I used to think the "cure" lay in reforming the standard methods course, shifting it from pious sermons about scientific method to hands-on data analysis. And some progress has been made here, thanks to computers, statistical packages, and data banks. But there has been little cross-fertilization to other courses—if only because we haven't had the courage to demand methods prerequisites for those courses.

Now, I think the time has come for a brand new attack, a combination of substance and method that blends the classical introductory and methods courses. And that, naturally, is what this book is all about. It is not a methods text with computerized examples, and it is not a standard "intro" text with a few tables thrown in. It is quantitative sociological substance, written for the beginner and drawing on the computer to give students the feel for conducting actual research.

Of course new approaches make new demands on instructors and on students—I do not wish to mislead you on that. Teaching with this text will require a great deal of work from you, and the first time you use it you should be prepared to spend as much or more time doing the laboratory assignments as do your students. In addition, the materials are not really suitable for multiple choice or true-false tests. You will probably have to read scores of essays to measure learning. But let me give you some good news. First, you yourself will find the materials interesting. The lab assignments are not Mickey Mouse, stripped-down exercises but actual data sets of the sort that produce journal articles. Second, you need not shy away from the materials because you are not a statistical whiz. The materials are self-contained, formal methodology is minimized, and the key skill required is "thinking like a sociologist." Third, the materials seem to generate much more lively class discussions than the standard "concept chopping" does. After a while you will find that you and your students are actually talking to each other in the same language—"the language of social research." Finally, a detailed instructor's manual is available from me in care of the Department of Sociology, Harvard University, Cambridge, MA 02138.

The Computer Program

"CHIPendale," the computer program to accompany this text, is an integral part of the course, not a supplement. It would be impossible to use the book and not the data sets. The program and data diskettes are available from TrueBASIC, Inc., 39 South Main Street, Hanover, NH 03755.

TrueBASIC can provide you with prices for diskettes and site licenses (highly recommended), as well as information on other curricular materials using the program. It will also send you a low-cost demonstration disk. I won't quote prices because they change. In general you will find them ridiculously low compared with commercial statistical packages but high if you compare them with the cost of a single supplementary textbook. Hence, I urge you to persuade your department to get a site license—for which you pay a one-time fee allowing you to copy as many diskettes as your students need.

TO THE STUDENT

I don't really have to persuade you to buy this book. The odds are that it has been assigned in a sociology class and you have no choice in the matter. Furthermore, Chapter One gives (in my opinion) an excellent introduction to the intellectual themes that make this text worthwhile. So let me take this space to give you some tips on how to get the most out of the book.

First, you have to do the computer assignments. They are not supplements or illustrations. They *are* the material. The main text asks questions, defines terms, explains data sets, and poses problems; but it (deliberately) contains little or no sociological information. You have to dig that out of the data sets.

Second, do not think of this as a workbook. *Social Differences* is about ideas, not about numbers. The object of each exercise is to help you grasp a sociological concept, not to find a specific number and write it down. The prose is Socratic. Its aim is to prod your thinking, and you will find many of the problems and questions ambiguous. That is also deliberate. Although each laboratory assignment has a specific goal, sometimes that goal is to give you practice in formulating research questions.

Third, don't work up a sweat over the math. There are only two or three equations in the entire book, and you don't have to "do anything" with them. While the materials are not easy and require thought and practice, they do not require any math or statistical preparation.

Fourth, hang in there. The main obstacle to success in the course will be your lack of practice in handling statistical tables. The text will give you that practice, but it can't be done in one lab session. Work all the assignments. Spend some extra time just playing around with the program. Go ahead and do the Tasks even if you aren't absolutely clear on the "theory." Most students experience a "breakthrough" in understanding after a few weeks even if their start was a bit shaky.

Finally, unless your teacher instructs you otherwise, work together on the lab assignments. Since our overall goal is mastery of ideas, not production of printout, you won't be cheating if you put your heads together to attack a problem. This is especially true when you are first getting used to the computer.

ACKNOWLEDGMENTS

A number of institutions gave me money for this project, and a number of people gave me feedback and encouragement. I needed both.

Dartmouth College, Harvard University, the National Opinion Research Center (NORC), and the Sloan Foundation funded various aspects of the project. And, although the National Science Foundation does not support curriculum development in the social sciences, it does grant funding for the General Social Survey, without which this project would have been impossible. Although no GSS funds were applied to this book, *Social Differences* stands as a fairly complete summary of what I have learned from the GSS in the last fifteen years.

I am also indebted to Beverly Douhan, Alice Mellian, and Suzanne Washington for their assistance in turning a first draft into a crisp manuscript.

In many ways this has been a lonely project for me, since few sociological researchers are interested in teaching and few sociology teachers are committed to empirical research. Consequently, personal support has meant a lot—for which I thank Ruth Bogart, Marcus Boggs, Karen Frederick, John Kemeny, Kent McClelland, Ed Meyers, Carol Mueller, Robert Muellner, Nick Mullins and his Sociology 1000 class, the students in my Sociology 115 classes at Harvard (especially Raul Cadena, Tack Chase, David Lee, and

Elizabeth Wirick), and all the fellows (male and female) from the Sloan Foundation Summer Workshops at which we put this thing together, took it apart, and put it together again.

James A. Davis

1
Introduction

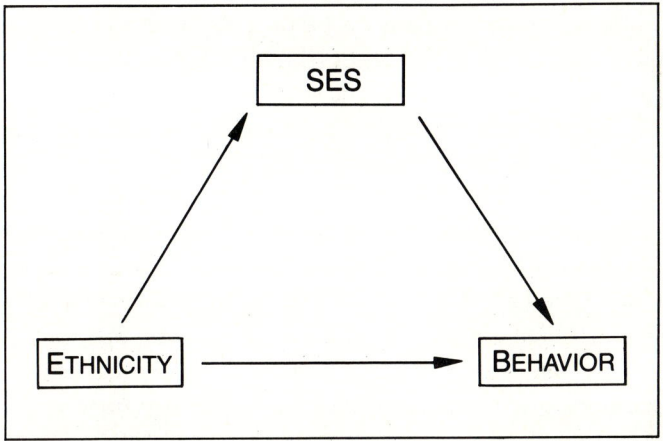

CHAPTER 1 INTRODUCTION

ABOUT *SOCIAL DIFFERENCES*

This is a data based, inquiry style, introductory book about the macro-sociology of the United States of America during the 1970s and early 1980s.

Macro-sociology means that we are concerned with national-level social structures (ethnic groups, social classes, religious denominations, regions, and major political parties, for example), not with individual people, small groups, business corporations, legislatures, TV networks, and so on.

Introductory means my aim is to teach you basic sociological knowledge, not the hottest new research hypotheses.

Data based simply means based on data. Every conclusion will be supportable by objective scientific data—not just opinions. My goal is to teach you what scientific sociological research has learned about American society, not to pass on the wisdom of the great (dead) theorists of the nineteenth century or the dozens of fuzzy "concepts" that make introductory sociology courses numbing.

Inquiry style means learning by investigation rather than memorization. Along with this book, you purchased, or were given, two micro computer "diskettes." They don't look very impressive and are really just glorified phonograph records, but they contain more than three hundred data sets with statistical information about contemporary America and a computer program you will use to analyze that data.

None of the important findings and conclusions are spelled out in the text of the book. Instead, the written text sets up research questions you will answer for yourself by analyzing the data. You will actually be "doing sociology" much the way the professional sociologist does it—by research rather than rote learning or free association. I have taught sociology this way for a decade now, and the vast majority of my students say they enjoy this way of doing business.

ABOUT COMPUTERS AND STATISTICS

The materials here are designed for personal computers. The program was designed by John G. Kemeny and written by Ruth Bogart and Chip Conner at TrueBASIC, Inc., Hanover, New

Hampshire for an IBM PC with a "256K memory." It has also been adapted for the Apple Macintosh. The program should work on many other brands or models "compatible" with these two market leaders.

You do not need to know anything about computers or computer programs, provided you can turn your machine on, insert a diskette, and type "CHIP2." (Its name is CHIPendale, "a program to hand craft tables"—which may well be the last element of levity in this book.) This book will tell you everything you need to know to run the program, but I have not included any *machine-specific* information (how to turn it on, which disk drive is which, how to print hard copies of your results, how to use your text editor to revise data sets, and so on) because these things vary model by model—and, it would seem, minute by minute.

You do not even have to type well. The program is *menu driven*. At the bottom of your screen there is always a numbered set of choices (the menu). You tell CHIP what to do next by punching the key for the number you prefer.

By the way, you can't break it. If all seems lost, just keep punching numbered keys. You will probably get to some safe place of refuge; at worst you will stop the program and have to begin again. (**Rare Exception**—you can erase data files from the diskette, but it would be very hard to do so by pure accident since it requires choosing the Unsave option in the Modify menu and typing in the title of the data set to be blitzed.) But pure accidents can happen. Make sure you, or your instructor, have backup copies of the diskettes before you begin working with the program.

This book does not assume *any* knowledge of statistics. The statistical tools you need and how to find them in CHIP are explained as we go along. The book is organized so the introductory sociological ideas and the relevant introductory statistical techniques are developed together. In addition, the assignments in each chapter start simply and become more complex. Beginners can cover the key ideas by merely doing initial assignments in each chapter. The main stumbling block here will probably be with *statistical inference* or the "margin of error due to sampling variation." Statistical inference is a beautiful idea and one of the more important tools of modern society; but beginners find it difficult, not because of the math, but because it seems to reverse common sense. The CHIP program can handle a variety of inference problems, and I draw on these features here and there. But exercises involving inference will be so indicated, and some teachers may wish to skip them. In no case is mastery of inference crucial for following the main ideas.

Regardless of its ease of use, however, CHIP is not a toy. It is a sophisticated statistical package for contingency table analysis which includes a number of features (multi-variate direct standardization, Haberman's standardized residuals, the "weighted least squares" approach to partial percentage differences, and direct calculation of $2 \times 2 \times 2$ interactions) of interest to advanced students.

QUANTITATIVE SOCIOLOGY

This is a sociology book, not a statistics book. It treats ideas about society, not ideas about numbers—*but* they are *quantitative* sociological ideas. This is so important that it merits explanation.

The case for quantitative sociology—aside from the snob value of the esoteric and inscrutable—might seem to rest on "quality control." Certainly sociologists have no monopoly on drawing conclusions about society. The Op Ed pages of major newspapers teem with weighty analysis, and any assistant professor of English can tell you loads of things about American society and values, drawing on the insights of (currently) immortal novelists and poets. The unique contribution of the sociologist then might seem to be documentation: we base our conclusions on scientific samples, objective measurement, and proper statistical calculations. But if that were all there is to it, I would not embroil myself in the hassle of hawking unmusical "phonograph records." If documentation were the only issue, I could merely assure you my credentials are in order, cite the appropriate references, and proceed to spin my yarn.

But quantitative ideas *are* ideas, not just stamps indicating the numbers have been slaughtered according to the correct rituals. Consider, for example, the notions of equality. They permeate sociology and they permeate this book. But what do they mean? How can you tell whether two people or groups are "equal"? If we are trying for something more substantial than Fourth of July oratory, we need such concepts as *variables, distributions*, and *controls*. I submit it is impossible to think seriously about equality without using quantitative ideas. And the same holds true for other sociological concepts such as *mobility, stratification, careers, parental influence, social class, norms*, and the like. Unless we can talk about them exactly (quantitatively), we are simply flailing our arms about while expressing our deep feelings.

Courses that avoid quantification are teaching "sociology appreciation" not sociology. Such teaching is analogous to program notes for a symphony concert. While good program notes enhance our listening, they are not a substitute for the music. Nobody ever said, "I'm not a trained musician, so I'll just the read the program notes and skip the concert."

In sum, quantitative sociology involves not only objective documentation of conclusions, but also a language for talking about sociological ideas. No fancy math is involved (and surprisingly little simple math), but you will need to develop a new way of thinking. This book is designed to help you in this, to get you to think like a sociologist, not just like a statistician.

THE DATA

Sociology likes to pretend it is very old, but it isn't. Depending on your professor's taste, the first lecture can begin with the Old Testament or Aristotle or August Comte or whomever you like; it doesn't make much difference since the great social philosophers have such a tenuous connection to modern sociological research that you can pick and choose at will.

Modern sociological research is a Johnny-come-lately on the intellectual scene. If you want to stretch things a bit you might go back as far as the turn of the century (Karl Pearson or Francis Galton), but the connection is through mathematical statistics, not social research ideas. A more likely beginning is the Department of Sociology at the University of Chicago where, in the 1920s and 1930s, empirical sociological research first took foothold in a university. But, in point of fact, the classic Chicago research consisted mostly of field observation, and surprisingly few contemporary research topics can be traced directly back to the Chicago School.

In my opinion the year 1950 (give or take five years) marks the abrupt beginning of scientific sociological studies of the United States. The U.S. Census, of course, goes back to 1970, but its content is narrow, inconsistent from year to year, and until very recently Census data were physically unavailable for reanalysis. The commercial polls (Gallup, Crossley, Roper, and so on) began in the mid-1930s, but their original *quota sampling* designs make it impossible

CHAPTER 1   INTRODUCTION

to take their data at face value; academic sociology prior to 1950 centered on community studies and classroom questionnaires, not the nation as a whole.

But shortly after the end of World War II several things happened to change sociological studies:

- The two leading academic survey organizations, the National Opinion Research Center (NORC) and the Survey Research Center (SRC), took root at the University of Chicago and Michigan (though neither is tied closely to their sociology departments). Since then, each has completed more than a thousand surveys.

- All major survey organizations adopted multi-stage area probability samples—the most scientifically desirable form of sampling. The obvious result was an upgrading in quality. Less obviously, this standardization meant that most studies by most survey organizations since 1950 could be compared because their samples represented the same national cross sections.

- The late Samuel A. Stouffer, a Harvard sociologist, in 1953 received (from the Ford Foundation) what I believe to be the first research grant for a sociological national opinion survey. The topic? McCarthyism and Free Speech.

- The Michigan SRC began its classic series of surveys of voters in national elections, running from 1952 to the present.

- The Bureau of the Census's Current Population Survey (started in 1940) expanded its sample points from 68 to 230 in 1954, and continually expanded its survey capacity so that by 1980 the CPS alone was interviewing about a million Americans a year.

It is almost impossible to convey the impact of these thirty years on sociology. I began my own graduate study in 1950, and, while my teachers found plenty of books for me to read, I think it is accurate to say, basic Census figures aside, neither students nor teachers knew a darned thing about the social contours of America—or, more exactly, what we thought we knew was not based on hard evidence. Consider these questions: Do Protestants and Catholics differ in their values? How many Americans are upwardly mobile? Are White Southerners really less liberal on racial issues? Is there a persistent class difference in political party preference? Such questions were debated endlessly using scraps of dubious evidence. Today, you can answer any of them in a minute or two using a computer that costs less (in real terms) than a 1950 adding machine!

What is the consequence of this knowledge explosion for sociology? I'd call it indigestion. The explosion has been so enormous and so quick that the discipline has been overwhelmed, unable to organize and assimilate its new riches. We know so much about so many things that we are in danger of losing the branches in the leaves, much less the forest in the trees. And yet, if you scan the zillions of research papers, books, and reports, you will begin to see some common denominators, variables and relationships that turn up time and time again, questions that always seem to yield interesting answers, themes that emerge regardless of the issue of the moment. This book is an attempt at such a synthesis. It isn't a "theory of society" (more about that later), but it isn't a collection of *curiosa* either. My aim has been to pull together the most persistent and reliable conclusions—the questions and answers that turn up over and over again as we sift through the fallout from the explosion.

Sorting all this out would be impossible were it not for the existence of a data set designed almost exactly for that purpose. It is called the NORC General Social Survey (GSS). Since virtually every data set on your diskettes comes from the GSS and every page of this book draws on it, let me explain the survey in some detail.

1. GSS is a collection of annual national surveys carried out from 1972 to 1978, in 1980, and from 1982 to 1985, and scheduled for additional years. The data on your diskette are drawn from the 1972 to 1984 surveys.
2. Each survey includes about 1,500 respondents (1,468 to 1,613).
3. The respondents are drawn through area probability methods (the 1972 through 1974 designs were of the *modified-probability* type with quota elements at the block level. Since 1978 the design has been multi-stage, full probability with predesignated respondents. In 1975 and 1976 half of the cases were drawn each way to allow comparisons.) and represent U.S., English-speaking adults, eighteen years of age and older, living in non-institutional quarters in the continental

CHAPTER 1   INTRODUCTION

United States (no cases from Hawaii, Puerto Rico, or Alaska, as is true in most national surveys, because of their very high costs. Extending the sample to Alaska and Hawaii would only add about ten cases per year; Puerto Rico would add about another twenty; and each of these cases would probably cost a thousand dollars or more).

4. The "universe" they represent is the standard one covered by national surveys. Nevertheless, it should be borne in mind that this definition excludes young people in college dormitories or living on military bases, as well as older people in hospitals or nursing homes.

5. Each survey is carried out in midwinter (February and March).

6. Completion rates (percentages of predesignated respondents who are actually interviewed) range from 74 percent (1978) to 79 percent (1983).

7. All respondents are personally interviewed, usually at home, by an NORC interviewer.

8. Interviews last an average of sixty-five to seventy-five minutes.

9. The content of the questionnaire (designed by a committee of leading sociologists) was planned to cover the spectrum of variables of interest to contemporary sociology—demographics, occupation, education, parental family characteristics, morale, a few political items, and dozens of attitude items on topics ranging from abortion to wire tapping.

10. About half of the items are *permanent*—asked each year using exactly the same wording and, where it seems important, in the same sequence. About a quarter of the items are *rotating*—asked regularly, but only two years out of three, which allows the questionnaire to include more items.

Repeated items allow one to monitor change over the GSS years, a decade running from the reelection of Richard Nixon to the reelection of Ronald Reagan. And, since most of the items were chosen because they had appeared in earlier studies, some GSS questions can be tracked back to the 1950s.

11. Repeated items also allow one to build up sample sizes by pooling (combining) surveys from several years. While a single GSS includes about 1,500 cases, the complete data file, 1972 to 1984:

    totals 16,698 cases and includes "whole surveys full" of Blacks (1,874 cases), retired people (1,754 cases), ex-cigarette-smokers (1,208 cases), people who are currently separated or divorced (1,758 cases), Methodists (1,985 cases), and so on.

12. Copies of the data tapes are disseminated widely at a modest cost. If you are a college or university student, your sociology department or computer center most likely has a copy of the cumulative file. If you wish to explore the data in this book in more detail or examine variables not included on the diskettes, your instructor can probably arrange for you to do so.

    NORC produces an annual codebook with detailed information on question wordings, sample design, prior studies using the same variables, and *marginal* (one-variable) distributions. You might find it a handy supplement to this book. The codebooks are sold—with or without the data tapes—by the Roper Public Opinion Research Center, Box U-164R, University of Connecticut, Storrs, CT 06268. Most college libraries have copies.

13. The GSS is funded by the National Science Foundation, the government agency that supports basic research in the social and natural sciences.

Strictly speaking, the data you will analyze come from just one of the thousands of studies that comprise the post-1950 information explosion. However, that study, the GSS, was designed to cover the spectrum of sociological interest, and its several hundred variables and slightly more than a decade span allow us enormous scope. The tough question is which variables to select.

THE SOCIOLOGICAL FRAMEWORK

Social Differences in Contemporary America is based on facts, but it is not a fact book or almanac. Once you get the hang of it, you can look up interesting facts and figures in the data sets. I hope you will,

CHAPTER 1 INTRODUCTION

but that isn't the main point. The main point is to go way beyond the "electric coloring books" currently hawked as educational software, to organize the facts as an *intellectual system* that represents mainline thinking in sociology.

What do I mean by intellectual system? It doesn't fall into any of the tidy categories such as theory, model, hypothesis, or explanation you read about in research methods' texts—although it is closer to *model* than to any of the others.

Think about it this way:

If a sociologist were suddenly set down in a strange country, call it Novelia, and asked to produce a sociological analysis of Novelia and the Novelians, he or she would have very little to draw on in the way of hard "theory"—if by theory we mean unambiguous predictions that increases in a measurable variable, X, produce increases in another measureable variable, Y. But the sociologist would not be hopelessly lost and would almost certainly not collect extensive data on meal times, favorite colors, national debt, pronunciations of vowels, or the available technology for manufacturing hats. (Other social scientists might collect such data, as might sociologists specializing in art or formal organization, but we are talking about a general analysis of the macro-society.) Instead, our visitor would ask: How do Novelians make their livings? Are there any rich people? Any poor people? Who lives with whom? Who marries whom? How old are they? Do they have churches?

Why these particular questions? Basically because the variables they tap are differences that make differences. If we only know that A's favorite color is red and B's favorite color is pink, there is little else we can guess about them (gender perhaps); but if we know A is a male and B is a female, we can predict lots of other differences—once we know a little bit about how things operate in Novelia. These core variables are hardly mysterious—they include sex, age, race, schooling, occupation, region, and so on. And their effects are not always whoppers—as you will see for yourselves. But they do tend to "work" in the sense that differences in these variables have a good track record of predicting differences in a wide variety of other variables.

And that is how this book is organized. First, we review the key variables, then we see what differences they do (and do not) produce across a wide range of attitudes, opinions, and behaviors. The key variables themselves form four groups: (1) the *horizontal* cluster of ethnicity (tribalism); (2) the *vertical* cluster of stratification (socioeconomic status); (3) the change variables—age, cohort, and year; and (4) gender (sex).

Ethnicity

In Canada there are the French and the English; in Italy, the Northerners and the Southerners. In Verona there were the Montagues and the Capulets; in Rockford, Illinois, when I was growing up, there was an East Side and a West Side. In virtually every community there is some sort of grouping into "us" and "them."

The most extreme version is the sorting into tribes—subgroups based on assumed descent from a common ancestor. If Novelia were small, one of the first things our hypothetical sociologist would investigate would be the presence or absence of tribes.

In a larger society (maybe I mean more modern, but there are too few, teeny weeny modern societies to check out the hypothesis), kin groups are too numerous to provide a framework. Even in Boston nobody knows who the "leading families" are these days. The tribal principle isn't genetic: religion will do the job (as in Germany), or language (Canada), or geography (Italy), or, in a pinch, skin color (maybe you can come up with an example here). What is important is the:

- **almost automatic similarity** between parents and children. (Northern parents tend to have Northern children; Yellow parents tend to have Yellow children; Jewish parents tend to have Jewish children.)

- **relative permanence.** People do not change color very often: how often they change regions, religions, and so on in the United States will be dealt with later.

- **absence of ranking.** When looking at socioeconomic strata (the next section) the main point is their arrangement in a pecking order of some sort. By definition, "everyone" agrees it is better to be upper class than middle class and better to be middle class than lower class. But when we consider French Canadians and English Canadians or Irish Protestants and Irish Catholics, each group believes it is the best, has higher morals, better food, better behaved children, more devoted families—you name it.

CHAPTER 1   INTRODUCTION

So, ethnic groups (tribes) may be defined as *horizontal* (unranked), self-satisfied groupings, defined early in life by inheritance (not necessarily genetic), which remain relatively permanent over one's lifetime.

But, how are America's tribes to be defined? There is no official register, and if you want to push the definition, Republicans and Democrats come close to being tribes, as do Red Sox and Yankee fans, or devotees of the, uh, Cleveland Indians. The main idea we will examine is that American ethnicity is not a single variable but a cluster based on several variables. My candidates are race, region, and religion. In the next chapter we will dissect their intricate interrelations, and throughout the book we will ask:

Does ethnicity make a difference? If so, which variables in the cluster seem most important?

Stratification (Socioeconomic Status)

If Novelia is larger than a few hundred people, it is quite probably stratified or "layered" into social classes. The classes may be clear-cut (as in the Indian caste system) or they may tend toward continuous shadings where class lines are drawn arbitrarily by the research worker; but either way our sociologist can expect a top and a bottom and quite probably one or more middle groups. Beyond that, sociological theory is rather shy: the top may consist of hereditary aristocrats or plutocratic industrialists or mandarin bureaucrats or great landowners or lots of things—exactly what characteristics put you on the top or on the bottom vary from country to country and time to time.

Sociologists seem obsessed by stratification (an unkind observer once noted this is probably because the economists pre-empted money and the psychologists pre-empted sex), and social class is one of the best-studied phenomena in modern America. In Chapter Three we will look at the basics of stratification. As in the case of ethnicity, we will not assume that a single variable is the key to everything (money for example). Instead, we will deal with a second cluster—schooling, occupation, and money—and see how they fit together.

A well-studied area generates concepts (jargon) and definitions. Among specialists, words such as *social class* and *stratification* have highly specialized meanings. To avoid false specificity, I will simply refer to the cluster of ranking variables as *socioeconomic status*, which is frequently abbreviated as SES.

The variables in the SES cluster (education, occupation, and money) differ in two important ways from the ethnic variables: first, by definition there is consensus on how their categories are ranked (this is obvious for money and schooling, and occupational ranking will be explained in Chapter Three). They are *vertical* variables in contrast to the *horizontal* ethnic variables. Second, there is less direct inheritance; although we take on our parents' races, regions and religions almost automatically, whether we will end up with the same schooling, jobs, and incomes as our parents is not automatic at all. This absence of automatic transmission leads to the important notion of *social mobility* (Chapter Six). It also leads to a *causal model*, the principle of which is fairly obvious: ethnicity might influence an adult's social stratum, but not vice versa (thus, race could well influence adult earnings, but adult earnings can not influence race). This may seem obvious, but it is complex enough to illustrate one of the main themes of this book, best seen, perhaps, as a diagram in which one-way arrows represent causal influence:

FIGURE 1-1
The Sociologist's Macro-Model in Diagram Form

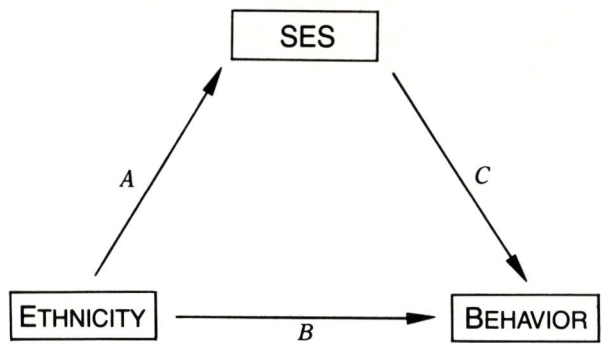

The arrows (A, B, and C,) represent possible causal relationships which reveal persistent questions of this book.

CHAPTER 1   INTRODUCTION

Ethnicity and SES (*A*)—The *A* arrow runs from Ethnicity to SES. The question we need to ask here is:

Do the various ethnic groups differ in their social standing? If so, which parts of the ethnic cluster produce which kinds of SES differences?

In a nation as diverse as the United States these are interesting and complicated questions. Furthermore, they have moral and policy overtones. The *American Creed* says one's social stratum (as an adult) should be mostly influenced by performance (talent, skill, hard work, character, and so on), not by ethnic background. To the extent we find strong ethnic differences in SES, we will be troubled (as Americans, not as "objective" sociologists) and moved to ask how these differences occur and whether they seem to show any diminution over time.

Ethnicity, SES and Behavior *(B,C)*—The *B* and *C* arrows run from Ethnicity and SES into the general purpose variable Behavior that stands for a variety of social phenomena (family structure, values, religion, politics, morale, and so on). We need to ask:

Does Ethnicity or SES seem to produce differences? If they do, which items in the cluster are more important? Which cluster, SES or Ethnicity, seems to have the bigger impact?

Consistent answers to these questions (and I'm not promising that) can suggest interpretations of our society.

If SES is the dominant variable, then we are a *class* society in which ethnic differences have been boiled away in the famous *melting pot,* and your most important social characteristic is your rung on the socioeconomic ladder. If so, there is a second question: do all aspects of SES contribute equally or is one dominant? Those who say, "Everything boils down to how much money you have" are betting on a single dimension; others use an *additive model* which assumes that each ranked variable produces part of the difference.

But we need not assume ethnicity is unimportant. Observers may claim that traditional regional, racial, and religious differences are increasingly passé in this era of jet planes, national TV networks, and fast food chains. But one look at the election strategies of contemporary presidential candidates will verify that the three R's—race, region, and religion—are still very much with us.

THE SOCIOLOGICAL FRAMEWORK

Those of you wise in the ways of academia have probably already figured out that there is no universal answer. Which cluster makes the biggest difference depends on the behavior (including attitudes) you are studying, though I'm a little more likely to go out on a limb and make a claim regarding factors *within* a cluster. (You'll seldom catch me betting that educational and racial differences are the least important variables.) The real question is which behaviors are highly SES related, and which heavily ethnic? You just might look at the topics of the later chapters and place your bets.

The Change Variables

Part One of *Social Differences* treats structure. Chapter Two explains the variables that define ethnicity; Chapter Three explains the components of SES; and Chapter Four helps you investigate how ethnicity and SES produce differences in the way we live and think. Although the data span the period from 1972 to 1984, Part One ignores social change.

Part Two (Chapters Five through Nine) focuses directly on change. Social change is at the forefront of contemporary sociological research, not so much because the pace of change is dizzying (you will probably be surprised how small year-to-year changes are for most of our variables) but because—thirty years into the modern era of sociological research—we now have a long enough span of data to ask sensible questions about change and continuity.

Social change is intimately tied to the human life cycle. We are born, we grow up, we marry, we begat, and we be gone. For the individual this means inexorable movement on the escalators of *career* and *life course*. For the analyst of social change it leads to questions about trends in career patterns (Chapter Five) and life-course stages (Chapter Nine). Since we all have parents who themselves moved on similar escalators, the life-cycle process leads to a special form of change sociologists call *intergenerational mobility* (Chapter Six), in which parents and children may differ in terms of SES and even some ethnicity variables.

While each individual gets exactly one ride on the escalator, a society is composed of people who got on their escalators in very different historical periods. Thus the oldest GSS respondents started school well before World War I, while the youngest adults in the early 1980s have no direct memory of Vietnam. This leads to the notion of *cohort* (a group of people who go through some process simultaneously) and of *cohort replacement* as a subtle form of change in which older generations are quietly but inexorably replaced by newcomers who may be quite different. Cohort processes turn up everywhere in Part Two of this text but receive special emphasis in Chapters Five, Seven, and Eight. Chapter Five contrasts the *careers* of *birth cohorts* spread over the last half century; Chapter Seven asks whether ethnic differences in achievement (SES) are narrowing in more recent cohorts; and Chapter Eight examines cohort replacement as an explanation of short-term social trends from 1973 to 1983, drawing on the classic research of the late Samuel A. Stouffer.

Gender (Sex)

Sex differences do not fall neatly into the previous categories. Although gender is permanent, unranked, and inherited, children do not resemble both their parents in gender, so sex cuts across ethnicity—every ethnic group has almost the same proportion of men and women. While there are sex differences on some SES variables (mainly workers' earnings), males and females are hardly ranked status groups like the rich and the poor. And since sex is about as permanent a characteristic as one can find, it hardly belongs with age and cohort in the generational change cluster. So it stands alone, and we shall frequently ask how and whether men and women differ on our variables. But be warned: sex is not one of the better predictor variables. Men and women do have their differences, yes indeed they do. But outside the classic areas of cultural sex typing (labor force participation for example), men and women are often remarkably similar. Therefore, there is no special chapter devoted to sex differences; they will be treated wherever their presence or absence is particularly interesting, in particular toward the end of Chapter Three and throughout Chapter Nine.

I
Social Structure

2
Ethnicity

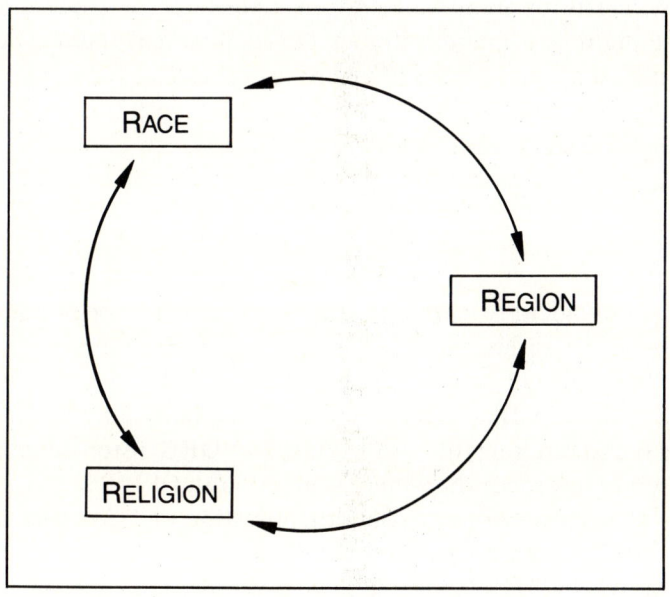

THE TRIBAL MOSAIC

America, a huge nation (only China, India, and Russia have larger populations) peopled over several centuries by immigrants of diverse cultural strains, does not have the tidy ethnic distinctions of, say Belgium, where the difference between French-speaking and Flemish-speaking people pretty well wraps it up. And a lot depends on how fine grain a detail you want. There are neighborhoods in the North End of Boston today where it makes a difference which town in Italy your family came from, not to mention whether you are Italian or Catholic or White or a New Englander or whatever.

If we settle for about half a dozen "tribes" (eight to be exact; not because eight is a magic number for sociological theory, but because the computer screen can handle eight groups comfortably), we can get a decent ethnic picture by working with three variables: *race*, *region*, and *religion*.

Race

In sociological research race means physical type or color (for example, Black or Negro), not national origin (Italian is not a race) or religion (Jewish is not a race). Race is socially, not biologically defined and many Blacks have lighter skins than many Whites. But it doesn't seem terribly ambiguous. NORC interviewers are supposed to ask race when there is any doubt. Of 17,052 cases (GSS 1972 to 1984) interviewers asked the question of 273 subjects. And despite all the possible hues, only 175 cases were coded other than Black or White (the 175 spread over twenty categories, the largest being Filipino with 21). In other words, for all practical purposes, contemporary Americans are either Black or White.

The data in this book are grouped as White-plus-Other vs. Black, but we will simply call the first group White as 99 percent of them are not Other.

What percent of contemporary U.S. adults are Black? I suspect you'll guess "10 percent" and if so, you'll be close, but let's use the CHIP program to find out exactly. First, however, you need to familiarize yourself with your computer's keyboard.

THE TRIBAL MOSAIC

> **The Computer**
>
> Your computer has a keyboard like a typewriter's. However, it (probably) has three sets of keys with the numbers one through nine on them. At the far left are two columns of keys labeled **F1, F2, F3 . . . F10.** These are "function keys." Any time a number appears in a CHIP menu you can choose that option by pushing one of the function keys. There is also a "normal" set of numbers, one through nine plus zero across the top of your keyboard. CHIP is programmed so that you can also treat these keys as function keys (use zero for ten). That is, you can choose from the menu with either function keys or top row keys. However, you must use the top row numbers when typing in information such as numerical file names. You can't use function keys for that. There is (probably) a third set of numbered keys at the right of the keyboard. Forget them when running CHIP.
>
> You need to be aware of one more key—the Enter key. On my computer it is a left-pointing arrow with a bent tail just right of the letter keys. The purpose of the Enter key is to tell the computer you are through entering data and it should go to work. Function keys (either set) have a built in Enter, but when you are typing in other information, a file name for example, the computer will sit idle if you don't follow up with a push of the Enter key.

Task 2-1: Race Marginals

1. Turn on your computer, insert the diskette and start the program, following instructions specific to your machine. Your diskette contains an introductory version of the program (CHIP1) and a more advanced, flexible version (CHIP2). This book assumes you are working with CHIP2.

2. When everything is tidy backstage, the screen lights up and delivers some propaganda. Next it asks about saving output in a file. Your instructor may or may not use this feature, so ask. Then it prints:

    1) Old   2) New

CHAPTER 2   ETHNICITY

This is a *menu*, though not a lavish one. The computer is asking you to select **1** (if you want it to fetch a previously saved data file from an inserted diskette) or **2** (if you wish to type in data of your own). You want one of the library data sets, so your choice is **1**. Push the **F1** key.

3. The computer screen will now read: **Name of file?**

    CHIP needs to know the name of the data file you wish to analyze. File names can be letters or numbers, or a combination of both. The data we want—GSS results on the ethnic variables—have the stark file name 2.1 (The first data set developed especially for Chapter Two). So type the number **2**, a period, then the number **1** (use the top row keys), and punch the Enter key.

4. CHIP now searches the diskette, finds the data set with this name, and displays a brief description (in this case, *The tribal trio*) and the number (*N*) of cases (13,750).

As you might guess from the *N*, these data are from the cumulative GSS surveys. Unless the text tells you otherwise, you can assume the same for all data files on the diskette.

You are now ready to analyze the data—that is, to find out what proportion of U.S. adults is Black. At this point the computer will display a new menu at the bottom of the screen. This is the *Command* menu and it includes the major commands. The menu looks like this:

**1) Info 2) Marginals 3) All Margs 4) Cross Tab 5) Whatif
6) Modify 7) No More**

For now we are only interested in possibilities 1, 2, and 3. They get us information about single variables. If you punch **F1**, the computer will tell you the names of the variables in the data set and the number of categories each has. These numbers tell you how many categories there are for each variable. For example, the "2" under Race says there are two different categories for the variable, Race. For the content of the categories, see this text and its appendices. For data set 2.1 we learn the variable names are *Race* (two categories), *Regin16* (five categories) and *Relig16* (six categories). We have learned that the variable we want, Race, is present in the data set and that two categories are present.

If you push **F2,** you can get *marginals* for a single item. Marginals is survey jargon for one-variable distributions, so called because in a two-variable cross-tab table, the one-variable figures turn up as row and column totals in the margins of the table. (See, for example, the *All Religions* row at the bottom of Table 2-1.) If you push **F2,** the program will print the names of the variables in this data set with a number next to each. Push the function key for Race (**F1**). The computer will now print the frequencies and percentages for each category of Race. It turns out that the Black percentage is 11.6. About 12 percent of U.S. adults are Black.

If you choose **F3,** CHIP will print the percentages for every variable in the data set. For single variables, **F1** is usually faster, but the percentages will be the same for **F2** and **F3.**

Now your assignment: repeat the steps explained above, check my 11.6 percent Marginal for Black, and find out exactly how many cases in the data set are Black.

Statistical Option

As I explained in Chapter One, CHIP has a number of statistical features that are optional in terms of grasping the sociology. The first of these is "confidence intervals for proportions." In Marginals, three numbers appear below each percentage. The middle one is 1 sigma (the estimated value of one standard deviation in the sampling distribution of this proportion, assuming the current N and simple random sampling). The bottom one is .05 limits. According to statistical theory you should be willing to bet nineteen to one that the true proportion is within brackets formed by adding or subtracting this number to the marginal percentage. The top one, .5 limits, gives you the bracket values for an even money bet. According to statistical theory, the .05 bracket value equals 1.96 sigmas, the .50 bracket value is .675 sigmas. A similar option is available in the % Across command in Cross Tab.

CHAPTER 2   ETHNICITY

Region and Religion

Geography creates the second axis of American ethnicity. In particular, regional differences—which once produced a civil war—are an important part of ethnicity. While Southerners and New England Yankees aren't quite tribes, regions meet our definition of ethnic variables. I will follow the U.S. Census definitions, grouping the states as follows:

Northeast
New England = Maine, Vermont, New Hampshire, Massachusetts, Connecticut, Rhode Island
Middle Atlantic = New York, New Jersey, Pennsylvania

Central
East North Central = Wisconsin, Illinois, Indiana, Michigan, Ohio
West North Central = Minnesota, Iowa, Missouri, North Dakota, South Dakota, Nebraska, Kansas

South
South Atlantic = Delaware, Maryland, West Virginia, Virginia, North Carolina, South Carolina, Georgia, Florida, District of Columbia
East South Central = Kentucky, Tennessee, Alabama, Mississippi
West South Central = Arkansas, Oklahoma, Louisiana, Texas

West
Mountain = Montana, Idaho, Wyoming, Nevada, Utah, Colorado, Arizona, New Mexico
Pacific = Washington, Oregon, California, Alaska, Hawaii

THE TRIBAL MOSAIC

Data set 2.1 includes a variable, Regin16, based on answers to "In what state or foreign country were you living when you were sixteen years old?" (Sociologists conventionally use Age 16 as a starting point since at Age zero family social influences have not yet had a chance to operate, but Age 16 is just before one makes crucial decisions about schooling, work, and marriage.) The data have five categories—the four major Census divisions and Foreign.

The third ethnic variable (Relig16 in data set 2.1) is *original religion* ("In what religion were you raised?"). The usual distinction is Protestant–Catholic–Jewish–Other–None, but this conceals several differences among the Protestant groups. The GSS codebook lists 120 distinct Protestant denominations, which is too rich a diet for CHIP. As a compromise, I divided the Protestants into Fundamentalist (Funprot) and Other (Othprot). To do so, I looked at a 1984 GSS question on whether the Bible is "the actual word of God," "an inspired word of God but not everything in it should be taken literally," or "an ancient book of fables, legends, history, and moral precepts recorded by men." Denominations whose current members had high proportions saying "actual word of God" I termed Fundamentalist. I ended up with Methodists, Lutherans, Presbyterians, and Episcopalians in Othprot and everyone else (mainly Baptists) in Funprot.

Task 2-2: Region and Religion Marginals

You can find the marginal proportions for the five regions and six religious groups in data set 2.1 the same way you found that 12 percent of Americans are Black.

1. Armed with these marginals, be prepared to answer the following:
   Which was the more frequent ethnic origin

   - Southern or Midwestern (Central)?
   - No Religion or Jewish?
   - Catholic or Protestant?
   - Catholic or Fundamentalist-Protestant?
   - Black or Foreign-born?

2. What sociological difference does it make if a group is large or small?

CHAPTER 2 ETHNICITY

HOW ETHNIC VARIABLES ARE RELATED

While race, region, and religion are distinct variables, they are not statistically independent of each other. Quite the opposite; they are linked together so that American ethnicity forms a complex pattern. In this section we will look at their relationships. This section will also introduce you to the CHIP feature you will use most—percentage tables.

First, race and region. At one time, the correlation was almost perfect. In 1860, just before the Civil War, 86 percent of America's Blacks were slaves living in the South, 6 percent were freemen living in the South, 5 percent were freemen living in the North, and 3 percent were slaves living in the North. One of the monumental events in American life has been the flow of the Black population out of the South, first as a trickle then as a flood (more on this in Chapter Six). We don't need CHIP to tell us the distribution is more even today, but the exact figures are interesting. We need to find the proportion of Blacks from the South and the proportion of Whites from the South, using data set 2.1. Here's how:

A. Retrieve data set 2.1 and wait for the *Command* menu to appear.

B. Push **F4** for the Cross Tab option (it makes tables).

   CHIP will now print out the names of the variables in the data set with a number next to each. Then it will ask you to type the function key numbers for the variables you want.

C. You know you want variables *1* (Race) and *2* (Regin16), but you have a further decision to make—which variable forms the columns (categories arranged from left to right across the screen) and which variable forms the rows (categories arranged up and down). If one of your variables is the dependent or "effect" variable, it should form columns and you type its number second. Hard to choose here, but I'd say it is more likely that Race affects Region than Region affects Race, so I'll punch **F1** and then **F2**. (In case of doubt enter them in the order on the screen. The data sets were constructed so as to put the

HOW ETHNIC VARIABLES ARE RELATED

variables in a reasonable causal order.) The computer will not blow up or anything if you enter them in the other order, and you will get perfectly sensible results. However, in later chapters we will be working with much more complicated problems where order is subtle and important. Get in the habit of typing them in *cause* first, *effect* second.

D. The screen will now show the *Cross Tab* menu:

1) Frequency 2) Percent 3) Chi Square 4) Control 5) Select Con 6) No More

If you punch **F1**, the computer will produce a table of frequencies (case counts). The top row will tell how many Whites hailed from which region, and the second row will give you the counts for Blacks. In data set 2.1, 3,749 Whites came from the South, as did 1,083 Blacks.

Such frequency tables are the meat and potatoes of sociological research, but they aren't digestable in raw form. To get anything out of them, you should transform them to percentages. To do so, push **F2**.

E. The screen will now show you the *Percent* menu, which gives four alternatives for calculating your percentages:

1) % Across (makes each *row* of numbers add up to 100 percent)
2) % Down (makes each column of numbers add up to 100 percent)
3) % Total (makes the various *cell* percentages add up to 100 percent over the total table. If you look at the row and column totals, you'll see where the word *marginals* comes from.)
4) % Diff (explained below)

Your best choice here (and whenever there is a dependent variable running across the page) is % Across. So push **F1**.

A new table will appear. The layout is the same as for the frequency table, but the percentages start to tell a story. Although there are more White *cases* from the South (3,749 vs. 1,083), Blacks have a higher Southern *percentage.* Two-thirds of U.S. Blacks (67.7 percent) grew up in the South, in contrast to about one-third (30.9 percent) of U.S. Whites. Their difference (67.7 − 30.9 = 36.8), called *d,* is a classic measure of the relationship between two variables. Big *d*'s mean strong relationships.

The percentage difference, *d,* is so useful that CHIP has an option to make the calculations for you. Push **F4** (% Diff) after **F2** (Percent) to get it.

F. The computer needs to know whether you wish to subtract the Black percentages from the White percentages or vice versa; that is, what the plus and minus values are for Race. (With more then two row categories it's more complicated than that—see the next section.) It will print the category numbers. I wished Black to be plus, hence positive values of *d* will mean disproportionately *more* Blacks from that Region, negative values of *d* will mean relatively *fewer* Blacks than Whites. So I answered the first question with **F2** and **F3** (No More), the latter being the equivalent of Enter. The second question evoked **F1**. (**F3** isn't necessary since all the possibilities have been used.)

A table then appeared on the screen giving all the *d*'s, like this:

	% Difference	d/Standard Error
Foreign	− .7	− 1.31
NEast	− 11.3	− 12.98
Central	− 15.3	− 15.81
South	36.8	29.65
West	− 9.5	− 17.64

The left-hand column is the set of *d*'s, the same numbers you would get by hand subtraction, comparing rows in the % Across data. The 36.8 for South is exactly what we got by hand.

The five *d*'s tell a concise story: South is the only positive *d.* Blacks are disproportionately (take that word apart and you'll have the main idea behind percentage

HOW ETHNIC VARIABLES ARE RELATED

tables) Southern, but relatively infrequent in all the other four origins. The d for Foreign is very small. Blacks and Whites don't differ much in the proportion growing up abroad.

The d's for the other three Census regions (-11.3, -15.3, -9.5) are pretty close. There seems to be no particular part of the North that is especially non-Black.

In sum, even today, Blacks are mostly and disproportionately Southern in origin.

Task 2-3: Race and Region, Race and Religion

1. Repeat my analysis of Race and Region step by step to confirm my results and acquaint yourself with the goodies on the Percent menu. Try various options until you feel you have the hang of it.

2. Use the variable Relig16 in data set 2.1 to look at Race (independent variable—rows) and Relig16 (dependent variable—columns). Use the percentage options and differences as I did above.

3. You now know two ways Blacks differ from Whites. What might be some of the sociological consequences?

Statistical Option
Just as a proportion has a sampling distribution, so does a d, as explained in most elementary statistics texts. In CHIP, the right-hand column in the % Diff tables gives d divided by *sigma d* (the estimated value of one standard deviation in the sampling distribution of d's for simple random samples of this size). According to normal-curve theory, 95 percent of sample d's should be within 1.96 sigmas of the true value. Therefore, if $d/sigma\ d$ exceeds 1.96 (in absolute value), it is an unlikely result in samples from a universe where the true value of d is zero. So, if the number in the right-hand column is larger than 1.96, the d is "statistically significant at the .05 level." CHIP automatically highlights

(continued)

> values of 1.96 or larger. For Race and Regin16, the four regional differences are significant (statistically reliable), but the *d* for Foreign is not.
>
> To find the value of sigma for the sampling distribution of *d*, divide the left-hand number by the one on its right; for example, for Race and South, 36.8/29.6 = 1.24. That's in percentages. In proportions it's .012.

Just as races differ on region and religion, these two variables are related to each other: people who grew up in different parts of the country were raised in different religions; people reared in different religions come from different parts of the country.

To see the data, we need a more complex table with thirty cells (five regions by six religions equals thirty combinations). To get it from the Command menu, punch **F4** (Cross Tab), **F3** (rows = Relig16), **F2** (columns = Regin16), **F2** (Percent), and then **F1** (% Across). CHIP then prints a table in which the rows are the five religions, the columns are the six regions and the cell entries are percentages. They tell us the regional distribution of each religion and sum to 100 percent across each row. (To get religious percents for each region, Enter **F4, F2, F3, F2,** and then **F1.** Make sure you see the difference.) Table 2-1 presents the results.

TABLE 2-1
Original Religion and Religion at Age 16

Religion	Foreign	Northeast	Region Central	South	West	Total%	(N)
Funprot	1.4%	8.8%	22.1%	57.4%	10.3%	100.0	(5,150)
Othprot	2.5	17.3	33.3	34.9	12.1	100.0	(3,524)
Catholic	7.3	37.4	31.2	12.4	11.6	100.0	(4,107)
Jewish	8.8	57.6	17.2	8.6	7.8	100.0	(373)
Other	37.6	26.8	17.2	7.0	11.5	100.0	(157)
None	3.9	12.1	32.6	21.2	30.3	100.0	(439)
All Religions	4.1	21.1	27.8	35.1	11.7	100.0	(13,750)

SOURCE: data set 2.1

HOW ETHNIC VARIABLES ARE RELATED

Percentage tables are the most popular way to handle sociological research results. You will interpret dozens of them before we finish the book. But they take a little getting used to.

First, make sure you can translate each percentage into literal English. For example, the 17.3 in the second row from the top, second column from the left says, "Of 3,524 respondents raised as Other Protestants, 17.3 percent grew up in the Northeast." (It *does not* say 17.3 percent of Northeasterns are Other Protestants or that 17.3 percent of the cases are Northeastern Protestants.)

The following ritual formula almost always works:

Among the (*row N*) cases who were/are (*row category*) in terms of (*row variable*), (X percent) were/are (*column category*) in terms of (*column variable*).

Use the formula until you get used to reading percentage tables.

Task 2-4: Reading and Graphing Tables

1. First, find the biggest and smallest cell (non-total) percentages in Table 2-1 and translate each into English.

   Second, spot the interesting differences. Basically, this amounts to comparing percentages in a given column. Thus, the 57.6 for Jewish-Northeast and the 8.8 for Fundamentalist-Northeast tell us that a greater proportion of Jews grew up in the Northeast than did Fundamentalists.

> When a table has more than a few rows and columns it is very difficult to tease out the main patterns by fishing around for big and small numbers. Graphics help enormously because it is easier for the eye to interpret a spatial distance than to compare the magnitudes of printed digits. We will make routine use of a particular graphic, a *telephone pole* graph (*tele-graph* for short).
>
> In a telephone pole graph one makes a *pole* for each column and draws in *rungs* (steps) for each of its
>
> *(continued)*

CHAPTER 2 ETHNICITY

> percentages. Let's create one step by step:
>
> a. Arrange the vertical scale on a piece of graph paper so the bottom value is zero and the highest is slightly larger than the highest percentage in your table.
> b. Draw in evenly spaced vertical lines (poles) for each column in your percentage table. (If the categories have no logical order, you might arrange them by the size of their marginals.)
> c. Indicate the overall (marginal) percentage for each pole by drawing in an asterisk.
> d. Indicate the various row percentages by drawing short horizontal lines across the poles at appropriate heights.
> e. If you wish to draw attention to one or two row categories, connect their rungs by lines running from pole to pole. But don't clutter the graph with too many of these.

2. Figure 2-1 presents the data in Table 2-1 in the form of a tele-graph. Use it to answer the following questions:

   a. Are there any religions where majorities grew up in a single region?
   b. Which religions are disproportionately high (above the asterisk) for which regions?
   c. Which regions seem to differ most and least from the overall national distribution?
   d. Which religions seem to differ most and least from the overall national distribution?
   e. What might be some of the sociological consequences of the regional pattern of religions? (What difference might it make if each region had the same religious distribution?)

3. Use CHIP to reanalyze the data in Figure 2-1 with Regions as your columns and Races as your rows. Display your results as a tele-graph with Regions as poles and Races as rungs.

FIGURE 2-1

Data in Table 2-1 in "Tele-graph" Form

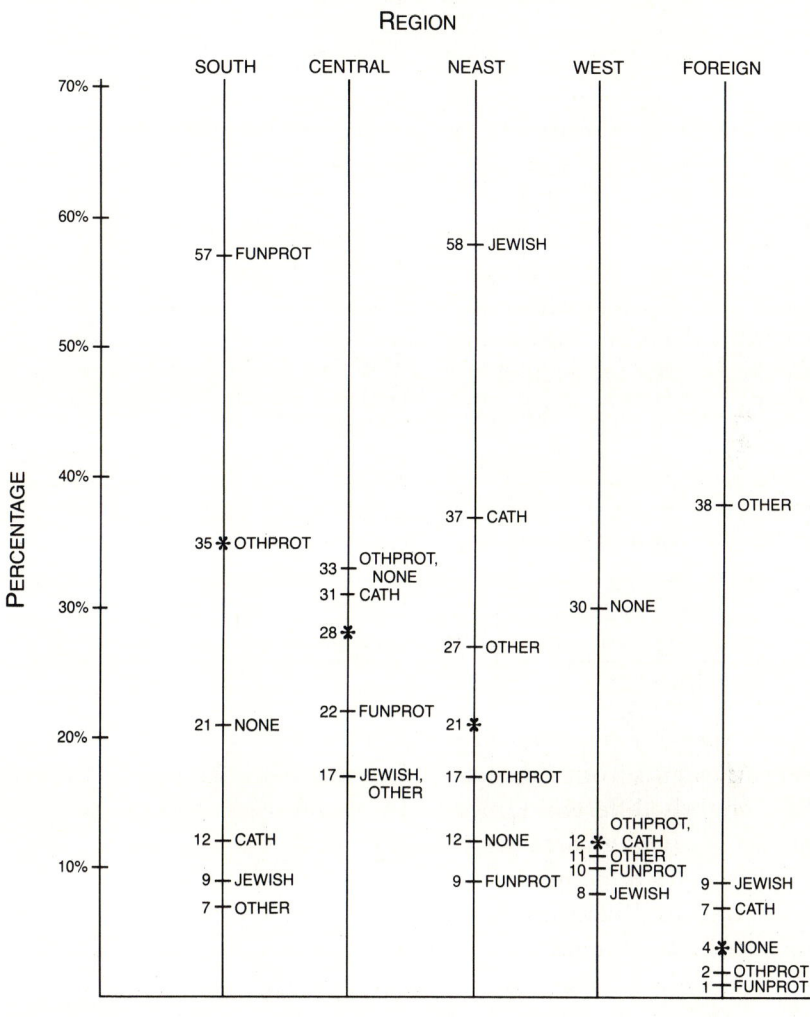

SOURCE: data set 2.1.

Race, Region, and Religion: An Ethnic Typology (Ethtype)

With two races, five regional origins, and six religious origins, we could define sixty different ethnic constellations (Blacks born in the Midwest and raised as Catholics for example). This is too many.

We can use the knowledge we have gained so far to come up with a more practical but sociologically sound array.

First, we divide Regin16 into South vs. All Other, since South stands out from the rest both racially and religiously. Then we Cross Tab the three variables and look at the largest cells in the table. There are twenty-four cells in the cross-tabulation, but 90 percent of Americans fall into one of the following (see Table 2-2):

TABLE 2-2
Ethnic Typology

Race	Regin16	Relig16	Label	Percent	Cumulative %
White	North	Catholic	WNCath	25.1	25.1
White	North	Othprot	WNProt	15.7	40.8
White	South	Funprot	WSFund	15.0	55.8
White	North	Funprot	WNFund	13.2	69.1
White	South	Othprot	WSProt	7.5	76.6
Black	South	Any	SBlack	9.2	85.8
Black	North	Any	NBlack	4.2	89.9
White	(Any other categories)		Othwite	10.1	100.0

100.0% ($N = 14{,}024$)

SOURCE: GSS 1972 to 1984

(*Note:* the percentages in Table 2-2 will not *exactly* match their logical equivalents from data set 2.1. This is because different data sets have slightly different numbers of missing cases; for example, "no answer," on *Other* variables.)

Among Whites, groups one through five are just the five largest combinations. Blacks are divided by Original Region but not by Religion since three-quarters of them were reared as Fundamentalists.

The Othwite (All Other Whites) is a grab bag. Roughly one-third are Jews, one-third Southern Catholics, and one-third Other/None on Original Religion.

Othwite doesn't make any particular sociological sense, but the other seven categories define the major ethnic *tribes* of modern America. Familiarize yourself with them because they turn up repeatedly throughout the rest of the book. In addition, with the % Diff option in CHIP you can make some interesting groupings.

If, for example, Region (North vs. South) is a major factor, then the same difference should turn up when we compare Northerners and Southerners among Blacks, Other Protestant Whites and Fundamentalist Whites. Similarly, when comparing Fundamentalists with Other Protestants we want to look at religious differences among people from the same race and region. We can do this by getting d's for Northern White Protestants vs. Northern White Fundamentalists and for Southern White Protestants vs. Southern White Fundamentalists.

Two familiar groups, Jews and Hispanics, are not broken out separately. Although both are highly visible on the national scene, they constitute very small minorities. Jews (as defined in data set 2.1) comprise about 3 percent of GSS respondents. While they do not appear in the ethnic typology (*Ethtype*), you will find data about them in the CHIP Library (see Appendix B). No one knows how many Hispanics there are because the definition is slippery, but the various estimates center around 3 to 5 percent. If you hail from, say, New York City or Los Angeles, these numbers may seem preposterous, but remember, although these are the two largest metropolitan areas in the nation, 87 percent of us do not live in either New York City or Los Angeles.

The Old Countries

The United States, like Argentina, Canada, Australia, and New Zealand, was formed rather recently by world standards, through the immigration of masses of foreigners into a thinly settled but promising territory. Immigration has not been steady. The original colonists, of course, were immigrants, but in the period from 1800 until the Civil War, immigration slowed considerably. The period between the Civil War and World War I saw the legendary flood of European immigrants one associates with Ellis Island and the Statue of Liberty. Then, during the Depression, World War II, and the early postwar years, immigration dropped (no mystery: we wrote highly discriminatory laws regulating the flow). Recently, it has picked up again.

The consequences are that at any given time Americans differ considerably in their *seniority*, ranging from "just off the boat" to "old old family"; different immigration streams have different religious backgrounds; and different immigration streams found different areas of the country open for settlement. As a consequence of these consequences, our eight ethnic tribes differ considerably in seniority and national origins.

CHAPTER 2   ETHNICITY

Data set 2.2 contains the Ethtype and two variables that shed light on immigration.

- *Grnborn* divides GSS respondents according to the number of their grandparents who were born abroad. Relatively few of us grew up abroad (4 percent according to data set 2.1); foreign-born parents are not that common (19 percent report one or both parents foreign-born, according to GSS 1972–84), but almost half of us (42 percent) report one or more foreign-born grandparents.

- *Famorig* is based on the question, "From what countries or part of the world did your ancestors come?" I grouped the answers as follows:

German = Germany, Austria
Britin = England, Wales, Scotland, Non-French Canada
SEEurp = Czechoslovakia, Greece, Hungary, Italy, Poland, Russia, Spain, Portugal, Lithuania, Yugoslavia, Rumania
Irelnd = Ireland
UNEurp = Africa, China, Japan, Mexico, Philippines, Puerto Rico, West Indies, Arabia, Other Spanish
Scndia = Denmark, Finland, Norway, Sweden
NWEurp = French Canada, France, Netherlands, Belgium
Noforn = American; Unable to name a country; Unable to choose one from several (333 respondents answering "American Indian" are excluded)

Task 2-5: Ethnicity and Immigration

Use data set 2.2 to answer these questions:

1. Find the Grnborn percentages for each ethnic type. Can you use them to arrange the ethnic types in terms of seniority? Use the Cat Order command in the Modify menu to experiment.

2. What ethnic groups have high and low proportions of Noforn on Famorig? What does this suggest about the melting pot hypothesis that eventually all nationality groups will be diluted into one?

3. What percent of U.S. adults are WASPS (White Anglo-Saxon Protestants)? *Hint:* You have to decide which nationalities

seem Anglo-Saxon. The % Total option in the Percent menu will be helpful.

Does that percentage seem high or low?

4. Which of the eight ethnic types is most WASP?

SOME ETHNIC DIFFERENCES

We have now defined the major ethnic configurations and have seen how they emerged from the irregular waves of immigration that peopled the United States. Chapter One seemed to promise you that ethnicity makes a difference, that people in different tribes differ systematically and nontrivially. But whether that promise is kept cannot be seen until we finish the book—especially since we have to consider socioeconomic status along with ethnicity (the SES variables will be explained in Chapter Three). But a preliminary scanning of the possibilities will give you some "feel" for social differences, experience working with the ethnic typology, and practice with CHIP.

This book uses two groups of data sets. Sets designed for specific problems in specific chapters (sets 2.1 and 2.2 for example) are stored on your CHIP diskette with names keyed to the chapters. Thus, set 2.2 is the second data set used in Chapter Two. In addition, you have (or will be told how to obtain) a second diskette comprising a general sociological library of 280 data sets. These CHIPLIB data sets are used in various chapters, so their names begin with an X, not a chapter number.

Appendix B at the back of this book explains the seventy different topics covered in CHIPLIB and the four different tables for each. Read it carefully. Study the introductory materials and then glance through the catalogue to familiarize yourself with the possibilities.

Appendix B also explains that each topic appears in four versions, (a, b, c, and d). The "a" version always contains the eight ethnic types, so that is the version you want for your next task.

Task 2-6: Ethnic Differences

1. Pick a general topic and three or four specific data sets relevant to it. (Take your theme from the classification in Appendix A or work out your own.)

2. Fetch the relevant X.a data sets. As you'll find explained in Appendix B, to fetch them off the second diskette in the "b" drive, you must tell CHIP the sets are in a library on a diskette in the "b" drive. I was interested in the ethnic difference in Ideal Number of Children, data set X.2, so I typed:

b:/lib/x.2a

3. Generate appropriate percentage tables, *d*'s and tele-graphs to illuminate ethnic differences (if any) in your variables.

Suggestion: Pick one of the seven major ethnic groups (not Othwite) as a focus both now and in later exercises throughout the book. If you do so, by the time you finish the book you will become an expert on this group.

To illustrate, I'll share what I found in the way of ethnic differences in fertility norms (data set X.2: "What do you think is the ideal number of children for a family to have?"). Figure 2-2 summarizes my cross-tab in a telephone pole graph.

Small families seem to be the norm: 57 percent of U.S. adults opt for two children or fewer (as explained in Appendix B, almost all respondents said "two"). But there is some spread around the norm. Figure 2-2 shows that:

- Blacks, especially the Southern-born, prefer larger families than do Whites. They are less likely to pick 0–2 and more likely to pick 4+.
- Among Whites, the White Northern Protestants seem the least "pro-natal." They are the highest group for 0–2 and the lowest for 4+.
- White Northern Catholics are relatively pro-natal—for Whites. They are the lowest White group on 0–2 and the highest White group for 4+.

So it looks as if Race (Black) and Religion (Roman Catholic) promote large family norms, while Regional and Fundamentalist-Other Protestant differences are not consistent. At the extremes, 62 percent of Southern-born Blacks say three or more children is ideal, in contrast to 37 percent of White Northern Other Protestants.

Now, go find your own tribal differences and similarities.

FIGURE 2-2

Ethnic Differences in Fertility Norms

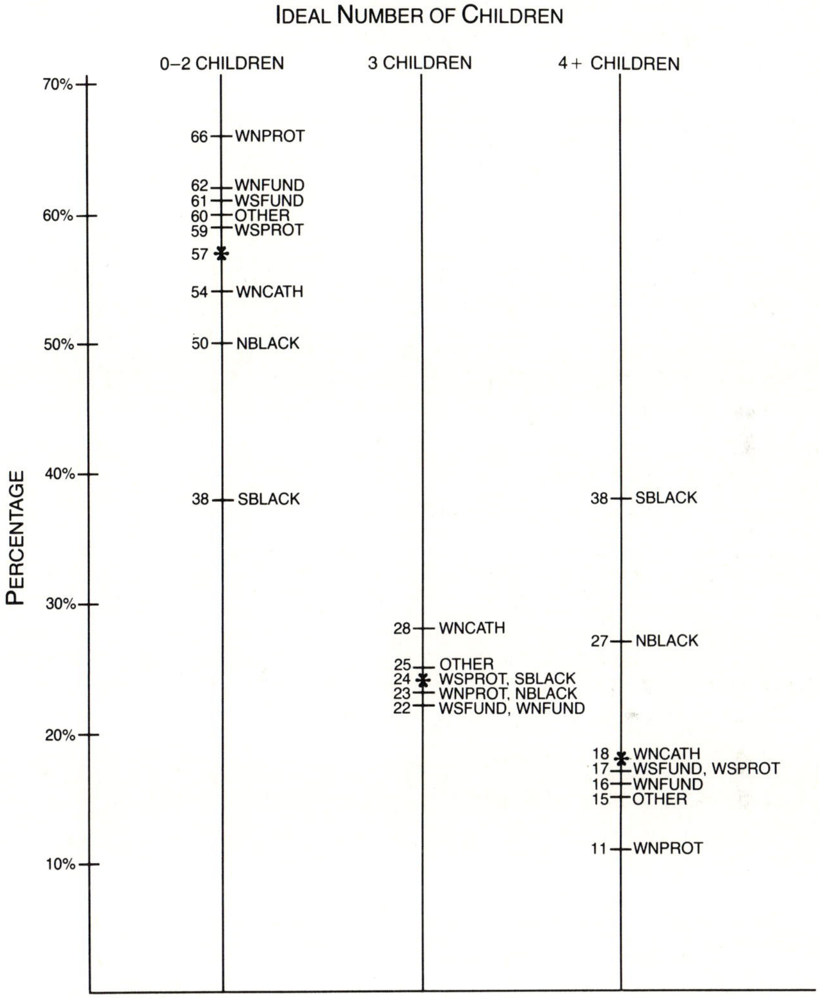

SOURCE: data set X.2a

SUMMARY

After completing Tasks 2-1 through 2-6 you should have a grasp of major ethnic configurations in modern America, their relative sizes, their non-U.S. origins, and some of the cultural and behavioral differences associated with ethnicity. You should also have some feel for the geographical patterning of ethnic differences.

On the technical side, you should now be able to use CHIP to (1) fetch a data set, (2) examine marginals, (3) run and interpret a bivariate percentage table and display it as a telephone pole graph, and (4) obtain and interpret bivariate percentage differences.

3
Socioeconomic Status

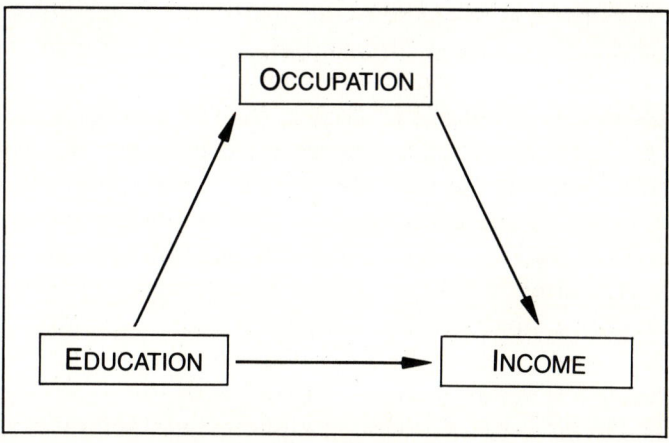

THE VERTICAL VARIABLES

Educational attainment (schooling), occupational prestige, and income comprise the second cluster of macro-level variables. Our hypothetical sociologist, if assigned to analyze the United States rather than Novelia, would probably conclude that these are the most important vertical variables.

As in the case of ethnicity, we shall look carefully at their relationships, but the perspective here is different. With ethnic variables we look at relationships to find important combinations; with the vertical variables we want to study how they affect each other. This perspective, known as the *Achievement Process* approach, is not the only way to go at things, but the dominance of the Achievement Process model is probably the most important intellectual development in sociology in the last two decades.

To gain perspective on this perspective, let's start with the "old fashioned" approach. In the old days we assumed there was some underlying vertical dimension called socioeconomic status (routinely referred to by the letters, SES) and that variables such as income, education, neighborhood, or how you got paid (salary vs. hourly wages) tapped the SES dimension in the same way individual items in an IQ test tap the underlying dimension of intelligence. (My first scientific publication—written with Joseph A. Kahl and published in 1955—put a dozen or so of these variables through the statistical sausage grinder to find out which were the "good" and which were the "bad" indicators.) But since there is no "true" measure of SES against which you can check the answers, this research ended up going around in circles.

Then in 1967, in perhaps the most influential sociological book of the twentieth century (*The American Occupational Structure.* John Wiley & Sons, Inc.), Peter M. Blau and Otis D. Duncan revolutionized things. The Blau-Duncan approach studies the same variables as its predecessors, but it views them differently. It sees SES variables as steps or stages in a life-cycle process; like this:

- First, we are born to parents with particular social characteristics that make us *advantaged* or *disadvantaged* from the beginning.

- Second, we trudge off to school, some of us staying there as long as twenty years, some departing well short of the standard twelve, with parental background playing a definite part in deciding who gets twenty and who gets less than twelve.
- Third, we go to work—the kind of job we get being influenced by our schooling and somewhat by our family background (how much so is treated in Chapter Six).
- Fourth, we get paid. The job is obviously a key factor in how much, but schooling plays a role, and some of us are suspicious that some people (not us, of course) are cashing in on our family backgrounds.

If we divide family background into ethnicity and family SES, the Blau-Duncan model allows us to elaborate Figure 1-1, as shown in Figure 3-1 below:

FIGURE 3-1
Macro-Model in Figure 1-1 Expanded

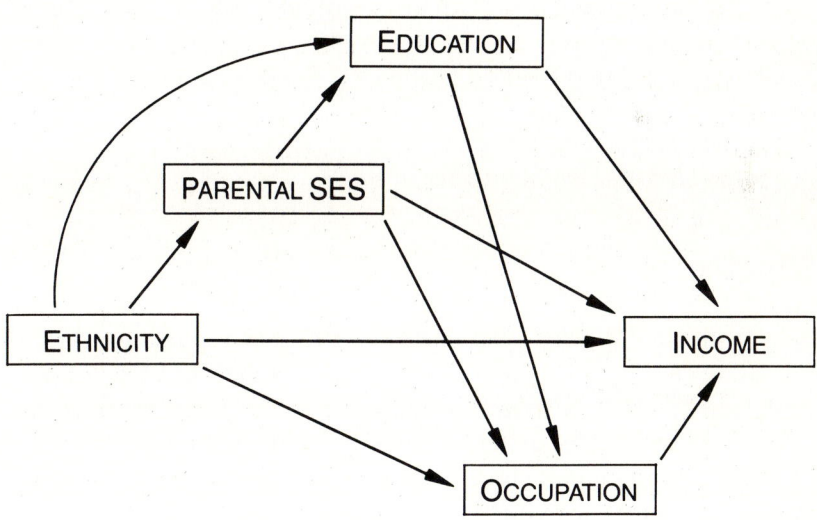

Figure 3-1 is certainly more complicated than the old approach of seeking the one perfect measure. But why is it better? Essentially, because it helps us frame causal questions. We can ask how

CHAPTER 3   SOCIOECONOMIC STATUS

variables earlier in the sequence influence variables "downstream." (Notice that Figure 3-1 is laid out so the earlier variables are toward the left, the downstream variables are to the right, and all arrows point from left to right.) And that, of course, is what you will do during this chapter.

This chapter focuses on the three variables of the SES triad; Chapters Six (Intergenerational Mobilities) and Seven (Trends in Inequality) expand the analysis to include family background. Chapter Three is organized as follows:

Part One: The Vertical Variables

- *Education:* the distribution of school years completed among U.S. adults . . . using the educational distribution to find the high and low hurdles.
- *Occupation:* the U.S. Census classification of occupations . . . sociological research on prestige, the HSR scale . . . does schooling pay off in better jobs?
- *Income:* objective and subjective measures.
- *All Three:* disentangling effects in a three-variable system . . . does schooling get you more money or "just" a better paying job? . . . an atheoretical but handy SES index.

Part Two: Some Pointed Questions about SES

- *Who are the Poor?*
- *Do Men and Women Differ in SES?*

Education

Of the 16,645 GSS respondents (1972–84) reporting years of schooling completed, 64 (0.4 percent) said "None," and 175 (1.1 percent) said "Twenty or more," leaving 98.5 percent strung out somewhere in between. The distribution of schooling years is far from the textbook normal curve since it contains big lumps at twelve (high school graduate), sixteen (college graduate) and eight (primary graduate).

Task 3-1 is designed to help you become familiar with the basic facts of the distribution.

THE VERTICAL VARIABLES

Task 3-1: The Distribution of Schooling

Data set 3.1 gives schooling, not in twenty individual years (which won't fit on the PC screen) but in seven clumps: 0–7, 8, 9–11, 12, 13–15, 16, and 17–20. They correspond to less than eighth grade, eighth grade, part high school, high school graduate, part college, bachelor's, and graduate school.

Use the Marginals command in CHIP to find the percentage distribution.

1. Can you divide the U.S. adult population into nearly equal thirds in terms of schooling?

2. Another way to look at these numbers is as a *cumulative* distribution—the percentage who have X or more years. This is not a formidable intellectual task, but ever helpful CHIP will do it for you with the Combine option in the Modify menu. It's a procedure you should know, so please use it to get your answers.
    a. What percentage of us have some graduate school? Easy, that's 6.1, as you can tell from the marginals.
    b. What percent have bachelor's degrees or more? That's the percentage with 16 plus the percentage with 17–20. If you Combine the two and run marginals, CHIP will give you the total (15 percent looks good to me).
    c. Now, use the same procedures to find the percentage who complete a year or more of college, are graduated from high school, and get beyond the eighth grade.

Task 3-2: Hurdle Heights

There is a third way to look at these numbers. We can ask, "Of the people who make it to level X, what percentage go on to the next level and what percentage stop there?" The Omit command in the Modify menu of CHIP works out these figures in a jiffy. If, for example, we Omit the 0–7 group, all the rest completed eight years or more. In the adjusted marginals the new proportion with eight years is the percentage who stopped there. They reached eighth grade but didn't get beyond it. One hundred minus that percentage is the proportion who went on.

1. Please work out the "stopped-at vs. went-beyond" percentages for the following: entered eighth grade; started high school; graduated from high school; started college; graduated from college.
2. If you think of schooling as a hurdle race, which hurdles seem especially high? Which seem low?

Task 3-3: Schooling and Vocabulary

Left-wing and right-wing critics of U.S. society share one opinion at least—cynicism about the effectiveness of our schools. In the absence of data, one might even argue that the years-completed measure is meaningless, since it lumps together schools of such varying quality and varying eras. The question of what schooling "really means" is difficult, and I don't purport to give any final answers here. However, since we will be using schooling over and over throughout the book, it may be a good idea to do a little checking.

The GSS is unique among national surveys in that it includes a vocabulary test. Respondents are asked to pick the correct synonyms for ten words taken from a standard test. Thus, they can have scores from zero to ten. The average correct is six. Data set 3.2 gives vocabulary scores for the seven schooling groups.

- Cross Tab Schooling (EDUC) and Vocabulary (WORDSUM). Are you surprised how (strongly or weakly) they are related?

Occupation

One's occupation is *kind of work* in contrast to *labor force status*—whether one is working full time, working part time, unemployed and seeking work, keeping house, going to school, or retired. Occupation is more complex than age, region, race, and the like, as can be seen by the set of questions required to get the data.

Here are the GSS occupation questions along with two verbatim answers from GSS respondents:

1. "What kind of work do you (did you) normally do? That is, what (is/was) your job called?"
   a. "Spooler"
   b. "Accounting"
2. "What (do/did) you actually do in that job? Tell me, what (are/were) some of your main duties?"
   a. "I take yarn off a bobbin and put it on a great big spool. This is mostly a hand operation."
   b. "I calculated the liabilities of life insurance companies according to the law, filed policies according to the law, answered complaints about life and health and accident policies."
3. "What kind of place (do/did) you work for?"
   a. "(name of firm) Woolen Mills"
   b. "State of (name of state)"
4. "What (do/did) they (make/do)?"
   a. "They make yarn used to knit or crochet sweaters, etc."
   b. "Handled the rules for all private insurance companies."

Questions three and four are used to code "industry," the character of the firm (agriculture, government, manufacturing, and communications, for example), and one and two tell us about occupation. (Frequently, information from the industry items helps to classify the occupation.) We will not deal much with industry in this book since there is little evidence it has much effect on one's life, once one allows for occupation.

Questions one and two are used to classify occupations. There are zillions of ways to do this. The GSS alone has eight. However, sociologically, two methods dominate: the Census classification into major occupational groups, and sociologists' *prestige scores*.

Census Occupations

The U.S. Census codes the answers into several hundred three-digit codes. For example:

Registered nurse	= 075
Bank teller	= 301

CHAPTER 3   SOCIOECONOMIC STATUS

Paper hanger	=512
Truck driver	=715
Midwife	=924

In our GSS example, respondent A was coded 672 (Spinners, Twisters, and Winders); respondent B was coded 034 (Actuaries). (For details on the fascinating craft of occupation coding, see Robert M. Hauser and David L. Featherman, *The Process of Stratification*, New York: Academic Press, 1977, pp. 61–80.)

In addition to the detailed, three-digit code, occupations are collected into nine major groups. (The classification was radically revised for the 1980 Census. For comparability with other sociological research we will stick with the more widely used 1970 version.)

As best I can tell, the Census has never given a formal definition of the groups, but the following labels and examples convey the flavor:

- *Professional, Technical, and Kindred* (require lengthy training, usually academic, and allow considerable latitude for judgment)
    Accountants, Chemists, Physicians, Dental hygienists, College teachers, Airplane pilots, Dancers
- *Managers and Administrators* (exercise authority inside organizations)
    Bank officers, Office managers, Purchasing agents, School administrators
- *Sales* (deal directly with customers)
    Insurance agents, Sales representatives, Sales clerks
- *Clerical* (symbol workers with little latitude)
    Bookkeepers, File clerks, Secretaries, Telephone operators
- *Craftsmen* ("skilled" workers who make or fix things)
    Bakers, Carpenters, Floor layers, Heat treaters, Shoe repairmen, Upholsterers
- *Operatives* ("semi-skilled" workers who tend machines)
    Assemblers, Garage workers, Bus drivers, Textile operatives
- *Laborers* ("unskilled" persons who work with their muscles)
    Carpenters' helpers, Fishermen, Garbage collectors, Vehicle washers
- *Service* (less skilled workers who help individual people or

THE VERTICAL VARIABLES

clean up after them)
Cleaners and Charwomen, Waiters, Nurses aides, Bootblacks, Ushers, Policemen, Firemen, Maids
- *Farm* (skilled, semi-skilled and less-skilled workers who grow food, tobacco, and cotton)
Farm owners and Tenants, Farm laborers

Table 3-1 shows how GSS respondents fit into the above categories.

TABLE 3-1
Major Census Groups

Census Group	In Labor Force		Total
	No	Yes	
Professional, Technical	11.2%	17.3%	15.2%
Managers and Administrators	6.5	11.1	9.5
Sales	5.2	6.0	5.7
Clerical	24.7	17.4	19.9
Craftsmen	8.8	14.3	12.4
Operatives	19.1	15.0	16.4
Laborers	2.8	4.1	3.6
Service	18.7	12.4	14.6
Farm	3.0	2.4	2.6
Total	100.0%	100.0%	99.9%
N	4,818	9,075	13,893
		NA =	1,332
			15,225

SOURCE: GSS 1972 to 1983

No = retired; in school; keeping house.
Yes = employed full time; employed part time; with a job but not at work because of illness, vacation or strike; unemployed; laid off.

Workers scatter *fairly* evenly across the nine categories, although the three largest (Clerical 19.9, Operatives 16.4, and Professional 15.2) comprise half the total (51.5 percent) while the three smallest (Farm 2.6, Laborers 3.6, and Sales 5.7) comprise just 11.9 percent.

Since the groups vary considerably in prestige or social standing (see below), it is conventional to group the categories in terms of "class" or "status."

TABLE 3-2
Data in Table 3-1 Collapsed (Total column)

Status Group

White-collar		50.3%
Upper (Professional, Managers)	24.7%	
Lower (Sales, Clerical)	25.6	
Blue-collar		47.0
Upper (Crafts)	12.4	
Lower (Operatives, Labor, Service)	34.6	
Farm		2.6
Total		99.9%

SOURCE: GSS 1972 to 1983

About half of us are white-collar workers, about half are blue-collar, only a handful are farm. White-collar jobs divide about fifty-fifty into upper and lower class, but among blue-collar workers, only a quarter are crafts workers.

Task 3-4: A Ladder of Occupations

Complete this task before reading the next section.

Listed below are fourteen occupations in alphabetical order:

    Coal Miner (MINER)
    College Professor (PROF)
    Fur Coat Tailor (TAILOR)
    Lawyer (LAWYER)
    Librarian (LIBRY)
    Mathematician (MATH)
    Secretary (SECY)
    Sewing Machine Operator (SEWMACH)
    Social Scientist (SOCSCI)
    Soda Fountain Clerk (SODA)
    Student Nurse (STUNURS)
    Superintendent of a Construction Job (SUPCON)
    Theater Usher (USHER)
    TV Repairman (TVREP)

1. Think of a "ladder of occupations" in terms of "your own personal opinion of the general standing that such a job has." If a job is at the very top, it has a score of one hundred. If a job is at the very bottom, it has a score of zero.

2. Please assign a score (no lower than zero, no higher than one hundred) for each of the fourteen jobs.
3. Jot your scores down and then read the next section.

Prestige (HSR Score)

Perhaps the only important "discovery" of modern sociological research is the remarkable agreement on occupational prestige. If you provide a list of occupations (architect, public school teacher, carpenter, automobile repairman, taxi driver, and so on) and ask *"your own personal opinion of the general standing that such a job has"* the results show remarkable (though not perfect) agreement:

- In studies from 1929 to date.
- Across fifty or more countries.
- Across occupations and class levels.
- Among men and women, young and old.

(There are hundreds of books and articles on this research. Two good places to start are Robert W. Hodge, Paul M. Siegel, and Peter H. Rossi (1964). Occupational prestige in the United States, 1925–63. *American Journal of Sociology 70,* 286–302; or Donald J. Treiman (1977). *Occupational prestige in comparative perspective.* New York: Academic Press.)

Since even such a seemingly ambiguous question as "general standing that such a job has" produces surprisingly reliable answers, sociologists have used the principle to develop scales to measure occupational prestige. The main problem is respondent fatigue—you simply can not ask people to rate hundreds of occupations—and a number of ingenious solutions have been invented. Among the better known scales are the *Duncan SEI* and the *Hodge-Siegel-Rossi (HSR).* The General Social Survey uses the HSR, so we will stick with that.

The HSR scale is based on national surveys in which respondents were asked to rate small batches of jobs by placing them on an arbitrary 0, 10, 20 . . . 100 scale. The batch results were combined to give ratings for each Census occupation. Consequently each GSS respondent with a "usual" job automatically *gets the HSR score associated with his or her Census job.* When interpreting HSR data,

TABLE 3-3
Illustrative HSR Scores

Score	Occupations	Score Group	Percent	Cumulative %
			Percentage of Respondents	
89–91 = 90	Member of the President's cabinet	85+	0	0
79–81 = 80	Ambassador to a foreign country, astronaut, nuclear physicist, physician, state governor	75–84	1.0	1.0
69–71 = 70	Aeronautical engineer, architect, clergyman, colonel in the army, department head in city government, electrical engineer, priest, psychologist	64–74	1.9	2.9
59–61 = 60	Advertising executive, building contractor, chiropractor, druggist, general manager of a telephone company branch office, grade school teacher, journalist, musician in a symphony orchestra, owner of a factory employing one hundred people, optician, religious education director, ship's captain, veterinarian	55–64	9.7	12.6
49–51 = 50	Bank teller, computer programmer, credit manager, merchandise buyer in a department store, musician, professional athlete, social worker, stock and bond salesman, supervisor on a construction job, undertaker	45–54	26.2	38.8

		Percentage of Respondents		
Score	Occupations	Score Group	Percent	Cumulative %
39–41 = 40	Enlisted man in the army, farm produce buyer, lens grinder, mail carrier, manager of a small store in a city, newspaper proofreader, owner of a filling station and garage, pattern maker, payroll clerk, photoengraver, photographer, plumber, powerlineman, railroad conductor, receptionist, tailor, telephone installer, telephone operator, traveling salesman for a wholesale concern, tree surgeon, typist, typesetter	35–44	22.4	61.2
29–31 = 30	Automobile worker, boilermaker, butcher, file clerk, house painter, loom fixer in a textile mill, lunch room operator, masseur, owner of a fixit shop, roofer, sales clerk in a store, sewing machine operator, shipping clerk, telegraph messenger, truck dispatcher, truck driver, used-car salesman	25–34	23.3	84.5
19–21 = 20	Bartender, beauty operator, butler, elevator operator, farm hand, filling station attendant, fruit packer in a cannery, janitor, restaurant waiter, stockroom attendant, taxi driver, waitress in a restaurant, worker in a dry-cleaning or laundry plant	15–24	14.3	98.8
9–11 = 10	Shoe shiner, soda jerk, street sweeper	Under 15	1.3	100.1
			N = 13,893	

SOURCE: GSS 1972 to 1983

remember that scores describe occupations in general, not the individual person. Some accountants are outstanding, some are way below par; but all GSS respondents whose job descriptions fit Census code 001, accountant, get an HSR score of 57.

In theory the HSR scores range from zero to one hundred, but the lowest that turns up in the GSS is 12 (cleaners and charwomen) and the highest is 82 (physicians). For respondents' fathers the lowest is 9, bootblack. The following tables give examples and show the distribution of GSS respondents. *You should study them carefully to get a feel for what HSR scores mean.*

TABLE 3-4
HSR Score Disbribution

	In Labor Force?		
Percentile	No	Yes	Both
Maximum = 100	82	82	82
75	46	50	48
67	45	47	46
Mean =	37	40	39
50 = Median	36	39	38
33	31	33	32
25	26	31	29
Minimum = 0	12	12	12
Standard Deviation	13.2	14.0	13.8
N	4,818	9,075	13,893

SOURCE: GSS 1972 to 1983

Percentiles are the percentages of people with scores at or below some value. Thus, for example, an HSR score of 46 means 67 percent of the people are equal to or below you. We can see from these percentiles that:

- Persons now in the labor force have slightly higher scores than others (mostly housewives and retired), but the difference is small.
- A score of 39 or higher puts you in the top half (a good number to remember).
- The middle half of the scores fall roughly in the 30–50 range.

- The groupings 12–32, 33–46, and 47–82 divide workers into roughly equal thirds.

Task 3-5: HSR Scores—Mine and Theirs

You now realize what was going on in Task 3-4. I asked you to be an HSR respondent for a subset of fifteen job titles from their study. Now you can see how your judgments compare with the overall results.

1. Start CHIP and retrieve the file HSR.1 (it is not a data file, but a trick to give you HSR scores). In the Command menu pick the **F2** (Marginals) option for frequencies. CHIP will print two digits for each job title. They are not its frequency; they are its HSR score. Jot down the seven scores and then do the same thing with the "data set" HSR.2.

2. You now have two HSR scores for each of the fourteen jobs, your own opinions and the U.S. national results. Lay out a sheet of graph paper with National as the horizontal axis, My Opinion as the vertical axis, and scales running from zero to one hundred. Now, plot each of the fourteen points on your graph.

3. What do you make of the results? What is the overall level of agreement or disagreement? Do you tend to "overrate," "underrate," or "neither?" Are there particular jobs where everyone is out of step except you?

Task 3-6: HSR vs. Census

Data set 3.3 gives the Census group and HSR score (in four categories) for 15, 272 respondents.

1. Find the HSR percentages for the eight Census groups. Assuming the HSR scores to be valid, do you think the Census groups are arranged in the correct order of prestige? If not, what is the correct order? Use Cat Order to experiment.

2. Use the Combine option in the Modify command to group the Census categories in the five status groups of Table 3-2. Cross Tab the collapsed measure against HSR.

CHAPTER 3 SOCIOECONOMIC STATUS

3. From all of this, what do you conclude about *white-collar vs. blue-collar* as an occupational prestige indicator?

4. Cross Tab Census and HSR but use % Down rather than % Across. In this book we will frequently divide HSR scores as 12–38 vs. 39–72 or 12–32, 33–46, and 47–82. What do these groupings "mean" in terms of Census categories?

Task 3-7: What Sorts of Jobs Get High Prestige?

By definition, high-prestige jobs are *better* than lower-prestige jobs, but research has not really nailed down the precise qualities that lead to high or low social standing. "Money," you say. We'll look at that in the next section. In the meantime, it is a good idea to look at some of the factors associated with HSR scores to get some feel for what this abstract number means in terms of what people do from nine to five. Data sets 3.4, 3.5, and 3.6 tell us about other variables that might be related to social standing.

1. Are higher-prestige jobs more secure and more in demand? Data set 3.4, based on full-time workers, allows you to Cross Tab HSR and Joblose ("Thinking about the next twelve months, how likely do you think it is you will lose your job or be laid off?" Unlikely = not at all likely; Likely = very likely, not too likely). Ditto for Jobfind ("About how easy would it be for you to find a job with another employer with approximately the same income and fringe benefits you have now?" Easy = very easy, somewhat easy; Not easy = not easy at all.)

2. What about HSR scores and the combination Unlikely + Easy? This will give you a chance to play with three variables. First, ask CHIP to Cross Tab Joblose by Jobfind. Then push **F4** (Control), **F1** (HSR), **F2** (Percent) and **F5** (% Subtable).

3. Are high-prestige jobs more satisfying? Cross Tab Satjob ("On the whole, how satisfied are you with the work you do?" Verysat = Very satisfied; Modrat = moderately satisfied; Dissat = a little dissatisfied, very dissatisfied) with HSR in data set 3.5, based on full-time workers.

THE VERTICAL VARIABLES

Sociological theorists have been intrigued with the proposition that authority and autonomy are related to job prestige. The nub of the idea is that the more control you have over other people and the less control others have over you, the better the job. Data set 3.6 contains two variables relevant to this proportion for persons with a current job. The two variables are constructed from GSS items about supervisors (in GSS codebook terms Wksub, Wksubs, Wksup, Wksups). The variable Peons is built from answers to "Do you supervise anyone who is directly responsible to you?" and "If yes, do any of those persons supervise anyone else?" None = supervises no one; 1Level = supervises someone who has no subordinates; More = supervises someone who supervises someone. The second variable, Bosses, is the reverse: Slfemp = self employed; Noboss = has no supervisor; 1Level = has an unsupervised supervisor; Layers = has a supervisor who has a supervisor.

4. Think of the two items (Peons and Bosses) as measures of the number of organizational echelons (layers) above and below the respondent. Do you think either, one, or both are related to prestige? Cross Tab them against HSR. Can you reconcile the results for the two measures of authority?

Task 3-8: Education and Job Prestige

I shall not demean either of us by asking you to guess whether or not there is an association between education (years of schooling) and occupational prestige. If college students (or their parents) didn't believe in this correlation, there would be more spaces available in campus parking lots. But the relationship is worth looking at in detail.

1. Data set 3.7 gives HSR scores for seven educational levels. Please plot Years-of-School against HSR scores. Plot one curve for HSR = 47–82, a second curve for HSR = 12–32. Put schooling from zero to twenty on the horizontal axis and HSR on the vertical axis (mean years of schooling for various EDUC groups are: 0–7 = 5.0 years; 9–11 = 10.1; 13–15 = 13.8; 17–20 = 18.2).

    Obviously the trend goes up. But is it a straight line or is it curved? What does that mean literally? What does it mean sociologically? What does this have to do with Task 3-2?

2. We now agree that education is strongly related to HSR scores. What does this mean sociologically? (*Hint:* what would the sociological consequences be if the correlation were to become much weaker . . . or much stronger?)

3. Is this correlation "fair" or "unfair" in terms of American values?

Income

The third and last of the secular trinity of socioeconomic standing is income, how much money you get. Income is very difficult to measure since it involves multiple sources (earnings, savings, investments, rents, welfare, and so on), although 91 percent of U.S. family income does come from earnings. If you are looking at data that spans several years, you also have to allow for inflation, and a realistic measure should take into consideration the number of earners and the number of mouths to feed. For sociological analysis, however, we will settle for something a lot less complicated, a single GSS item, called **FINRELA** in the codebook. It reads, "Compared with American families in general, would you say your family income is far below average, below average, average, above average, or far above average?"

Table 3-5 gives the marginals (GSS 1972–84):

TABLE 3-5

Perceived Income

Answer	Percent	
Far above average	1.5	18.7
Above average	17.2	
Average	53.5	
Below average	23.1	27.7
Far below average	4.6	
Total	99.9%	
$N = 16{,}542$		

SOURCE: GSS 1972 to 1984

Slightly more people see themselves below average (28 percent) than above average (19 percent); but the striking result is that half of us (54 percent) see our family incomes as average, neither above nor below the middle. (Interestingly, a 1984 British survey using a similar question came up with 3 percent above, 47 percent middle, and 50 percent below.)

Task 3-9: Income—*Objective* and *Subjective*

1. Data set 3.8 gives perceived income (FINRELA) and family income (Income82) for GSS 1982–84 in six categories (0–7K = $6,999 or less; 7–12K = $7,000 to $12,499; 12–20K = $12,500 to $19,999; 20–24K = $20,000 to $24,999; 25–35K = $25,000 to $34,999; 35K = $35,000 or more). Please Cross Tab them.
2. Are objective and subjective measures in good, fair, or poor agreement?
3. How large must family income be (in the early 1980s) before you think you are above average? How small must it be before you think you are below average?

Task 3-10: An SES Index

While we view education, occupation, and income as a sequence of variables rather than reflections of an underlying dimension, it is true that people tend to be high, middle, or low on several SES variables at the same time. Those who are at the top in education turn out disproportionately to be the same people who are at the top on HSR and income, and so on. Therefore, it is handy to have a single index combining the three. It can be useful in exploring data—if the SES index is related to something, we can come back to see which of the three is doing what; if it is unrelated, it is hardly worthwhile to look for educational, occupational, or income associations. I constructed such an index, dividing the population into low, medium, and high SES on the basis of the three variables.

Data set 3.10 contains the three SES variables (EDUC, HSR, and Income) and the three-category SES index constructed with

CHAPTER 3   SOCIOECONOMIC STATUS

them. These data are not limited to full-time workers. Nonworkers are coded in terms of the work they "normally do"; persons with no normal job (8 percent of the total; mostly older females) are given the HSR score of their spouse, where available.

1. Cross Tab the bivariates, SES/EDUC, SES/HSR, SES/Income. Inspect the data so you have some feel for the salient characteristics of those with high, medium, and low SES scores.

2. I purposely didn't tell you how I made up the index, because, now that we are working with multivariate (more than two variables) data sets, you should learn to operate the Control option in Cross Tab.

When it is outside the Whatif menu, CHIP tends to think of multivariate data as bivariate tables in a variety of "conditions." For example, CHIP will treat a Sex-Occupation-Income data set as two Occupation-by-Income tables (one for males, one for females), or several Sex-by-Income tables (one for each Occupation) or Sex-by-Occupation tables (among various Income categories). You can pick your two bivariates any way you like and then choose your conditional variables with the option **F4** Control.

Let's try an example first. Retrieve data set 3.9 and select Cross Tab. Cross Tab HSR (rows) and Income (columns). Then punch **F4** for Control and choose EDUC as your conditional or control variable. (That's the only possibility here, but with larger data sets you can choose from several or you can have multiple controls—the conditions will be combinations of categories from control variables.) Create three tables: HSR and Income among the 0–11s, HSR and Income among the 12s, and HSR among the 13–20s. CHIP will ask you the necessary questions on its own.

Now, your task: retrieve data set 3.10. Use SES as the dependent (column) variable, Income as the independent (row) variable, and HSR and EDUC as your controls. You will get nine conditional tables for Income and SES. Use them to figure out how I constructed the SES index. (*Note:* There is no trick here. The principle is very simple, so don't spend more than ten or fifteen minutes on it. This task is designed to get you used to the Control option.)

Task 3-11: Correlates of SES

In Task 2-6 you explored ethnic differences in selected behaviors and opinions. We are now ready to ask similar questions about SES differences.

- Cross Tab the variables you analyzed in Task 2-6 with SES as the independent variable, using data in the X.a series in CHIPLIB. How do SES differences seem to compare with ethnic differences? (We will follow this up in more detail in Chapter Four.)

Education, Occupation, and Income

So far—in Chapter Two and in our introduction to the SES variables—we have looked at single variables (marginals) and two-variable cross-tabulations, a sort of Noah's Ark, of sociological findings. But the central insight of modern sociological research is that a bivariate relationship is just the exposed part of the iceberg. Down below, where they are hard to see, third, fourth, fifth, ... nth variables may be operating to confuse things. Unless we control these outside factors, our bivariate findings may be quite misleading (famous example: a University of Michigan study found that tall workers earn more than short workers, which suggested all sorts of things about the psychology of work—until the researchers controlled for sex. When the outside variable, sex, was controlled, the difference went away. Why? Because male workers were taller and males earned more than females, regardless of height).

The SES triad is a nice example of the necessity for control.

Data set 3.9 includes Education, HSR scores, and Comparative Income. The cases are limited to full-time workers and households with only one earner. This ties the Income measure to the respondent rather than a spouse, parent, or roommate. We will use data set 3.9 to see how schooling and jobs influence income.

First, we must think a bit about *causal order*. You will remember that when studying two variables, we pick one as dependent (the item that forms the columns and produces the categories to be percentaged) and one as independent (the item that forms the rows and produces the categories we contrast). With three items, we think of them in a 1,2,3 order. Please skip back to the figure on the title page of Chapter Three. It shows the usual causal order for looking at the three SES variables. Variable *1* is Education, variable *2* is HSR, and variable *3* is Income. In other words, the author/artist assumed education influences occupation rather than vice versa, and education and occupation are more likely to influence income than vice versa.

So, we view income as dependent on education and occupational prestige: we will wish to see the income percentages for the various levels of schooling and prestige, not schooling percentages for levels of income and prestige.

Second, having chosen our dependent variable, we should look at the bivariate relationships; for example, Education and Income as displayed in Table 3-6, which gives data for full-time workers in single family households (data set 3.9).

TABLE 3-6
Education and Income

Education	Below	Income Average	Above	Total	(N)
13–20	22.6%	42.5%	35.0%	100.1%	(1,610)
12	31.0	54.6	14.4	100.0	(1,266)
0–11	41.2	50.1	8.9	100.2	(1,071)
Total	30.3%	48.4%	21.3%	100.0%	(3,947)
d (13–20 vs. 0–11)	−18.6	−7.6	+26.1		

SOURCE: data set 3.9

Do better-educated workers make more money? Of course they do. Table 3-6 shows the percentage Above increases with schooling while the percentage Below declines. Only 8.9 percent of the 0–11s are in the top income category, in contrast to 35.0 percent of the 13–20s. This gives a d of $35.0 - 8.9 = 26.1$ for 13–20 years vs. 0–11 for Above. "Why" do better-educated workers make more? This chapter suggests an obvious possibility: maybe the better educated earn more because they have better jobs and it is these jobs, not education itself, that make the difference. We certainly know that schooling has a powerful effect on occupational level (Task 3-8). According to the methods textbook, we should carry out an experiment in which workers in each educational group are given random

THE VERTICAL VARIABLES

jobs and their incomes compared. Not very practical, but CHIP has a branch that enables you to carry out a pseudo-experiment by adjusting the data so the education-occupation relationship disappears. Then you can look at the adjusted results to see if the education–income relationship changes.

For now, don't worry about the computer operations: we'll explain them later. Instead, assume the data have been adjusted so *each of the three schooling levels has the same HSR percentages*. That done, let's make a second Cross Tab of Education and Income, as shown in Table 3-7.

TABLE 3-7
Education and Income (Adjusted Data)

Education	Below	Income Average	Above	Total	(N)
13–20	27.3%	45.1%	27.6%	100.0%	(1,610)
12	30.2	54.8	15.0	100.0	(1,266)
0–11	34.4	50.7	14.9	100.0	(1,071)
Total	30.2%	49.7%	20.1%	100.0%	(3,947)
d (13–20 vs. 0–11)	−7.1	−5.6	+12.7		

SOURCE: data set 3.9

Compare Table 3-6 and 3-7, starting with the college group (13–20). In the adjusted data they have a lower percentage Above (27.6 percent vs. 35.0 percent) and a higher percentage Below (27.3 percent vs. 22.6 percent). If college-level workers had the same jobs as everyone else, their incomes would go down (in these data. In the real world such a profound social change would set off many powerful and unpredictable causal chains). The results for the least-educated (0–11) are the opposite: if they had the same HSR levels as everyone else, their incomes would go up. If the 13–20s' incomes go down and the 0–11s' incomes go up, this is the same as saying the relationship between education and income is reduced in the adjusted data. To see this, compare the d's in the bottom rows of Tables 3-6 and 3-7.

Skipping back and forth comparing several numbers from similar rows in different tables can be confusing. So, let's present the same information graphically (see Figure 3-2). In this figure, I display the percentages as six telephone poles (see discussion of

FIGURE 3-2

Data in Tables 3-6 and 3-7 as "Rickety Ladder" Graphs

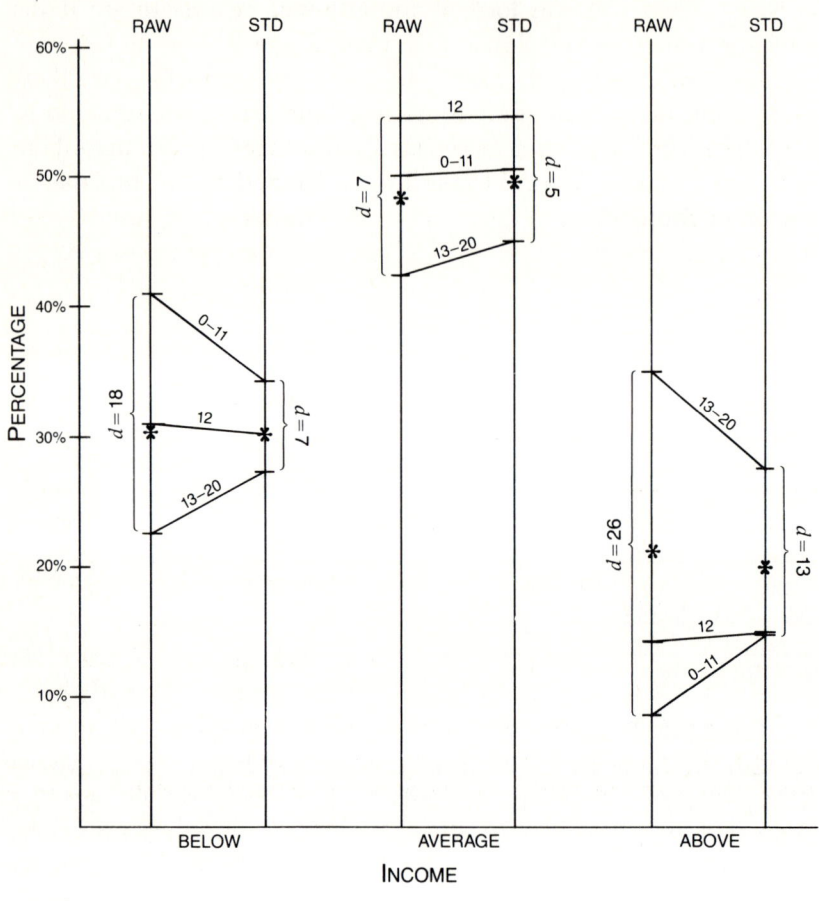

SOURCE: data set 3.9

Figure 2-1 in Chapter Two) with the raw and adjusted poles next to each other. (STD means *standardized*—the technical term for the data adjustment). Then I connected the raw and standardized percentages, producing three "rickety ladders" one for each category of the dependent variable.

The angles for the rungs of the rickety ladders tell the stories. For Below Average and Above Average the rungs form funnels—the results are closer in the adjusted data than in the raw data. Thus, education makes less difference after HSR has been standardized.

But the funnels never quite close: even after standardization there is a seven-point spread on Below and a thirteen-point spread on Above. Note, however, that for Above, the 0–11 and 12 rungs touch in the STD pole. Thus, the original difference between high school completers and dropouts in Above Average was solely due to differences in their HSR scores.

We can now state our major sociological conclusion: occupational prestige explains about half of the educational difference in incomes (compare the 7 and 18 for Below and the 13 and 26 for Above in Figure 3-2). The main reason better-educated workers have higher incomes is their HSR scores; but even after we adjust the data to remove this difference, the greater the schooling, the greater the income.

Whatif Procedures: To Standardize Three Variables

1. Choose your dependent variable and your two independent variables.

2. Use Cross Tab to get two bivariate tables, showing the relationships between each independent variable and the dependent variable.

3. Order your variables. The standardization procedure is extremely sensitive to assumptions about the causal order—what is dependent on what. The Info command (**F1** in the Command menu) will tell you the current order—CHIP assumes variables are dependent on those to their left. You want your dependent variable in position three and your independent variables in positions one and two.
    a. The concept behind this is a difficult one for most students. My experience has been that you should not drop everything and ponder its full meaning now. Learn to "do by rote" what has to be done, and after you have had practice applying the procedures to research problems, the concept will become clearer. (If you feel completely lost, I recommend reading James A. Davis (1985). *The logic of causal order.* Sage Publications.)
    b. Actually, it doesn't make any difference which *independent* variable is first and which is second, as

(continued)

long as the *dependent* variable is third. Thus, if variable *C* is dependent on variables *A* and *B*, the orders *A-B-C* and *B-A-C* will give you the same answers, provided you Change position two. Why? Because making *B* statistically independent of *A* is logically equivalent to making *A* independent of *B*.

4. Change variable *2*. Move to the Whatif branch (**F5** in Command) and choose **F1**, Change. CHIP will now print a list of your variables in causal order. Punch **F2** to tell the program you wish to adjust percentages for the second variable.

   The computer will now print the category names of your change variable (*2*). Answer each question by pushing the Enter key. That's all there is to it. The computer will now return to the Whatif menu. Punch the key for No More to return to the Command menu.

   What happened? Each category prompt asks for a variable *2* percentage. CHIP will then give that percentage to *each* category of variable *1*. For example, if Education is *1* and HSR is *2* and you type "50" when CHIP prints "12–32?", the computer will adjust the underlying frequencies so that 50 percent of the 0–11s are low HSR, 50 percent of the 12s are low HSR and 50 percent of the 13–20s are low HSR. You can reset to any percentages you wish, but when you always answer with Enters, CHIP uses the original marginals. That is, whenever you Change *2* by pushing Enter-Enter-Enter-Enter . . . CHIP proceeds to alter the frequencies in the data set so each and every category of variable *1* has the marginal distribution on *2*. This, of course eliminates any correlation between *1* and *2*. Categories of *1* no longer differ in the slightest on any of the percentages for *2*.

   Whatif, like many simple but powerful tools, takes a little getting used to. If you are interested in further details, see Appendix D. But the procedures are not complicated at all. They boil down to this: If you Change variable *2* with Enter-Enter-Enter . . . you create a data set where variables *1* and *2* are unrelated but each has the original marginals.

5. Cross Tab *2* by *1* to make sure the adjustment "worked."

(continued)

THE VERTICAL VARIABLES

> 6. Now repeat the Cross Tabs in step two on the adjusted data.
>
> 7. Present your results in a rickety ladder graph.
>
> *Remember:* If you change variable *2* with Enter-Enter-Enter . . . you alter the data set so that each category of variable *1* has the marginal percentages for variable *2* and vice versa.

Task 3-12: Occupational Prestige and Income

In Tables 3-6 and 3-7 and Figure 3-2, I worked out the raw and adjusted effects of Education on Income. What about HSR? Do higher-prestige jobs bring in more money? Is any of this because workers at different job levels have different formal credentials (educations)?

1. Work out the seven Whatif steps with data set 3.9 to get your answer.

2. When you are doing step six, Cross Tab Education and Income to see whether we agree on the numbers.

3. On the basis of these results, return to the arrow diagram at the beginning of this chapter and modify it by thickening the arrows for any relationship that seems particularly strong and, if necessary, removing any arrow that seems weak or negligible.

4. Is the system you drew "fair"? If not, what would a fair system look like? What does your arrow system suggest about "the American dream," "equal opportunity," "affirmative action"? Would the system be fairer if some or all of these selections were made by "lottery"?

Task 3-13: Which SES Variables Do What?

Pick a pair of SES variables (Education and Occupation, Education and Income, or Occupation and Income) and compare

CHAPTER 3   SOCIOECONOMIC STATUS

their impact on some dependent variable where SES makes a difference, using the Whatif procedures explained in this chapter.

GENDER, SES, AND POVERTY

SES, and social differences in SES, show up throughout the rest of the book; but two facets, *Gender* and *Poverty,* merit special attention here because you need to know the basic facts about these highly charged issues before considering other correlates.

Do the Sexes Differ in SES?

In Chapter Two (Ethnicity) we ignored differences between males and females. Since every ethnic group—White, Black, Protestant, Jewish, Northern, Southern—has about equal proportions of boy babies and girls babies, sex and ethnicity are uncorrelated. But when we shift from the ascribed ethnic variables to the achievement triad there are no biological dice to guarantee fifty-fifty splits on schooling, jobs, and incomes.

Only the most old-fashioned male chauvinists or the most avant-garde feminists would argue that one sex is generally superior to the other, but the Achievement Process model of SES suggests we might find differences on some SES variables and not others. So, let us consider gender differences in the SES triad.

Task 3-14: Gender and SES

1. Which sex is better educated? Jot down your prediction and then Cross Tab Sex and Education in data set 3.1.

2. Are sex differences in education changing? Data set 3.11 gives some clues. The variable Birthyr divides the respondents into seven birth cohorts: *1* = 1883–1903; *2* = 1904–1913; *3* = 1914–1923; *4* = 1924–1933; *5* = 1934–1943; *6* = 1944–1953; *7* = 1954–1964. The data are limited to persons twenty-five and older. If you Cross Tab Sex and Education and use the Control option for Birthyr, you can compare sex differentials in schooling for Americans born at various times during the first

half of this century. Are the gaps closing, opening, or staying about the same? (*Suggestion:* calculate the *d*'s for Sex and Education in each cohort group and plot the results on a graph in which Year is the horizontal axis and *d* the vertical one, one curve for each schooling category.)

CHIP can calculate all those *d*'s for you: Cross Tab (**F4**) Sex and Education (**F2, F3**), Control (**F4**) Birthyr (**F1**), and calculate the percentage differences (**F2, F4, F2, F3, F1**). After a pause, CHIP will print a partial *d* (weighted average of the *d*'s in various cohorts). Ignore the partial *d*. CHIP will then ask you, "**Subtables**?" Choose **Yes** (**F1**) and the program will print out Sex by Education *d*'s for each cohort.

Omit 0–11 years of schooling and repeat the analysis. Why? See Task 3-2.

3. Jobs and Gender. Do men and women have the same kinds of jobs? Which sex has the better jobs?
   a. Cross Tab Census by Sex in data set 3.3 (use % Down and % Diff). Which Census occupation groups show the highest percentages of males? The highest percentage of females? The least sex difference?
   b. Now Cross Tab HSR by Sex in the same data set. Are you impressed by how big the differences are or how small they are?
   c. How can you reconcile the two results?

4. Sex and Earnings. Data set 3.12 gives the annual earnings (less than $12,500, $12,500–$22,499, $22,500 or more) for full-time workers in GSS 1982–84 by Education, HSR, and Sex.
   a. Cross Tab Sex and Earnings (Earns). Are you impressed by how big the differences are or how small they are?
   b. Do the prior variables Education and HSR account for the sex difference in earnings? Can we "justify" the earnings gap on the basis of training or differential social value of the jobs? Well, Whatif men and women had exactly the same schooling and HSR scores? If it isn't fresh in your mind, review the discussion of standardization in Task 3-2. Then Reorder your data so Sex = *1*, Education = *2*, HSR = *3*, Earns = *4*, and Cohort = *5*; apply the change command and Enter-Enter-Enter to *2*; do the same to *3*. You now have a data set where males and females have

identical schooling percentages and where males and females in each educational category have the same HSR percentages. Now, leave the Whatif menu and Cross Tab Sex and Earns in the adjusted data.

c. How much of the sex differential in earnings in the early 1980s is justifiable on the basis of education and occupational level?

d. Task 3-14.3 showed us that occupational prestige and Census occupation group, while closely related, are not exactly the same. Men and women show strong job differences that are not captured by the notion of level ("general standing"). With that in mind, let's turn to data set 3.12a. It is exactly like data set 3.12 except that Census occupation group has been inserted as the third variable. Repeat your multivariate analysis of Sex, Education, Occupation, and Earnings, substituting Census Occupation for HSR.

5. Given all of the above, do you think that the sexes differ in SES?

Standardization in Larger Systems

The exercise you just completed had a dependent variable, Earns, preceded by three independent variables, Sex, Education, and HSR. Thus, the situation is a bit more complicated than Task 3-10, where you only had two independent variables. Figure 3-3 may help you see the common principle in the two exercises, as well as show you how to apply it later in this book.

Figure 3-3 shows a hypothetical, four-variable system, with arrows indicating relationships between pairs of variables.

The key is this: when you apply the change command to any variable, the data are adjusted so that that variable becomes statistically independent of any and all preceding variables (because it creates a data set where all categories and combinations of categories of the preceding variables have the same percentages for the changed variable).

(continued)

FIGURE 3-3

The Logic of Standardization as Control

A. The raw data

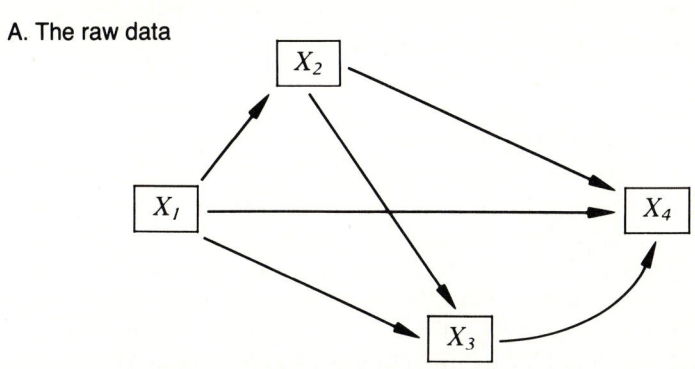

B. After Change 2

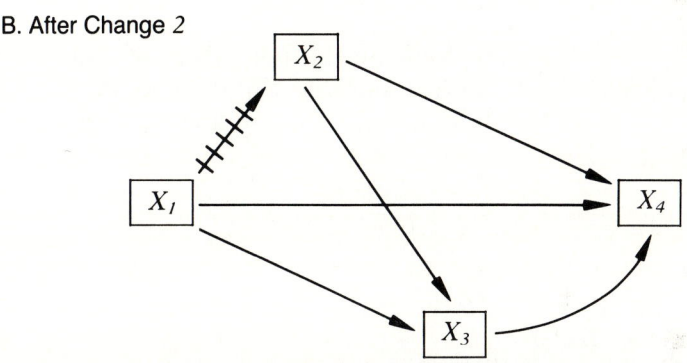

C. After Change 3

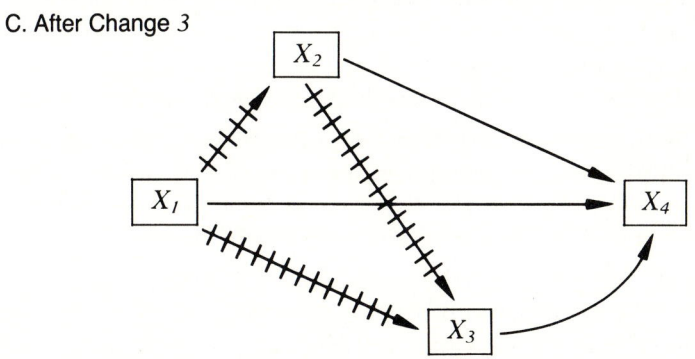

Note: ┼┼┼┼┼┼► = statistical association set to zero by the adjustment.

> Thus, in Figure 3-3b we see that after Changing X_2, variables X_1 and X_2 are no longer related. That's exactly what we did when X_1 was Education, X_2 HSR, and X_3 Income. But look at X_4 in Figure 3-3b. Since X_1 and X_2 are still related to X_3 it is possible that X_3 is distorting things—perhaps X_1 and X_2 only appear to affect X_4 because they are related to X_3.
>
> If, however, we also change X_3 (Figure 3-3c), X_1, X_2 and X_3 are now totally independent of each other. Any association between one of them and X_4 can not be produced by their associations with each other.
>
> And that is what I asked you to do in the last exercise, Change X_2 and then Change X_3 to produce a data set in which Gender was unrelated to Education or HSR, where men and women had the same educations and the same occupational prestige.
>
> ***General Rule:*** **To look at the net effect of independent variables on dependent variable X_N, Change X_2, X_3, X_4 ... X_{N-1} and Cross Tab the predictors against X_N in the adjusted data.**

Who Are The (Semi) Poor?

Obviously, the distinguishing characteristic of poor people is low income. The proposition almost sounds like a cynical joke, yet the question of where to draw the poverty line is extremely important in terms of national policies, and extremely difficult in terms of social science.

The federal government has a formula which is the most common, objective yardstick. In a nutshell, since research shows that families spend about one-third of their income on food, the basic poverty level is three times the cost of purchasing a nutritionally adequate diet. This basic number is adjusted for family size and changes in the cost of living. In 1983, the poverty line was about $5,000 per year for a single individual, about $6,500 for a couple, and about $10,000 for a family of four. By this yardstick about 12 to 15 percent of the U.S. population were below poverty level in the GSS years 1972 to 1984.

Task 3-15: Who Are The (Semi) Poor?

Are most poor people:

- Elderly?
- Blacks?
- Widows and divorcees?
- Poorly educated?
- Rural Southerners?
- Residents of the "inner city"?

All of these? Some of these? Nobody alleges that middle-aged, White, college graduate males living in the suburbs are mired in poverty, but beyond that speculation and stereotypes run wild.

The GSS does not purport to give the federal definition of poverty (this would require much more detailed income data than the GSS collects), but it can give us a picture of the 27 percent of U.S. adults who say their family incomes are below average. This semi-poverty measure gives about twice the proportion of poor as the government definition, but I feel confident it points in the same directions in terms of social differences. And should the two disagree, it might not be amiss to know how property is defined *subjectively* as well as *objectively*.

Data set 3.13 comprises seven dichotomized independent variables and the dependent dichotomy (Below Average vs. Average or Above Average for Family Income). The independent variables are:

- Age (18–64 vs. 65–89)
- Race (Black vs. White)
- Sex (Male vs. Female)
- Education (0–11 vs. 12–20)
- Region (South vs. Other)
- Marital Status (Separated, Divorced, Widowed vs. Married, Single–Never Married)
- City (Central City in metropolitan area of 250,000 or more vs. All Other vs. Open Country or City under 2,500)

1. Cross Tab each of these predictors against Semi-poverty. Which are the strongest and weakest predictors (use % Diff)?
2. Which *combinations of categories* from two or three variables do the best job of spotting groups with high rates of poverty?

CHAPTER 3 SOCIOECONOMIC STATUS

3. Use Omit in the Modify menu to exclude the Average and Above, that is, limit your data to the semi-poor. Use All Margs and if you wish details, Cross Tab with Control and % Total to describe the social composition of the semi-poor in contemporary America.

4. Assuming the poor are concentrated in the same categories as the semi-poor, what do these findings suggest about social policies for dealing with poverty?

SUMMARY

After reading this chapter and doing the exercises you should:

1. know how today's adult population is divided in terms of schooling and where the key *hurdles* occur in the educational sorting process.

2. know how the HSR prestige scale was constructed. (It might be handy to memorize some yardstick scores: 82 for Physician, 9 for Bootblacks, 39 for the average, 30 to 50 for the middle half.)

3. feel comfortable thinking of the three SES variables in terms of the arrow diagram at the beginning of this chapter.

4. be able to use the association between education and occupational prestige as a *landmark* for evaluating other associations.

5. be able to back up your discussions of sex discrimination and poverty with the basic facts.

On the technical side you should now be able to:

1. run and interpret percentage tables with control conditions.

2. standardize two or more independent variables with Whatif to get at their net associations with a dependent variable.

3. present standardization problems as a "rickety ladder" graph and interpret the slopes of the "rungs."

4
Culture, Class, and Behavior

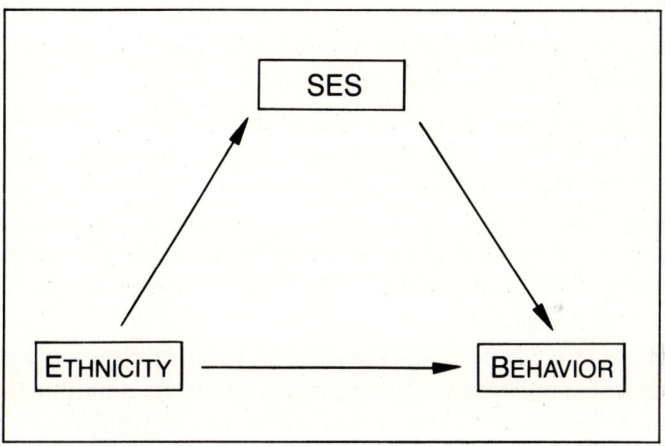

CHAPTER 4   CULTURE, CLASS, AND BEHAVIOR

THE RESEARCH PROBLEM

We have now disassembled and inspected the working parts for two clusters of variables, Ethnicity (Chapter Two) and SES (Chapter Three). Interesting (at least I think so), but something is lacking. We have yet to show what happens when both sets of variables operate together. This chapter, the third and final section on social structure, deals with the central question of the book: do horizontal and vertical social differences make any differences?

Obviously, it is nicer to be in the "upper crust" than the "bottom of the barrel," but does this mean that socioeconomic status shapes our attitudes, opinions, politics, leisure, family life, and so on, to the point that people at different social levels are seen as being fundamentally different? Or is it the case that we are all pretty much alike, only some of us have cushier niches than others? Social stereotypes such as "hard hat mentality," "middle-class conformity," and "noveau riche taste" suggest that class shapes American lives profoundly. Yet one may argue that our national system of education, the powerful impact of mass media, and the American strain of egalitarianism work the other way, reducing and eliminating SES differences. In a nation where 90 percent of the families own color televisions, one would not be astounded to find class levels surprisingly undifferentiated.

Exactly the same questions apply to ethnicity. If you knew about America only through its fiction, you might conclude that the North and South were completely different cultures. Both Protestants and Catholics would be astounded if told their religions had little impact outside narrowly devotional areas. And every college campus with more than a handful of minority students experiences continual questioning of what it means to be Black. Yet, the Civil War was over a century ago; you can't tell what region you are in from the speech of local radio announcers; Catholics, Protestants, and Jews watch the same network news, and a number of sociologists argue that class differences among the Black population are beginning to outweigh racial differences per se. So, for ethnicity, as for SES, it is not obvious whether we should expect large, medium, or small differences in impact.

Task 4-1: Theorizing

Give your predictions for the following. Across a wide variety of matters (attitudes, opinions, family life and politics):

- Do macro-variables generally produce small d's (say, less than five), medium ones (say, five to twenty-five), or large differences between the highest and lowest groups?
- Which cluster produces the bigger differences, Ethnicity or SES, or neither?
- Which produces the biggest differences—Race, Region, or Religion?
- Which produces the biggest differences—Education, Occupation or Income?
- If more than one macro-variable is "working," about how large (in percentage points) is the typical gap between the joint categories with the highest and lowest percentages? (For example, if both Race and SES affect the dependent variables, what is the "point spread" between high SES Whites and low SES Blacks?)

ETHNICITY AND SES

Ethnic differences in SES complicate matters. While I have stressed the theoretical distinctions between the two clusters of variables, this does not guarantee that each ethnic group has the same percentages in high, medium, and low SES categories.

Task 4-2: Ethnic Differences in SES

Data set X.8a allows you to Cross Tab Ethtype against the SES index explained in Chapter Three. (The dependent variable in X.8a is Household Size. There are no "no answer" cases on this variable because it was used by NORC before the interview to select cases. So it is a good data set for looking at relations among the independent variables.)

1. Cross Tab the two variables and display your results as a tele-graph.

2. Are there any groups that are consistently high on high SES and low on low SES? Any that show the opposite pattern?
3. Do these data seem to support or refute social stereotypes?

Keep these results for reference. (For a much more detailed discussion of this topic see Chapter Seven.)

———

Task 4-2 tells us much about equality and inequality in the contemporary United States. It also raises a technical issue that is central to this chapter. In exploring our problem—the relative strength of the two structural clusters—we clearly have to allow for their correlation. As in the SES triad (education, occupation, and income) we must view the data as a multivariate system, not a pair of bivariate cross-tabs. The standardization techniques explained in Chapter Three are designed exactly for that. As you explore the correlates you should look at the effects before and after giving each ethnic group the same SES levels. You will use the procedures explained in Chapter Three (Whatif Procedures: To Standardize Three Variables), but since these techniques are probably fairly new to you, in the next section, I will work through one dependent variable—Ideal Number of Children—to give you an example.

ETHNICITY, SES, AND FERTILITY NORMS

The social norm of the two-child family (a boy named Dick and a girl named Jane—the dog, Spot, is optional) is certainly the most common, as shown in Table 4-1.

Half of us (52.5 percent) give the standard answer "two," but the figures trail up so that a total of 20 percent say four or more. Figure 2-2 in Chapter Two revealed some ethnic variation in this norm: White Northern Protestants strongly endorse the small-family norm (66 percent chose 0–2), while among Southern Blacks this is a minority position (38 percent).

But what about SES? Does it affect these norms? Two contradictory themes run through the literature: high SES people can afford more children, so they tend to be pro-natal. Conversely, however, some argue that high SES people got where they got by inhibiting their reproductive proclivities, and so, the higher the SES, the lower the fertility norm. Which hypothesis seems right to you?

ETHNICITY, SES, AND FERTILITY NORMS

TABLE 4-1

Distribution of Answers to "Ideal number of children for a family to have?"

Answer	Percent
7+	0.6
6	1.2
5	2.2
4	15.5
3	24.5
2	52.5
1	2.2
0	1.4
Total	100.1
N = 11,177	

SOURCE: GSS 1972 to 1984

Also, if you compare Figure 2-2 with your tele-graph for SES, you will note that higher fertility groups tend to be lower on SES. What does that imply about the results when we adjust the data to eliminate ethnic differences in SES? If SES raises fertility norms, our ethnic differences will become even stronger (the ethnic differences were dampened by SES influences operating in the opposite direction). If SES inhibits fertility norms, it is possible that the ethnic differences will decline or even go away (if the "real reason" for the differences is SES).

Data set X.2a contains Ethtype, the SES index, and Ideal Number of Children *(Chldidel)*. Following my own advice (Chapter Three—Whatif Procedures: To Standardize Three Variables), I

- Cross Tabbed SES and Chldidel, Ethtype and Chldidel.
- Reordered the system, putting Ethtype first, SES second, and Chldidel third.
- Used Change in Whatif to give each ethnic group the same (marginal) distribution by typing Enter-Enter-Enter.
- Repeated step 1 and
- Displayed the results in the two rickety ladder graphs shown in Figure 4-1 (to keep things simple I used Combine to divide answers into 0–2 vs. 3 or more).

FIGURE 4-1
Ethtype and SES Differences

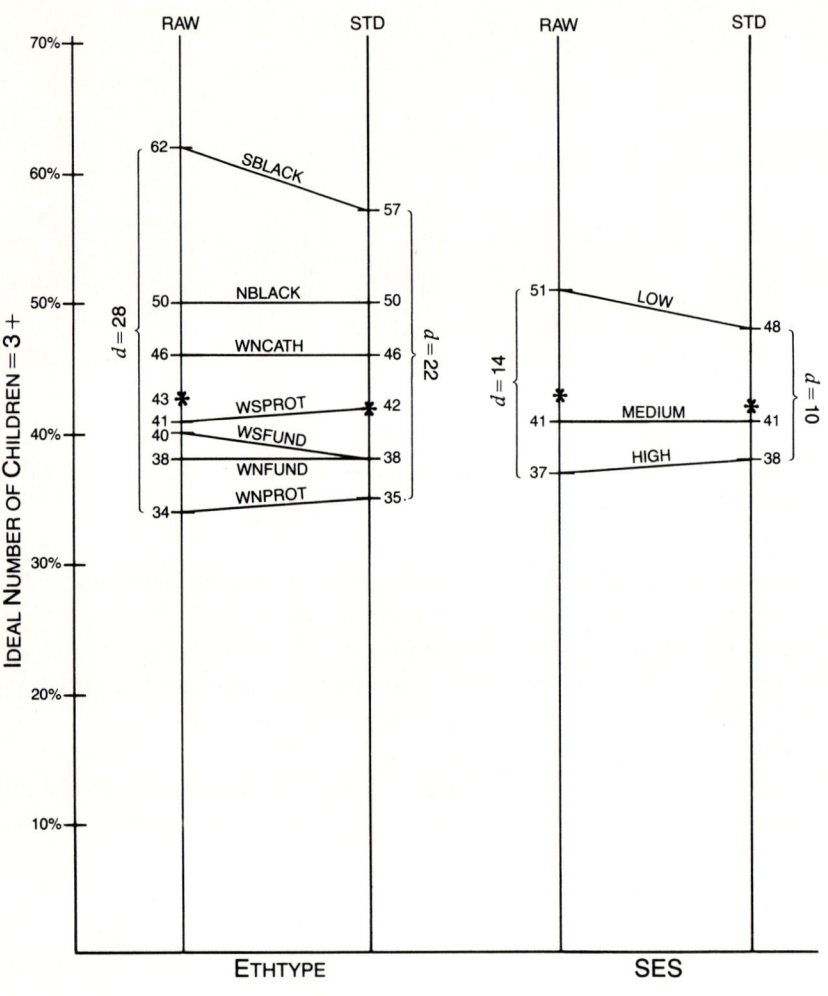

SOURCE: data set X.20

The left-hand ladder (ethnicity) doesn't look very rickety. Most of the rungs are parallel. Ethnic groups have pretty much the same positions before and after standardization. Southern-reared Blacks do drop five points (part of their very high pro-natalism was due to SES), but that's about it. Our original inference—Blacks and White

Northern Catholics are more favorable to big families, White Northern Protestants are less favorable—holds true when SES is controlled.

Score one for a *cultural* as opposed to a *class* perspective.

The right-hand ladder in Figure 4-1 shows SES differences, before and after controlling for ethnicity. The relationship is negative. The higher the SES score, the lower the fertility norm. There is a bit of funnelling (the percentage of low SES respondents opting for three or more children drops from fifty-one to forty-eight when ethnicity is controlled), but not much.

Score one for the *class* perspective.

So, it seems subculture (race, religion) *and* SES influence our notions of desirable family size. We can see both at work with a new graph, a *fishnet*. While tele-graphs display bivariate relations and rickety ladders display the raw and net effects of particular variables, fishnets help us see the simultaneous contributions of two independent variables to a dependent percentage. The rules for constructing a fishnet graph are presented in the box below.

---

1. Pick a single percentage to summarize the dependent variable (combining Chldidel as 0–2 vs. 3 or more for example).
2. Cross Tab one of your independents against the dependent, using the other as a control. It doesn't make any difference which is the control, but the output is tidier if you use the one with fewer categories. (With a three-variable problem, it doesn't make any difference whether you have standardized or not. Appendix D explains why.)
3. Lay out a sheet of graph paper with a vertical axis running from 0 percent up to some number higher than the largest dependent percentage in your cross-tab.
4. Pick one of your independents as telephone poles (but don't draw the poles). For the other, pick a different

(continued)

graphic character (dots, asterisks, boxes, or circles) to represent each category.

5. Plot the percentages at appropriate heights on the (invisible) telephone poles.

6. Connect symbols from pole to pole with solid lines; connect the highest and lowest symbol on each pole with a broken line.

The solid lines tell us the statistical effects of the pole variable for each category of the symbol variable; the broken lines tell us the effect of the symbol variable for each category of the pole variable. The horizontal and vertical lines meeting at the dots look like a fishnet—or enough so that you will remember the concept.

Figure 4-2 shows a fishnet graph for ethnicity, SES, and fertility norms (I combined all the White Protestants since their internal differences aren't very interesting). Table 4-2 shows the original table for Figure 4-2.

TABLE 4-2

Influences on "Ideal Number of Children"

SES	Ethnic Type*	Ideal 0–2	3plus	Total %	(N)
High	White North Catholic	52.1%	47.9%	100.0	(430)
	White Protestant	68.1%	31.9%	100.0	(956)
	Black	55.2%	44.8%	100.0	(96)
Middle	White North Catholic	55.4%	44.6%	100.0	(1,237)
	White Protestant	63.4%	36.6%	100.0	(2,301)
	Black	46.7%	53.3%	100.0	(467)
Low	White North Catholic	51.9%	48.1%	100.0	(449)
	White Protestant	54.7%	45.3%	100.0	(989)
	Black	34.7%	65.3%	100.0	(479)

SOURCE: data set X.2a
*Othwite (N = 776) excluded.

In general, of course, the graph confirms our conclusion that both ethnicity and SES produce differences in fertility norms, but we see something new here. For Blacks and White Protestants the solid lines slope down—the higher the SES, the smaller the percentage recommending big families. But for Catholics (White,

FIGURE 4-2

Influences on Ideal Number of Children

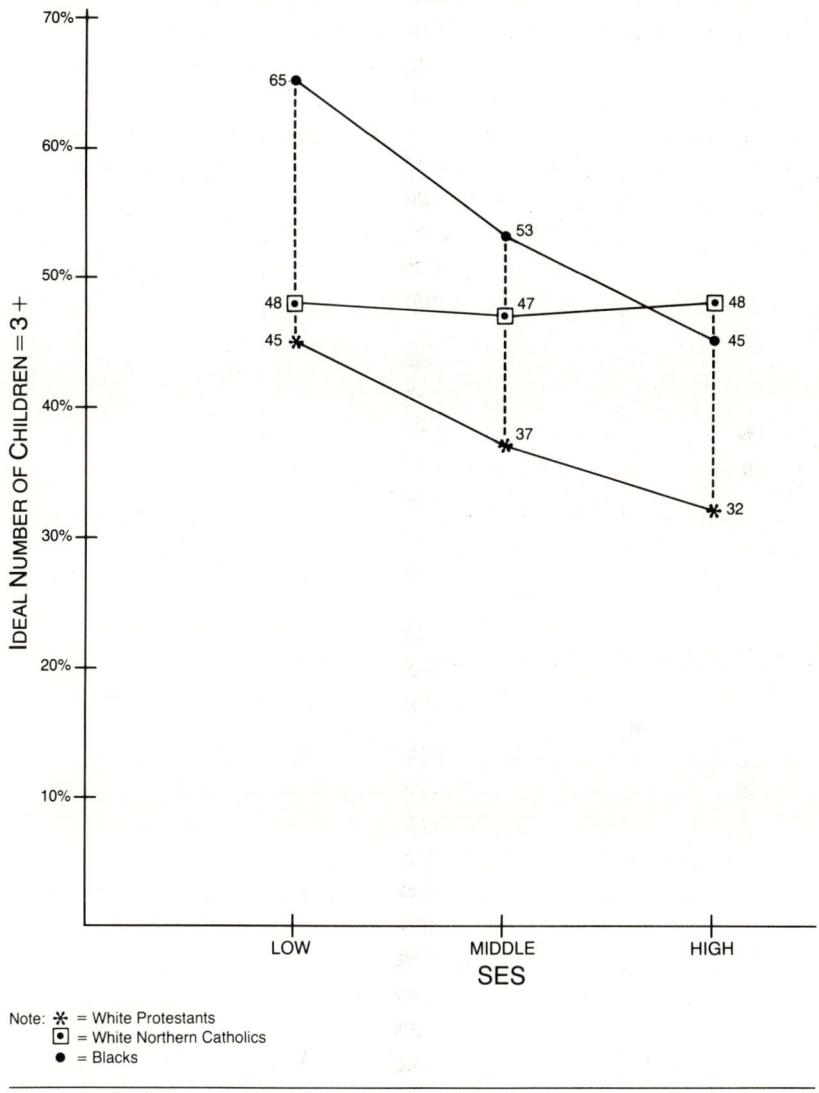

Note: ✳ = White Protestants
⊡ = White Northern Catholics
● = Blacks

SOURCE: data set X.20

Northern ones) there is no slope. SES doesn't seem to make any difference among Catholics: about 48 percent of them prefer big families at every SES level. As a result, the purely ethnic differences depend on what SES level and ethnic group you have in mind. At every SES level, Blacks are higher than White Protestants; but while Catholics are the most pro-natal among high SES White Americans, they are little different from White Protestants among the low SES.

At the extremes, 65 percent of low SES Blacks recommend three or more children in contrast to 32 percent of high SES White Protestants.

Fishnets not only point up the cumulative impact of the independent variables (for example, 65 percent vs. 32 percent) they also draw our attention to what statisticians call *interactions*—situations where the effect of one independent variable differs according to the category of the other.

We have learned that high SES Americans prefer smaller families, but since SES is a grab bag, not a meaningful variable, we can only learn more by dissecting it. In the CHIPLIB data sets the "b" series of tables contains the SES constitutents: Education, Occupation, and Income. So, data set X.2b helps us see what is going on with SES.

Following the advice in the section on "Standardization in Larger Systems" (Chapter Three), I

- Cross Tabbed each of the three SES variables against Chldidel (dichotomized again as 0–2 vs. 3 or more)
- Reordered the system to put Education first, HSR second, Income third, and Chldidel fourth
- Changed HSR and then Income to their marginals by two sets of Enter-Enter-Enters, producing a data set in which the three SES variables are statistically unrelated.
- Repeated step one and
- Produced the rickety ladders shown in Figure 4-3.

I see two funnels and one non-rickety ladder. For Schooling, the graph at the left, there is a definite effect on fertility norms—the higher the schooling the smaller the family-size norm, and I'd say the rungs are almost parallel. That is, the negative relationship between Education and fertility norm is not influenced by the other two SES variables. For the HSR and Income, however, the original differences (ten points for HSR, six for Income) almost disappear in the adjusted data. That is, in the standardized data, Occupational Prestige and Income don't make any difference. My conclusion:

FIGURE 4-3
SES in Detail

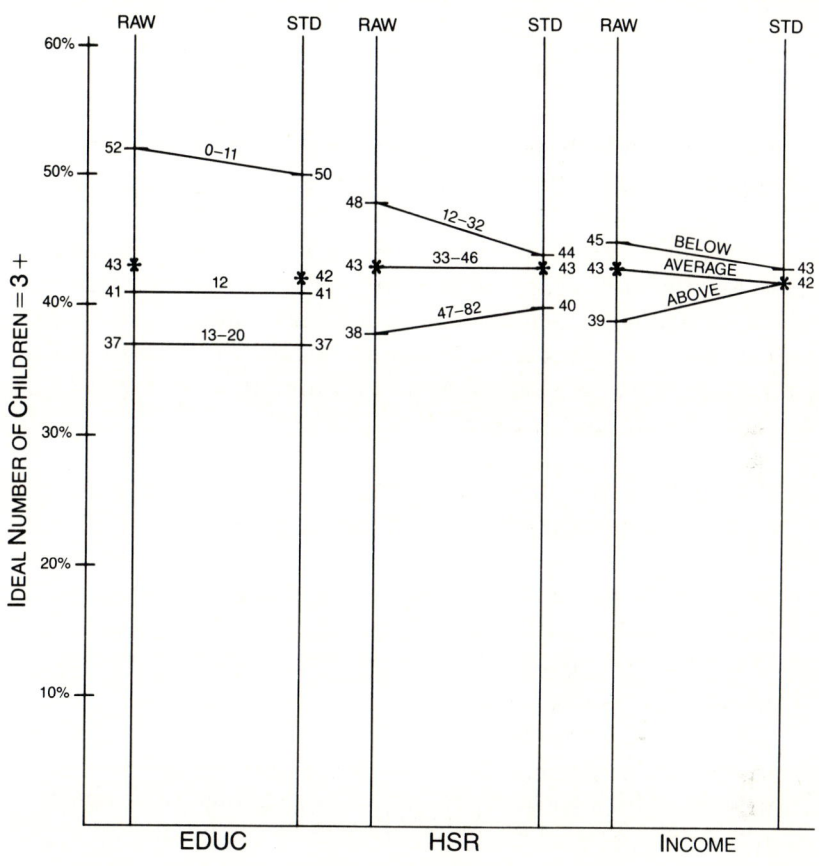

SOURCE: data set X.26

what appeared to be a general SES effect is really an educational difference. Schooling, but not higher-prestige jobs or greater income, lowers our fertility norms.

We can now summarize our findings:

1. The differences in fertility norms seem medium (for example, a twenty-eight-point gap between Southern Blacks and White Northern Protestants, and a fourteen-point gap between high and low SES in the raw data).

2. I'd say ethnicity makes the bigger difference, but the point is arguable.
3. Race and religion produce bigger differences than region.
4. Education is the only SES variable which makes an independent contribution.
5. The gap between low SES Blacks (65 percent favoring large families) and high SES White Protestants (32 percent) is thirty-three points.

In terms of larger theoretical issues, I'd lean more toward the "cultural" than the "class" interpretation here. It appears to me that where you stand on the desirability of large families is due more to the values and traditions of your subgroup than to how high you are on the socioeconomic ladder. At a minimum, the hypothesis "it all depends on how rich you are" comes off badly.

Task 4-3: Ethnicity, SES, and Behavior

The CHIPLIB diskette is a data library with seventy dependent variables, of which Chldidel is just one. You were exposed to them in Tasks 2-6 and 3-11. Now, you are ready to make much more systematic use of the information.

Read the introduction to Appendix B and browse through the items. Your actual assignment here will depend on your teacher. Perhaps you will be asked to choose one dependent variable and scrutinize the effects of ethnicity and SES. Perhaps your instructor will assign a different variable to each person in the class—this would enrich the discussions. If you are free to choose, I'd suggest you pick a theme of special interest to yourself, run off some bivariates, and then dig into one or two of the more promising ones using rickety ladders and fishnets. If the ethnic or SES differences seem intriguing, use the b and c tables for deeper exploration. In any case the aim of the project is to allow you to explore the question of whether the variables explained in Chapters Two and Three really do seem to affect our lives, and if so, which variables are doing what?

SUMMARY

This entire chapter has been "summary." It should have given you the chance to (a) dig into specific topics (dependent variables) to see how our positions are influenced by where we are in the social structure, and (b) explore the broader question of which structural variables make the biggest differences. By now you should be able to deal with such questions as "How important is SES?" or "Which aspect of ethnicity makes the biggest differences?" and be able to back your claims with data.

On the technical side you should be able to present three-variable results as a fishnet graph which shows the total impact of the two independent variables and helps spot peculiarities in specific categories (which statisticians call *interactions*).

II
Social Process

5
The Big Change

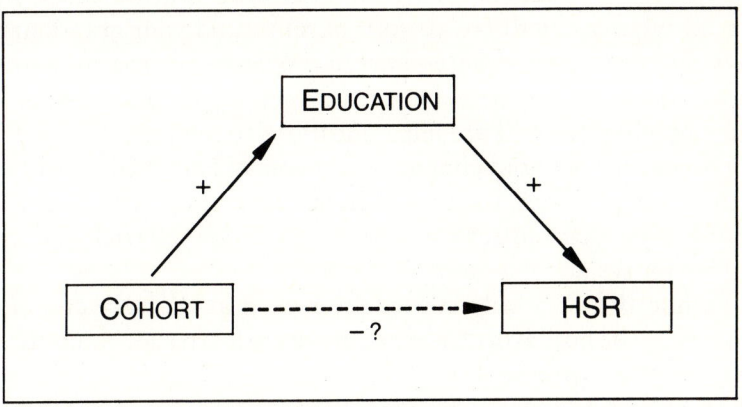

CHAPTER 5   THE BIG CHANGE

ON AND OFF THE FARM

Historians believe agriculture, the deliberate cultivation of plants and animals, began in Southeast Asia around 10,000 B.C. This transition from wandering hunter to settled farmer is one of the two or three most important episodes in the history of human beings. And for several thousand years we were pretty much farmers or people who sold things to farmers.

As late as 1870, almost half the labor force in the United States was in farm-related work, while today around 3 to 4 percent is. Thus, in just about one century, a 12,000-year pattern was turned around. Call it urbanization, the industrial revolution, modernization, or what you will—you, your parents, and your grandparents grew up in radically different worlds. Whether your grandparents and great-grandparents experienced such a gap and whether you and your children will are hard questions to answer.

Any grasp of social change, the theme of Part Two, must begin with this *Big Change,* the three-generational shift from an agricultural to a postagricultural society (I will dodge the tricky question of whether we are also postindustrial).

While the GSS only covers the period at the very end of the transition, the notion of *cohort* enables us to learn a lot about the Big Change from contemporary data.

A cohort is defined as persons who undergo some process together. Everyone who got married in 1970 belongs to the *marriage cohort of 1970*; everyone who entered college in 1980 is in the *college entrance cohort of 1980,* and so on. So, all the people born at the same time form a *birth cohort.* To find out one's cohort, subtract Age from Year (two digits) and add 1900. If I was interviewed in the GSS 1980 and reported my age to be fifty-one, my birth cohort would be 80 − 51 = 29 + 1900 = 1929. (I wasn't, but I am.) We can formalize this equation:

$$Cohort = (Year - Age) + 1900$$

There is no magic in single years, and research workers generally group ages into intervals. Since U.S. Censuses are carried out in *00* years (1790, 1800, 1810 . . . 1980, 1900, and so on), it is conventional to group ages so they all come out neatly across decades. The GSS did not begin in a nice *00* year, so the data sets in this book were constructed to give convenient comparisons across the ten-year span 1972–74 to 1982–84, as in the X.d tables in CHIPLIB. Table 5-1 provides a handy reference guide.

TABLE 5-1

Cohort Groupings for *Social Differences* Data Sets

Cohort (Birthyr)	Year of Birth			Age in	
	Interval	Mean		1973	1983
1	1883–1903	1898		70+	80+
2	1904–1913	1909		60–69	70–79
3	1914–1923	1919		50–59	60–69
4	1924–1933	1928		40–49	50–59
5	1934–1943	1939		30–39	40–49
6	1944–1953	1949	(1948)*	20–29	30–39
7	1954–1964	1957	(1956)*	10–19**	20–29

SOURCE: GSS 1972 to 1984

*Mean in data sets limited to persons twenty-five and older
**Only eighteen and nineteen year olds were eligible for GSS samples

For example: row three says Cohort 3 comprises persons born between 1914 and 1923. In the cumulative GSS 1982–84 their mean (average) year of birth is 1919; in 1973 they were Ages fifty to fifty-nine; in 1983 the survivors were sixty to sixty-nine.

Task 5-1: Cohorts

1. Study Table 5-1 so something will come to mind when you see the category labels 1 through 7 for data sets with the variable Birthyr.

2. In which cohorts are you, your parents, and your grandparents?

3. Studies of the GSS give a mean age of father at respondent's birth of thirty and a mean age of twenty-eight for mothers. Are the three generations in your family spaced about thirty years apart?

CHAPTER 5   THE BIG CHANGE

GROWING UP IN 1900 AND 1950

A good way to grasp the Big Change is by comparing the family situations of people growing up in different eras; that is, by comparing birth cohorts on characteristics of their parental families. Data set 5.1 is designed for that purpose. Its variables are

- *Birthyr* = cohorts 1–7
- *Pared* = parental education (Either = mother or father completed 12 years; Neither = both parents 0–11. Persons from single-parent families were coded in terms of the parent present, almost always the mother.)
- *Dad* = characteristics of the father (see description in data set X.60, Appendix B). This is a rich but complex variable. Make sure you see how it was constructed.
- *Sibs* = number of brothers and sisters (0–3 vs. 4 or more)
- *Mawork* = mother's employment for money after marriage (Yes vs. No). See description in data set X.32, Appendix B.

Task 5-2: The Big Change in Families

1. Graph the percentage *Dad = Farm* (vertical) against Birth Cohort (horizontal). (The category labels for Birthyr give the mean year of birth in each category as in Table 5-1. Use them for plotting.) Obviously, the trend is *down*—but do you see any particular pattern to the decline?

2. Now, let's look at trends in family structure. Three categories tell us a lot: Nodad tracks changes in *intact* households and *single parents*, 0–3 Sibs tracks changes in fertility, and *Mawork = Yes* tells us a lot about the sexual division of labor. Plot these percentages on a graph where the horizontal axis is Year of Birth. Any trends? Any exceptions? Does the exception surprise you? What probably accounts for it?

   If you compare these charts it is quite likely that this hypothesis will come to mind: the shift from agriculture to industry and services leads to more modern family structures. Let's check it out.

3. Cross Tab Dad against Pared, Sibs, and Mawork. Do these bivariates support the hypothesis?

4. For a more direct test, let's ask Whatif each cohort had the same percentage Farm fathers? Whatif there were no historical trend in agriculture? Would the family structure variables still change the same way? Here we will use Change in a slightly different way since we wish to give every cohort the same percentage Farmer, 16.7, the marginal value, but not fix the other components of Dad. CHIP allows you to do this—if you Change one percentage, it will adjust the others to maintain their relative sizes. Since we wish to allow cohorts to vary on other components of Dad, we will use Change2 instead of Change. To do so, enter Whatif and choose Change2 and the variable Dad (the items are already in the proper order—unless you have been fooling around with them). CHIP will then present you with combinations of cohorts and Pareds. Answer each with Enter-16.7-Enter-Enter. This will give both educational levels in each cohort group 16.7 percent Farmer fathers while allowing the other categories to follow their inclinations from the raw data.

    Repeat your bivariate cross-tabs of cohort against Sibs and Mawork. Plot your adjusted data as curves, as in (2) above. Then draw the raw data points on, below, or above the curves. Connect the standardized and raw data points by vertical lines. (This is really just a twist on the rickety ladder graph.)

5. Given all of this, what do you infer about the impact of declining agriculture, the women's movement, wars and depressions, and so on on the Big Change?

Tabulation by Birth Cohort can be extremely revealing. It gives one an odd feeling to be working with "live" data about people born around the time of the Civil War (the parents of Cohort 1). However, some qualifications and quirks must be borne in mind.

First, there is mortality. Americans born in 1900 had an expected life at birth of 47.3 years (for cohorts born in the 1950s and

CHAPTER 5 THE BIG CHANGE

1960s it's around seventy years). That is, about half of them died before reaching fifty, the vast majority of the deaths being among infants. Consequently, older GSS respondents represent only minorities of total birth cohorts. This bias, of course, only causes serious difficulties if our variables are correlated with mortality. For example, if persons from farm origins have a higher mortality rate, they will be under-represented among older GSS respondents. I don't think such biases affect the data in set 5.1 much, but the numbers should not be taken as absolute truth.

Second, you may remember (Task 2-2) that 4 percent of GSS respondents grew up abroad. The parental families they tell us about were not living in the United States. But, since the Big Change has been basically similar in all countries, this is not a major problem.

Third, and this is tricky, the parents of persons in a cohort are not a representative sample of adult persons living then. Consider farmers. Data set 5.1 tells us that 38 percent of persons in Cohort 1 had farmer fathers. This does not mean 38 percent of the adult males in 1898 were farmers. Why not? Partly because not all adults are parents (bachelor farm hands for example), but mainly because of differential fertility. Highly fertile groups (such as farmers) have many more offspring to report them in later GSS's. Similarly, while 68 percent of persons in Cohort 1 report four or more Sibs, it does not follow that 68 percent of parents in 1898 had four or more children. Consider the following hypothetical case: Mom A has one child, Mom B has nine, so mothers average five children; but the average child comes from a family with 8.2 children!

COHORTS AND STATUS INFLATION

Tabulating Ethnicity against Cohort isn't very interesting since the Ethtype composition of the United States hasn't changed remarkably in this century (it did in the nineteenth). But trends revealed in the SES variables will repay your close scrutiny. Tabulating Cohort, Ethnicity, and SES, moreover, is so interesting that Chapter Seven is devoted entirely to it.

Task 5-3: Cohorts and SES

Have prestige levels changed much in this century? The question is controversial. The left wing says jobs are becoming degraded, the right wing says they are being upgraded. Let's see what the GSS data say.

Data Set 5.1 is a good place to start. Farmers tend to be middling in the HSR prestige scale (Task 3-6.1), so the shrinkage of agricultural employment shouldn't by itself do anything much to HSR levels; although their decline is so precipitous it makes all the other categories increase their shares by default. To get around this we can look at trends in HSR levels in the non-farm population.

1. In data set 5.1, Omit the categories Nodad and Farmer from the Dad variable. Then Cross Tab the modified Dad variable against Cohort. Plot the results and the percentage Either for Pared on a graph. As they say on exam questions, please "compare and contrast" the two curves.

If educational levels have been increasing faster than occupational prestige levels, what is implied about the relationship between the two?

Data set 3.11 shifts us back from parental families to individual respondents.

2. Plot Educational attainment by Cohort using data set 3.11. Plot the proportions 0–11, 12, and 13–20. Then Omit 0–11 and plot the proportion 13–20 by Cohort (you might review task 3-2 here). How would you characterize trends in educational attainment during the Big Change? What do these figures imply about trends in the American dream?

3. One reading of the figures so far is *status inflation*. If educational levels have risen considerably and HSR levels haven't, it would seem that the HSR obtainable with a given level of schooling has declined—just as the purchasing power of the dollar has.

Data set 5.6 is designed to help you test this hypothesis. We are back to fathers again (we get a longer time span and we dampen "age" factors, since, within cohorts, fathers of sixteen-year-olds tend to be similar in age—roughly forty-five years old). The data set contains Father's Education, HSR scores, and Cohort (Birthyr), and is limited to nonfarm fathers.

CHAPTER 5   THE BIG CHANGE

To test the hypothesis:

a. Cross Tab Daded (independent), DadHSR (dependent), with Birthyr as Control, choosing the % Across option.
b. Lay out three graphs, one for 0–11 fathers, one for 12s, and one for 13–20s. The horizontal axis will be Birth Year, the vertical axis will be Percentages.
c. On each graph you will draw two "curves," one for trends in the percentage with high-prestige jobs (47–82) and one for trends in the percentage with low-prestige jobs (9–32).
d. Before drawing the curves, decide how they would look if the "inflation hypothesis" is true.

4. Do you think the correlation between Education and HSR has changed during the twentieth century? If so, has it become stronger, weaker, or what? Test your predictions by finding % Diff for Education and HSR within each Cohort in data set 5.6.

A NOTE ON INCOME TRENDS

GSS cohort data are of little use when we ask about trends in income. While our relative income item (below, average, above) works well for cross-sectional (one-time data) differences, it is a bad question for looking at trends. When one adds problems stemming from memory (more of us know our parents' schooling than their incomes), short-run changes (incomes in 1935 were not the same as 1925 even for the same family), and inflation, it is hopeless to look at income in the same way as we explored the Big Changes in family structure, education, and occupation.

The absence of data does not mean the absence of change. The change has been enormous! Since media discussions of incomes are saturated with politics and we are highly sensitized to short-term movements in the business cycle, it is easy to forget the big picture. Figure 5-1 shows that big picture. It graphs disposable (after-tax) personal income per capita in 1972 dollars against time.

Disposable, per capita, and *1972 dollars* make the numbers look esoteric but they are necessary as a sort of Whatifing to remove the effects of changing tax rates, increased population, and inflation. The picture in Figure 5-1 is unambiguous: income has risen steadily and precipitously since the 1930s. In 1955, twenty-five years after the Great Depression, we were 1.6 times as rich, and in 1980, another twenty-five years down the line, 1.8 times as rich as in 1955. In 1983, the average real income was almost three times that of 1930.

Federal economic data on disposable personal income per capita do not go back before 1929. But there is every reason to assume that the period from 1900 to 1929 saw similar growth.

This is not to say that the distribution of income is totally fair (or totally unfair), that poverty has been wiped out (see Task 3-15), that unemployment isn't a persistent problem, or that recessions

FIGURE 5-1

Disposable Personal Income Per Capita in Thousands of 1972 Dollars

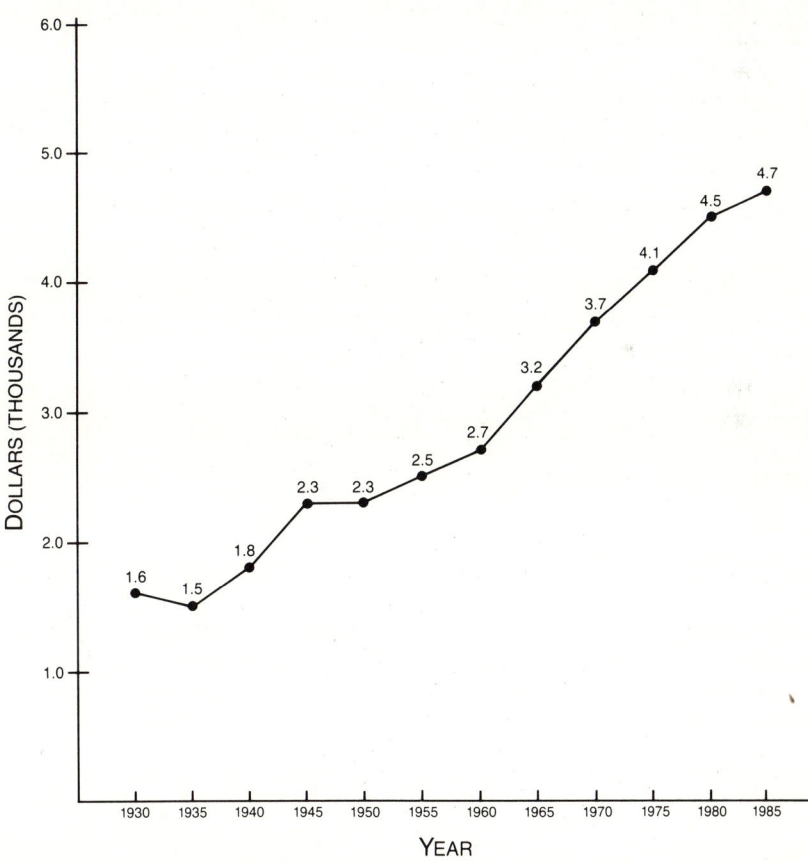

SOURCE: *Statistical Abstract*, 1985

are not real. But it is important to remember that the period of the Big Change also includes a spectacular and steady increase in real incomes.

SUMMARY

The goals of this chapter have been (1) to help you grasp the sheer size of the social changes in the first half of the twentieth century, (2) to warn you off overly simple explanations of social change, and (3) to expose you to the tempting, but far from rock solid, status-inflation hypothesis.

On the technical side, the aim has been to acquaint you with the concept of birth cohort, its powerful potential, and some of its complexities and ambiguities.

6
Intergenerational Mobilities

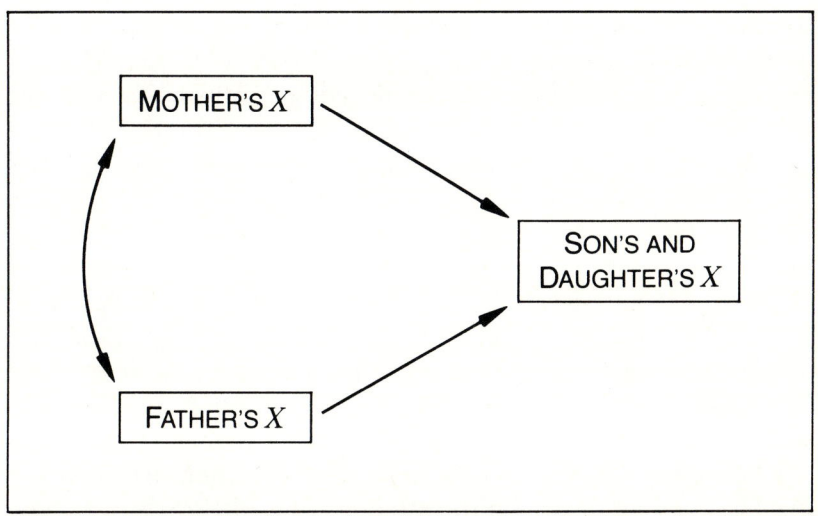

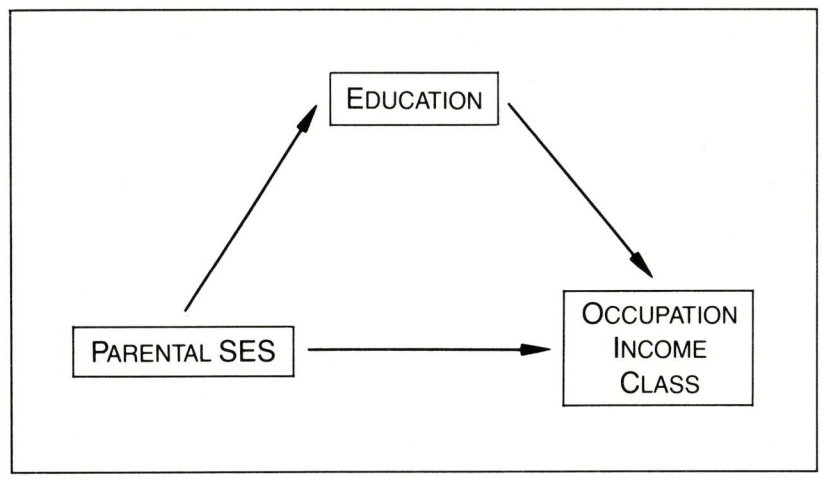

CHAPTER 6   INTERGENERATIONAL MOBILITIES

MOBILITY

Change and *mobility* sound like the same thing, but sociologists reserve the word mobility for *before* and *after* measures on the same person (or group). In Chapter Five we saw a great deal of change when we contrasted various cohorts, but we did not track members of a given cohort through time. In Chapter Five we studied change but not mobility.

The before and after measures can be close (changes in voting preference before and after a campaign for example) or spread out over a lifetime. Sociologists have been particularly interested in the latter, and when sociologists become interested in something, a flood of new terminology is never far behind. This leads us to the terms *inter*generational mobility and *intra*generational mobility.

We usually divide lives into three phases: (1) In the early years of childhood and adolescence, by and large, we share our parent's social characteristics. Children either mirror parental characteristics (ethnicity for example) or have none of their own (income for example). (2) In our teens or early twenties we leave home, finish school, and get our first jobs, personal earnings, voting experience, independent religious choices, and so on. (3) Later in life we have some "final" occupation, income, political position, religion, and so on.

When we compare parental and current characteristics, we are in effect conducting a mobility study in which before is phase one and after is phase three. This is called intergenerational mobility ("inter" means "between").

When we compare adult characteristics ("first job" vs. "current job" for example) we are studying intragenerational mobility ("intra" means "within").

Sociologists have become specialists on intergenerational mobility; indeed, it is one of the few topics where sociologists "know more" than other social scientists. But the topic also has a *value* side that makes it worth your attention. The American dream is about intergenerational mobility—the proposition that "In America even a poor boy can get ahead [of his father]." Research on mobility helps us see how much of the American dream is myth and how much is reality.

Mobility Tables

Since the basic data of mobility research consist of before and after measures on the same variables, the meat and potatoes of mobility research is the study of *mobility tables*, cross-tabs of before against after. Since you know a lot about cross-tabs, mobility tables should not pose much of a problem for you. But they have some unique features because the rows and columns have the same categories.

Table 6-1 crosses Region at Age 16 by Current Region. (The convention has emerged that phase one data in mobility studies focuses on Age 16 because early childhood memories are unreliable, but Age 16 generally precedes leaving home, finishing school, getting a full-time job, entering the military, and so on.) The figures come from data set 6.3. I omitted Foreign as a before category to simplify matters.

TABLE 6-1
Region, Current and Age 16 (GSS 1972–84)

	Current					
Age 16	Northeast	Central	South	West	Total	N
Northeast	(83.0)	3.5	8.5	5.0	100.0%	3,492
Central	1.9	(82.5)	6.5	9.1	100.0	4,899
South	3.9	6.5	(83.6)	5.9	99.9	5,346
West	1.4	3.0	4.7	(90.9)	100.0	1,837
All	20.7	29.3	33.2	16.8	100.0%	15,574

SOURCE: data set 6.3, (Age 16 = Foreign excluded)

Table 6-1 may be read as any percentage table: 83 percent of Northeastern-reared are currently in the Northeast, 3.5 percent are in the Central region, 8.5 percent in the South, and so on (for regional definitions, see Chapter Two). Note the cells in the diagonal running from upper left (Northeast–Northeast) to lower right (West–West). They have huge percentages, each over 80 percent, and have the same categories for row and column. The other cells have smaller percentages and non-matching pairs of category

CHAPTER 6   INTERGENERATIONAL MOBILITIES

labels. Thus, in a mobility table, the cells can be divided into two classes: cells in one diagonal that tap stability, and other cells that tap mobility. (If the variables have a natural order, cells on one side of the mobility diagonal define *upward mobility,* cells on the other side define *downward mobility.* This will become important when we get to mobility in SES.)

The bottom row of Table 6-1, labeled "All" gives the marginal percentages for Current Region. If before and after were unrelated (statistically independent), we would get these same percentages in every row. (This is what the Change command Enter-Enter-Enter does in Whatif. It resets the percentages in every row to the marginals, producing a table where the row and column variables are unrelated.) Statisticians call these *expected values* as they are the numbers one would expect in each row if the variables were statistically independent. Consequently, one way to look at a percentage table is to ask whether the various row percentages are bigger, smaller, or the same as the expected (marginal) percentages.

With the expected values serving as yardsticks, let's look at the percentages in Table 6-1. The pattern is simple: we get more than expected values in every stability cell and less than expected values in every mobility cell. This is no fluke; it is virtually guaranteed in mobility tables. Want an empirical sociological law with no known exceptions? Try this: *every mobility table shows less-than-chance mobility.* Sociological laws are not so common we can afford to be snooty about this one, but it actually creates problems: the stability effect is usually so strong that it swamps the data and makes it hard to study the change cells.

Because the data tend to pile up in the stable cells, it is useful to divide mobility analyses into two parts: "Who changes?" and then, "Among the changers, who goes where?"

Assessing Differences in Stability
Cross Tab before by after (with after dependent), percentage across, and compare figures for cells in the stability diagonal, preferably with a tele-graph. (For more detailed analyses with an independent variable influencing mobility, use the Merge command to rearrange the table so it boils down to a dichotomy, Stable vs. Mobile.)

Figure 6-1 shows the results for regional mobility in the U.S.

adult population. All the figures are high—84 percent of us are living in the same region where we grew up. There is very little difference in stability rates among the South, Northeast, and Midwest, but the West is a bit higher. Westerners are more likely to stay put.

The question "Who changes?" is easy to answer. Usually the stability proportions almost leap out of the tables. The second question, "Among the changers, who goes where?" is very tricky, so tricky there are entire books on the topic. (See for example, Michael Hout's, *Mobility Tables*, Sage University Paper Series 07-031. Sage Publications, Beverly Hills, CA, 1983.) I will show you a simplified technique using CHIP. It takes a little work, but it helps you see things in your mobility table that would be invisible in the usual cross-tab analysis.

We proceed in these three steps:

- First, get rid of the stability effects.
- Second, find the big flows with a telegraph.
- Third, diagram the results.

FIGURE 6-1

Stability by Original Region in Table 6-1

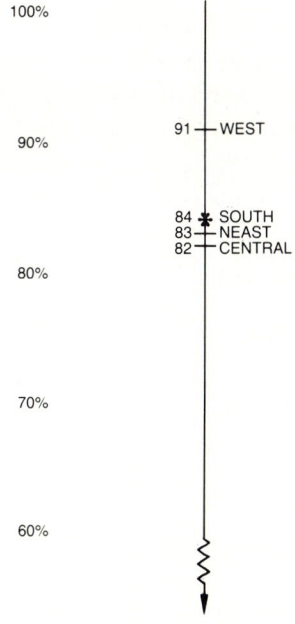

Step One. A simple way to tune out the effects of the stability cells is to limit the table to movers, cases that are not in stability cells. In other words, adjust the data so the stability cells have frequencies of zero but nothing else is changed. This is easy with the Edit function in the Modify menu of CHIP. Even easier, I have done it for you already in data sets 6.1a, 6.3a, 6.6a, 6.9a, and 6.9b. Table 6-2 shows the regional data after editing each stability cell to zero (and putting the foreign-born back in since all of them are mobile).

TABLE 6-2

Table 6-1 with Non-mobile Cells Set to Zero and Foreign-born Added

Age 16	Northeast	Central	Current South	West	Total	N
Northeast	(0.0)	20.7	49.9	29.4	100.0%	595
Central	10.7	(0.0)	37.1	52.2	100.0	858
South	23.9	40.0	(0.0)	36.2	100.1	876
West	15.6	32.9	51.5	(0.0)	100.0	167
Foreign	44.5	15.6	15.0	24.9	100.0	687
All	19.9	19.9	25.3	34.9	100.0%	3,183

SOURCE: data set 6.3

The off-diagonal numbers are all larger than in Table 6-1, and some subtle differences appear. Consider, for example, migration to the Midwest (central): 3.5 percent of Northeasterners and 3.0 percent of Westerners in Table 6-1 ended up in the heartland. Now look at Table 6-2: there we get 20.7 percent for Northeast and 32.9 for West. For the total data (Table 6-1) Northeasterners are a tad more likely to end up in the Central region, but among Changers, the persons in the mobile cells, (Table 6-2) Western changers are more likely to do so. The "paradox" is due to the differences in stability. Relatively few Westerners migrate to the Midwest—but this is mainly because few of them go anywhere. Among Changers, the rate for Westerners is higher than that of Northeasterners. This finding is of no great importance, but it illustrates how a two-step (first, "who stays?," then, "which movers go where?") analysis can pay off.

Step Two. Given a table of movers, find the biggest percentage in each column. The rule is:

1. Pick the single largest percentage in each column

2. Unless
   a. they are all very close to each other, in which case don't pick any.
   b. two of them are close to each other and there is a gap between number 2 and the rest; in which case, pick the two largest.

FIGURE 6-2

Table 6-2 as a Tele-graph

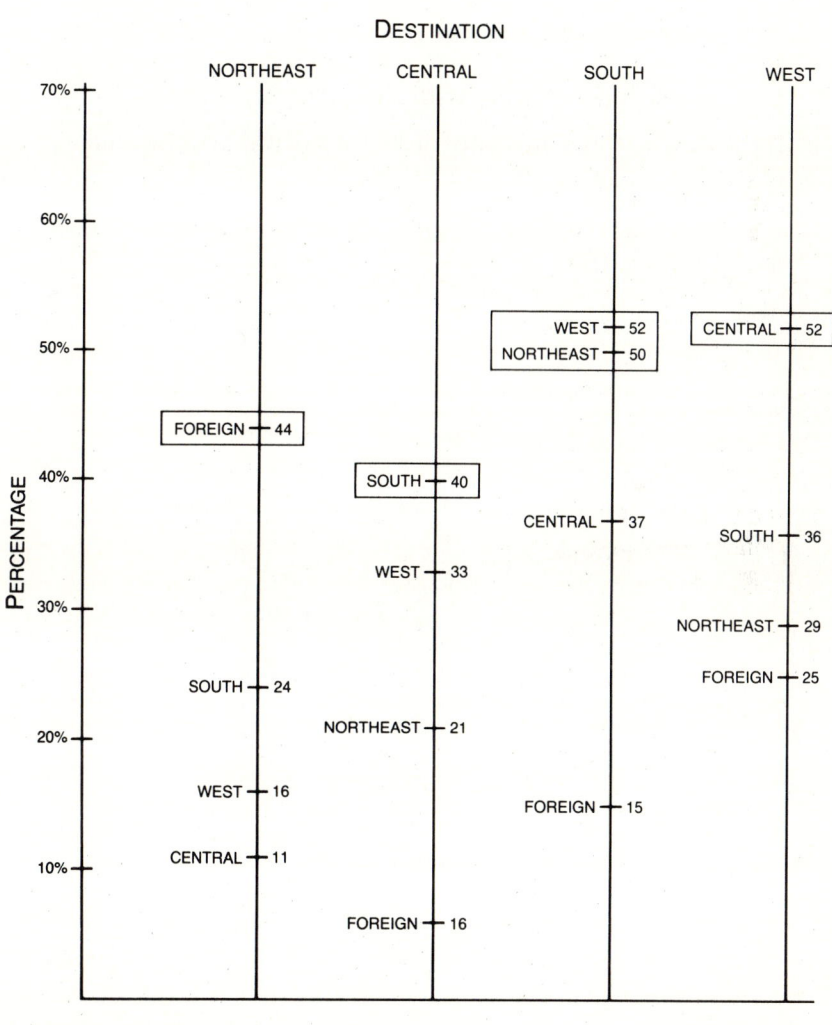

SOURCE: data set 6.3

I strongly recommend using a tele-graph here because, as we have seen repeatedly, it is hard to judge relative closeness in a table of numbers. Figure 6-2 presents the data in Table 6-2 as a tele-graph.

For Northeast, Foreign has the highest percentage (44 percent); for Central, it is South (40 percent); and for West, it is Central (52 percent). For the destination South, however, West and Northeast are close to each other (52 percent and 50 percent) and they are separated from the pack, so I chose both.

We now have a list of the largest flows.

Step Three. To diagram the results:

1. Indicate each destination with a labeled circle or box.
2. If the destinations have any order or natural arrangement place the circles to reflect it.
3. Draw arrows connecting the origins and destinations singled out in Step Two.

Figure 6-3 illustrates.

FIGURE 6-3
Directional Change in Region

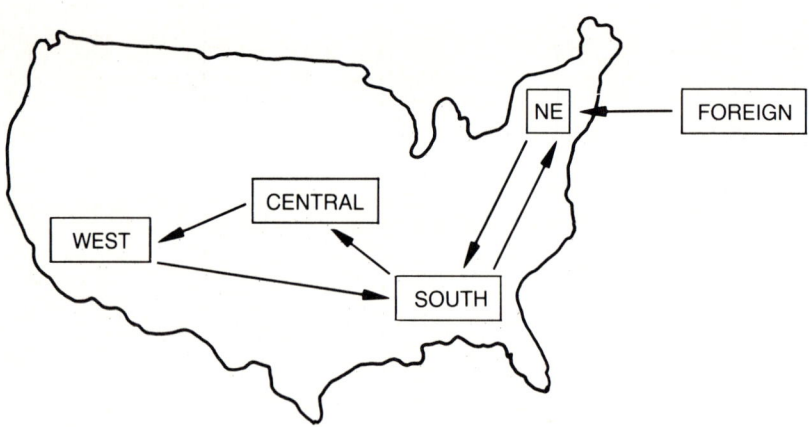

There are no firm rules for interpreting such diagrams, but you might keep the following ideas in mind:

MOBILITY

- Is the system "connected" or does it break down into clumps? (Figure 6-3 is connected; every region is linked to every other region, directly or indirectly.)
- If there is an underlying order or arrangement, are all the arrows between "neighbors" or are there some "long jumps"? (In Figure 6-3, the "neighbor" rule applies—that is, migration is roughly inverse to spatial distance.)

To See "Who Went Where"
1. Edit your mobility table so each stable cell has a zero frequency.
2. Cross Tab and percentage the adjusted table and find the biggest percentage in each column.
3. Diagram the results, connecting the biggest flows from step 2 with arrows.

But there's more (you can see why sociologists find mobility tables so intriguing). Since the row and column marginals treat the same categories on the same cases before and after, we can compare them to find the "net change." The All Margs option in the Command menu gets the information; and a rickety ladder, one side for before, the other for after, is a good way to see what has happened. Figure 6-4 gives the net changes for region in the data from set 6.3.

Three regions (South, Central, and Northeast) show one- or two-point declines, while West shows a five-point increase. Thus, more U.S. adults live in the West now than did so as children.

You may be surprised by the small size of the shifts. Two explanations come to mind. First, we are talking about net shifts. Although about 16 percent of us shifted regions (Figure 6-1), inflows tend to offset outflows, and outflows tend to compensate for inflows (*Change = Inflow − Outflow*) so the net effects will be smaller than the total mobility percentage. Second, we are a large nation and media discussions of migration are usually given in absolute terms. A shift of a million people will get your data in the newspaper (if not on television), but it means less than half a percentage point (the total U.S. population in 1983 was about 234 million, and the population eighteen and older was about 172 million). Conversely, even a tiny blip in the GSS indicates something happening to scads of Americans, as each GSS respondent represents approximately a million U.S. adults.

> To Spot Net Shifts in Categories
> 1. Compare the marginals for before and after.
> 2. Display them in a rickety ladder graph.

FIGURE 6-4

Net Change for Regions

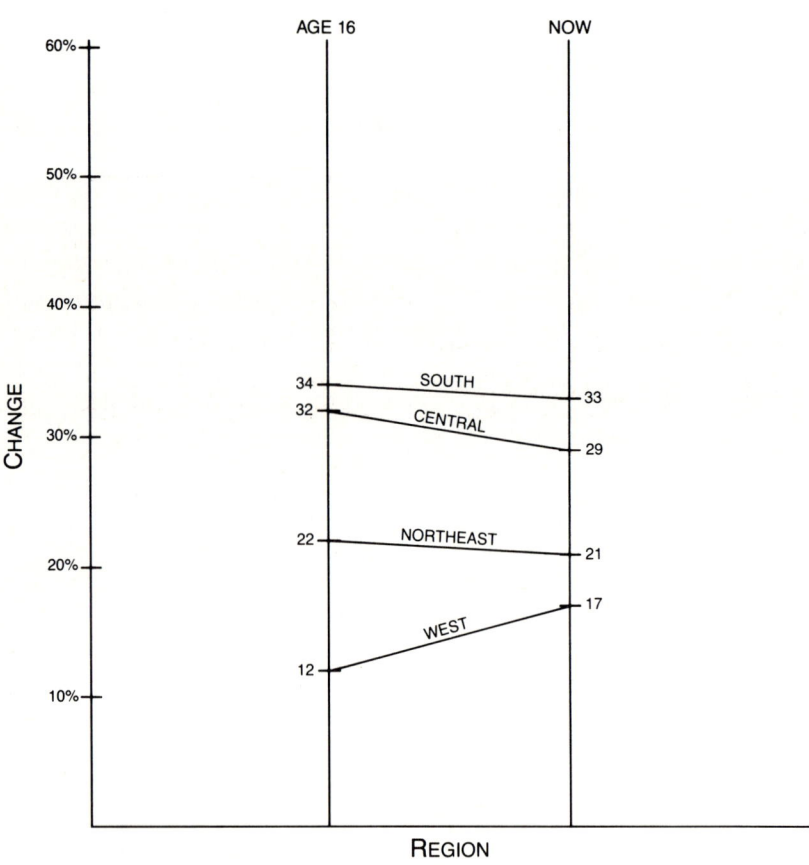

SOURCE: data set 6.3

Task 6-1: Practice at Mobility Analysis

Data sets 6.1 and 6.1a give size-of-place data analogous to the regional figures we just discussed. The categories are:

- Country = open country
- Town = community of less than 50,000
- City = community of 50,000 to 250,000
- Metburb = suburb of a city of 250,000 or more
- Metro = central city of 250,000 or more

Data are limited to respondents twenty-five and older. In data set 6.1, stable cells have been edited to zero. Analyze:

- Relative stability of communities
- Patterns of flow between community types
- Net shifts in community size using the techniques explained above

(In interpreting your data, bear in mind that respondents may have stayed put while the community grew.)

Ethnic Mobility

Ethnic mobility may sound odd, and for the theoretically inclined, it may seem like a contradiction in terms. In Chapter One I argued that *relative permanence* is part of ethnicity's definition. But notice the weasel word *relative*. I didn't say ethnic characteristics never change, I said they change less than other important variables. Such ambiguous statements deserve empirical testing.

Obviously racial "mobility" happens. While social skin color is black or white (see Chapter Two), physical skin color in both races shows enormous variation. At the extremes (the darkest Whites and lightest Blacks) options exist and doubtless a number of Americans "change race." But we have no good data (the GSS does not ask its respondents, "What was your race when you were Age 16?"), and there is no reason to believe that the proportions—even if known—are large enough to be sociologically important. So we will skip racial mobility.

What about regional mobility? Task 6-1 confirmed the theoretical hypothesis that it is rare; but it becomes more interesting if you divide respondents by race. Tasks 6-2 to 6-4 will give you a chance to dig into racial patterns of migration and some of their sociological implications.

As for the third ethnic variable, religion, religious mobility begins to sound less preposterous when we realize that questions such as "Is the younger generation less religious?", "Are fundamentalists gaining spectacular numbers of converts?", and "What does intermarriage do to religious preference?" become researchable when we translate them into questions about mobility tables. In Tasks 6-5, 6-6, and 6-7, you will do just that.

Regional Mobility of Blacks and Whites

In 1860, 92 percent of all Blacks lived in the South (Chapter Two) while today the figure is close to 50 percent. Over the last century, Blacks have not only shifted from chattels to freemen, they have experienced an epochal migration that has changed the social geography of the nation. Tasks 6-2 through 6-4 allow you to scrutinize the extent of this migration, its regional pattern, the relation between race and urbanism, and the "payoff" in SES terms.

Task 6-2: Race and Regional Mobility

Data set 6.3 gives Region at Age 16 (*Reg16*) and Current Region (*Regnow*) by Race. We have already looked at the total pattern. Now let's compare regional mobility patterns for Blacks and Whites.

1. Compare the stability percentages for each region and race, ignoring Foreign.

2. In theory you could use data set 6.3a to make flow diagrams for the two races. In fact, however, there aren't enough Black cases starting in Northeast, Central, or West to give reliable figures. But you can compare the destinations of Southern Blacks and Whites. (Select Control helps here). A percentage table shows what's going on, and *d*'s will tell the story exactly.

3. Use data set 6.3 to find the net shifts in region for each Race.

4. Given all this, how do Black and White regional mobility patterns differ? Why might that be?

Task 6-3: Race and Urbanism

Historically, Blacks were not only Southern, they were rural laborers on commercial farms. Yet today, our image of Blacks has the urban flavor of Harlem, Chicago's South Side, and Motown. Data set 6.4 allows us to check this image against empirical data with the variables *Res16* (Size of Place at Age 16—LT250K = less than 250,000, Metburb = suburb of city of 250,000 or more, Metro = central city of 250,000 or more) and *XNORCSIZ* (Current Size of Place with the same categories as Res16).

1. Cross Tab Res16 by XNORCSIZ with Race as a control and the % Subtable option.
2. Compare the races on Res16.
3. Compare the net shift in marginals for Blacks and Whites.
4. Use data set 6.4 to find the percent Black in each of the six possible combinations of Current Region and Current Size of Place, for example, in North/Metro, South/LT250k, and so on.
5. How do Whites distribute among the six combinations? And Blacks? (*Hint:* use % Subtable)
6. Suggest several sociological implications of all these findings.

Task 6-4: Did Migration Pay Off?

Black migrants from the South, like White migrants from Europe (or anywhere else) left to find a better way of life. In the past this meant, if not racial equality, at least escape from the famous Southern "etiquette of race relations" (and, White Southerners might add, escape from the benefits of Southern White paternalism). Important as this may be, we shall not try to measure racial climates. (In 1982, the GSS asked Blacks a series of items about perceived discrimination. Regional differences were very small. But 1982 is pretty late in the history of Black migration.)

We do, however, have relevant data on SES variables, and we can ask whether migration paid off in terms of the SES variables, occupation and income. Education is more ambiguous since the GSS doesn't ask whether migrants completed school before or after their moves.

CHAPTER 6 INTERGENERATIONAL MOBILITIES

1. Use data set 6.4 to find out what percentages of Blacks are
   a. nonmigrant Southerners
   b. Southern-reared but now living in the North—that is, migrants from South to North,
   c. Northern-reared nonmigrants, and
   d. Northern-reared but now living in the South—that is, migrants from North to South.

   Data set 6.5a contains the variables Birth Cohort, Race, Region at Age 16, Education, Current Region, HSR score, and Income. To simplify your work, the variables Race, Reg16, and Current Region have been collapsed into four groups (use data set 6.5 if you want more detail):

   NWhite = White; Current Region = North.
   NBlack = Black; Original Region = North.
   SNBlack = Black; Original Region = South;
                    Current Region = North.
   SSBlack = Black; Original Region = South;
                    Current Region = South.
   SWhite = White; Current Region = South.

   The typology enables us to compare migrant Blacks with nonmigrant Blacks in both regions and to contrast each of the three Black groups with Whites in the North and South.

2. Migration theorists claim that OUTmigrants are not the "losers" at the bottom of the heap, but persons with better than average SES. Is this true for Blacks? You can test the hypothesis by comparing the educations of the SSBlacks and SNBlacks in data set 6.5a. Since migrants are older (among Blacks 28 percent of the 83–23 Cohort are SNBlack compared with 12 percent in the 44–64 Cohort), you should make these comparisons within Cohorts to control for the "Big Change." Display your data as a tele-graph in which the poles are Cohorts, the rungs are the five Migr groups and the scale is the percentage with 12–20 years of schooling.
   Note: From the GSS we can not tell for sure whether the migrants completed their schoolings in the South or the North. But, since the Reg16 question asks about residence at Age 16, the SNBlack group does not include persons brought North as young children.

3. Clearly, task 2 tells us we must allow for educational differences when we examine the HSR and Income patterns of the migration groups. Standardization (Whatifing) is in order here, but with a new wrinkle. Since Schooling is related to both Cohort and Migration category, let us try a more complex mental experiment. What if Cohorts varied in Schooling but within each of the three Cohorts, the migration groups had identical Schooling? The Change2 option in Whatif allows you to carry out this experiment. Simply choose **F2** in Whatif (rather than the familiar **F1**) and ask to Change EDUC. With data set 6.5a, the program will ask you to enter the Educations (percent 0–11) of each of the fifteen Cohort-Migr combinations. Set each of the 83–23s to 52.1 percent 0–11, each of the 24-43s to 28.1 percent 0–11, and each of the 44-64s to 14.6 percent. Remember, with two categories you can give Whatif the first percentage and hit Enter. The program will get the other percentage by subtraction.

   You now have a data set where the Big Change in Education still holds but the five racial/migration groups are equated on Schooling. Now look at (a) the HSR scores by Cohort and Migration status and (b) Income levels by Cohort and Migration status. I suggest displaying the standardized data in two telephone pole graphs with Cohorts for poles, Migr groups for rungs, and the HSR and Income percentages as vertical scales.

4. From all of this, be prepared to discuss "Did the great migration pay off for Black Americans?"

Religious Mobility

Because *none* is a legitimate category for *religious preference*, religious mobility tables (Age 16 by Current Religion) give insight into movements to and from religion in general as well as patterns of flow between faiths. Hypotheses are plentiful:

- For flow between religions, the leading hypothesis is the *triple melting pot* (Will Herberg, (1960). *Protestant-Catholic-Jew.* New York: Anchor Books). It says (among other things) to expect lots of movement between

Protestant denominations, but very little between the big-three faiths.
- The *secularization* hypothesis predicts that science, rationalism and skepticism tend to erode religious faith. If so, two predictions would seem to follow: newer cohorts should be less religious, and the better-educated should be less religious. But these hypotheses are not unchallenged: some argue that modern technology, television, for example, has made religious proselytizing more effective and the complexity of modern life has increased the need for religious faith; others argue that the better-educated, since they have a firmer grasp of the abstract principles of their faiths, are more steady in their adherence.
- And, of course, the "line" of *this* book is that ethnic variables such as religious persuasion are quite sticky.

Tasks 6-5, 6-6, and 6-7 will allow you to test these hypotheses.

Task 6-5: Religious Stability and Change

Data sets 6.6 and 6.6a allow you to examine mobility tables for Original and Current Religion. (*Other Religions* have been excluded because of the small number of cases and the ambiguity of the category).

1. Use the three standard analyses (stability percentages, flow in zero-adjusted tables, and net shift in marginals) to assess the overall patterns of religious stability and change.
2. Which, if any, of the hypotheses receive support?

Task 6-6: Secularism

The hypothesis about secularism suggests, to me at least, that one might find more shifts from organized religion to *None* among members of new cohorts and the better-educated. These ideas may be tested with data set 6.6, which includes three birth cohort categories (1883–1923, 1924–1943, and 1944–1964) and three educational levels.

1. Cross Tab Cohort and Education against Religion to test the hypothesis.

    Note: To simplify the output, Combine Relig16 and Relignow so each has two categories, Some and None. Then look at (a) the percentage of Somes who become None and (b) the percentage of Nones who stay None—in the six combinations of Cohort and Education.

2. In the non-merged data look at the percentage Stable by Original Religion and Cohort (simultaneously—with a fishnet graph). Do the five groups show similar trends in "holding power"?

3. Whenever we see a cohort difference we should bear in mind the possibility that the differences really stem from aging. Does this change your interpretation?

4. Does American religiosity appear to be faltering or flourishing?

Task 6-7: Religious Intermarriage

No religion "likes" intermarriage, the union of couples whose faiths differ. Rather than seeing intermarriage as an opportunity for conversion, most believe that mixed marriages tend to erode faith. Thus, organized religions tend to develop their own schools, sports organizations, and social clubs, at least in part to encourage marriages within the fold.

The sociologist's term for marriage between brides and grooms with similar characteristics is *homogamy;* its opposite is *heterogamy.*

1. How much religious homogamy do we see in the U.S. adult population in the 1970s and early 1980s? You can find out by Cross Tabbing respondent's Original Religion (*Self 16*) and spouse's Original Religion (*Spouse16*) in data set 6.7. Find the overall rate and the rates for the five religious categories.

2. What is the trend? Compare homogamy percentages in the two cohorts of data set 6.7 (1883–1934 vs. 1935–1964).

3. Are those who enter mixed marriages especially likely to shift to No Religion? To find out, Cross Tab Spouse16 and Relnow

CHAPTER 6   INTERGENERATIONAL MOBILITIES

with Self16 as a control and find the percentage None. (*Hint:* you can cut down the irrelevant numbers by using Combine in the Modify menu to divide Relnow as None vs. Some.)

———

Task 6-8: Tribal Trends

Let us try to put the disassembled parts back together again.

1. Data set 6.2 gives before (Age 16) and after (Current) scores for the eight ethnic types defined in Chapter Two. Cross Tab them. Do you think the theorizing in the introduction to this book overstated, understated, or correctly stated the stability of *tribal* characteristics in the contemporary United States? (*Note:* Given the typology, these data tell us nothing about religious stability among Black Americans. GSS data not available on your diskette suggest Black religion is quite stable. Among original Fundamentalist Protestants, 91 percent of the Blacks are still in that category in comparison with 80 percent of Whites reared as Fundamentalists. Two-thirds, 68 percent, of Blacks were reared as and still are Fundamentalist Protestants.)

2. All in all, what evidence can you advance to both support and refute the argument that tribal characteristics are melting away under the advance of modernization?

———

VERTICAL MOBILITY (AND STATUS INHERITANCE)

Educational Mobility

While babies have a definite race, home location, and often religion, their educational attainments are meager, zero to be exact. We are all upwardly mobile educationally if we think of the starting point as zero years. But sociologists prefer to use parental education as the before measure and then compare the schooling of parents and offspring. If we think of parental schooling as a measure of the

VERTICAL MOBILITY (AND STATUS INHERITANCE)

educational climate in which we were reared, the convention makes a lot of sense. So, when we study educational mobility, the before scores are parental and the after scores are the respondent's current attainment. Simple enough, until we remember we generally have two parents (81 percent of GSS respondents 1972–84 report that they were living with both mother/stepmother and father/stepfather at Age 16).

Task 6-9: Educational Mobility Patterns

1. Please review Task 5-2.3—what do the results there imply about educational mobility?

2. Data set 6.8 contains the variables Birth Cohort (1883–1923 vs. 1924–1943), Sex, Mother's Education, Father's Education, and Respondent's Education. Use Select Control and % Subtable to find out (a) how many sons have more, the same, and less schooling than their fathers and (b) how many daughters have more, the same, and less schooling than their mothers.

3. What might be some sociological consequences of such rates of educational mobility?

   Remember the facetious "law" about stability diagonals? The high rates of mobility you see in this task do not rule out stickiness in the system. When intergenerational variables have high and low ends, concentration in the stable diagonals means the offspring of highs tend to remain high, the offspring of middles tend to remain middle, and the offspring of lows tend to remain low. With vertical (SES variables) the stability-diagonal principle implies *interitance* of status, in that parents in a given level are especially likely to have offspring ending up in that level, and also implies that children from higher levels have a better chance of ending up in higher levels than children from families farther down the ladder. I am not asking you to approve or disapprove of the proposition; but you should see how it follows logically when the stability-diagonal principle is applied to vertical variables.

4. Repeat the cross-tabulations in 6-9.2 using % Across rather than % Subtable. Does this change your impressions?

CHAPTER 6   INTERGENERATIONAL MOBILITIES

Task 6-10: Parental Influences on Schooling

Since we have two parents, we come in two sexes, and education is a cumulative variable (see Task 3-2), some intricate questions come to mind:

- Are mothers and fathers equally influential, or does one parent have a stronger effect on offspring's schooling?
- Is there a cross-sex/same-sex effect? Do, perhaps, mothers have a relatively greater influence on daughters than sons?
- Do parental influences seem to work the same way for completing high school (0–11 vs. 12–20) and entering college (12 vs. 13–20)?

1. Data set 6.8 allows you to explore these questions. You will need two Cross Tabs with Respondent's Education percentaged as the dependent variable. In each, you will have as prior variables Sex, Father's Education, and Mother's Education (which of these is independent and which are controls doesn't matter here). One table should present Respondent's Education as the percentage 12–20 (either Combine or subtract the 0–11 figures from 100 percent). The other table should Omit 0–11 so you can look at college vs. high school only.

    Fishnet graphs (see Chapter Four) can be helpful here. You will need four of them: the two educational attainments (12+, and 13–20 among the 12+) for the two sexes. Your rows and columns will be Mother's and Father's Schooling and the percentages will be Respondent's Education.

2. Task 6-9 revealed a considerable amount of educational inheritance along with the educational mobility discerned in Task 6-9.2—do you think the pattern has changed during this century? If so, is the degree of inheritance increasing or declining?

    Data set 6.8 allows you to check your predictions by looking at the association beween parental and respondent schoolings. Since we now know that both parents must be considered, and since we don't want as much output as turned up in Task 6-9.2, and since you should practice the useful Merge command, begin by making an index with three categories:

I = mother or father has some college;
II = neither parent has any college but mother or father is a high-school graduate;
III = neither parent is a high-school graduate.

Call the result Pared for Parental Educations.
   Cross Tab Respondent's Education by Pared in each of the three birth cohort groups in data set 6.8. Again, look at both high-school completion and college entrance among high-school completers.
   What seem to be the trends—if any?

3. Homogamy and Dynasty: In Task 6-7 you encountered the term *homogamy*. It isn't limited to religion by any means. Even though it is said that "opposites attract," when we shift from biology to sociology, "homogamy holds," as, for instance, schooling.
   a. Cross Tab Mother's and Father's Schoolings in data set 6.8 to see whether I misled you on the degree of educational homogamy. While you're at it, use % Total to find out what proportions of women and men *marry up* and *marry down*.
   b. Now Cross Tab Father's and Respondent's Schooling (or Mother's and Respondent's), and find the percents graduating from high school and entering college in each parental level.
   c. Reorder the data Father-Mother-Respondent (or Mother-Father-Respondent) and use Whatif to eliminate homogamy.
   d. Repeat (b) and compare the two sets of data on occupational inheritance.
   e. Keeping all this in mind, be prepared to comment on the following: "Radical critics of U.S. society maintain that the family system tends to perpetuate inequality." Are there any data to support this notion? If so, what are the major social mechanisms involved?

CHAPTER 6   INTERGENERATIONAL MOBILITIES

Occupational Mobility

Intergenerational occupational mobility (in plain English, a comparison of fathers' jobs and respondents' jobs) is perhaps the most studied topic in modern sociology. In fact, when sociologists talk about *social mobility* they generally mean intergenerational occupational mobility—even though we have already notched four other kinds: size-of-place, region, religion, and education. We need to look at:

- The classic patterns in a mobility table.
- The linking variables that connect generations.
- Variations by sex, time, and space.
- Mobility and "fairness."

You will notice two "conventions." First, mobility analysis is traditionally carried out in terms of Census jobs (Task 3-6) rather than HSR scores, although the main conclusions come out the same with either measure. Second, the analysis is generally limited to fathers and sons rather than fathers and sons *or* daughters. Before berating sociologists for their obvious sexism, review Task 5-2 and the historical trend for the variable Mawork. We will, however, look at both men and women in Task 6-13.

Task 6-11: Patterns of Mobility and Inheritance

Data set 6.9 (Birth Cohort, Sex, Father's Occupation, Respondent's Occupation) presents Father's and Respondent's Occupation in the eight Census occupation groups (Task 3-6). The data are limited to GSS respondents twenty-five and older to make sure respondents are finished with their schooling.

1. Cross Tab the occupations of fathers and sons (use Select Control to get sons). What occupational groups have the highest and lowest stability percentages? Overall, do the stability percentages seem especially high or low to you?

2. Look at the net shift from father to son. (If you use Select Control to find males and % Subtable, the percentages you need will appear in the row and column totals of your table.) What shift dominates the data? What does that reflect? Use

VERTICAL MOBILITY (AND STATUS INHERITANCE)

Omit to remove Farm as an origin and destination and repeat the net shift analysis. What implications do these results have for stability and mobility in occupations?

Combining categories: The eight occupations in data set 6.9 are really too many to grasp clearly. Therefore, mobility researchers frequently combine them into the five groups of Table 3-2 (this would be a good time to review the section on occupations in Chapter Three). This has been done for you in data set 6.9b. Please use it for assignments 6-11.3, 6-11.4, and 6-11.5.

3. Use data set 6.9 to draw a flow chart for origins and destinations of mobile men. In data set 6.9 the stability cells have not been reset to zero so you will have to do this on your own. The easiest way is to produce a frequency table and then type it in CHIP using the the "New" command and substituting zeros for the actual frequencies in the stability cells. If you have not entered data on your own previously, your instructor or the user's manual can provide coaching. In laying out your chart, bear in mind the prestige levels of the five groups. (For men in GSS 1972–84, the mean HSR scores by group are: Hiwhite = 56, Craft = 40, Lowhite = 37, Farm = 36, Loblue = 27, All Men = 39.)

   What are the most interesting flows and nonflows?

4. For another perspective on the table make the cells inside add up to 100 percent. To do so, limit your data to men with Select Control and then use the % Subtable option. Find and mark the cells that show stability, upward mobility, and downward mobility. (I'd treat Craft, Lowhite, and Farm as having essentially the same prestige levels.) The Cat Order command might be helpful here.

   How much upward mobility do you get? How much downward mobility do you get? How do these results square with your conclusions in 6-11.2 above?

5. Use the data in data set 6.9 (keeping the original stability cell frequencies) to make a tele-graph in which the poles are sons' occupations and the rungs on each pole are the paternal occupations. Use the graph to support four propositions about occupational mobility in the contemporary United States.

CHAPTER 6   INTERGENERATIONAL MOBILITIES

Task 6-12: The Linking Variables

The stability-diagonal "law" says there is a more-than-chance level of occupational "inheritance." How does this work? How do high-level fathers manage to "get" high-level jobs for their sons? What keeps sons from low-status families from getting top-ranked jobs? It is rarely the exact inheritance of specific occupations. Studies in which fathers and sons with identical jobs are removed from the table still show the stability-diagonal law at work. Sociological researchers point to educational attainment as the key linking variable. They argue that high-prestige fathers have better-educated sons and better-educated sons get better jobs.

From everything we have seen in this book it would be astounding if there were nothing to these propositions. The real question is whether the effects are powerful. Are they so strong as to account for the similarity between fathers' and sons' occupational levels? Or is sons'/daughters' schooling just one of many small influences on mobility? Our Whatif logic was designed for exactly such questions, and data set 6.10 gives us Birth Cohort, Father's Occupation, Education, and Respondent's Job, with occupations in five categories, for GSS respondents twenty-five and older (both sexes are included).

1. Do fathers with higher status jobs really have better-educated sons and daughters?

2. Cross Tab Father's and Respondent's Occupation with the raw data. Then use Whatif to reorder (1 = Dadsjob; 2 = EDUC; 3 = Ownjob; 4 = Cohort) and then give each cohort and paternal job stratum identical distributions for offspring's schooling (use Change1 on EDUC), repeat the cross-tab, and present the results as rickety ladder graphs. To what extent does schooling explain intergenerational occupational mobility and inheritance? Are its effects pretty much the same for each occupational stratum?

3. For another perspective on education as a linking variable, we can compare it with other possible linkers. Data set 6.11 has Father's and Respondent's HSR (dichotomized, with the breaking point, 46–47, toward the high end) and seven potential linking variables: Birth Cohort (1883–1934 vs. 1935–1964), Sex, Race, Region at Age 16 (South vs. All Other), Parental Education (Either parent completed 12 years vs.

VERTICAL MOBILITY (AND STATUS INHERITANCE)

Neither), Siblings (0–3 vs. 4–31), and Education (0–12 vs. 13–20).

a. If you Cross Tab Father's and Respondent's HSR scores and ask CHIP to calculate the % Diff, you will get a *d* of 20.5. High SES offspring have a twenty-point advantage in getting top jobs. If you ask CHIP to introduce the control variable, EDUC, and then get a % Diff, CHIP will produce a *partial d*, one controlling for education. It does this by working out the *d* within each category of the control variable, (within each educational level, for example) and averaging them in a sophisticated fashion. The calculations are complicated, but the logic is simple: *d*'s calculated *within* control categories can not be explained away by differences *between* control categories. I introduced EDUC as a control and got a partial *d* of 8.3. What should one make of that? The following table may help:

Father/Respondent *d*			
No control	=	20.5	
Education controlled	=	8.3	
Difference (20.5 − 8.3)	=	12.2	= 60 percent of 20.5

If the relationship drops from 20.5 to 8.3 when Education is controlled, then 20.5 − 8.3 = 12.2 points are due to Education. In other words, 60 percent of the occupational inheritance *d* can be explained by the linking variable, Education.

Repeat my analysis of the contribution of education just to see whether you get the same numbers.

b. Now we have a yardstick. With education we can reduce the partial *d* to 8.3. Try some of the other linking variables. Does the mobility-inheritance *d* drop from 20.5 when you introduce one of them as a control? If so, does it drop to 8.3 or less?

c. Overall, how would you evaluate the role of schooling in promoting status continuity/status mobility across the generations?

CHAPTER 6 INTERGENERATIONAL MOBILITIES

Task 6-13: Variations on Our Theme

You are now familiar with the main relationships in the classic, contemporary U.S., father–son mobility table and the role of schooling in coupling and uncoupling the generations. In this task we will look at variations on this theme—between the sexes, over time, and across nations (well, across three nations).

1. *Gender.* As noted above, we have no data on mother–daughter, intergenerational occupational mobility; and when we Cross Tab Father's Job by Daughter's Job we get noise from Sex differences in Occupation. In particular, we get a very large flow into clerical-sales daughter from non-clerical–sales fathers. Nevertheless, two exercises repay the effort.
   a. On the whole, do you expect women's intergenerational mobility is much like men's or different in important ways? Why?
   b. Compare and contrast men's and women's occupational mobility. Which sex is more stable? (Use data sets 6.9 and 6.9b.) Among the movers, are the flows similar? (First make two flow tables, one for women and one for men, using data set 6.9b, a la Task 6-11.3. Second, graph the results. Make the *X* axis women's percentages, the *Y* axis men's percentages. Your graph will display 24 points, one for each possible origin/destination among movers.)

   Use Merge on the two occupations in data set 6.9b to divide the respondents into upwardly mobile, stable, and downwardly mobile. Are there any sex differences in your mobility index?
   c. Does schooling link the generations to the same degree for men and women? Why might it show different effects for men and women? Use data set 6.11 to find the mobility/inheritance *d*'s before and after controlling for Education—separately for men and women.
   d. Given all of the above, do you find the intergenerational occupational mobility of men and women essentially similar or interestingly different?
2. *Time.* Has mobility increased, decreased, or shown no trend during the twentieth century? Ideologists have definite answers; leftists say mobility is declining, rightists say it is

VERTICAL MOBILITY (AND STATUS INHERITANCE)

increasing. Sociological researchers find it difficult to say for sure because we don't have extensive data from the distant past. But, with the data available we can do better than mere guessing. We can explore answers by comparing birth cohorts in the GSS and by comparing adult samples taken at different times.

a. What is your prediction? Have inheritance-mobility d's increased, decreased, changed little, or shown trendless fluctuation since the turn of the century?

b. Data set 6.9b has occupational mobility data (by sex) for GSS respondents twenty-five and older in three birth cohorts (1883–1923, 1924–1943, and 1944–1964). Find the percentage in white-collar jobs for respondents with White-collar, Blue-collar, and Farm Fathers in each cohort. Do this separately for men and women. Present your results as tele-graphs in which the poles are birth cohorts. Are the gaps closing, widening, holding steady, or fluctuating?

Data sets 6.14a, 6.14b, 6.14c, 6.14d, and 6.14e give father-son mobility data from classic mobility studies conducted in 1962, 1940, 1925, 1910, and 1840 to 1889.

c. Find the percentage with white-collar jobs for sons with White-collar, Blue-collar, and Farm Fathers in each of these data sets plus set 6.9b. (The all-urban sample in data set 6.14e excludes Farm Fathers.) Plot these percentages against Year in a graph. (For data set 6.14e you may use 1865 for Year; for set 6.9b use 1978.) Remembering that the studies are noncomparable in many ways, which *trend* hypothesis do they seem to support?

d. Given all of the above, what is your hypothesis regarding changes in occupational mobility and inheritance during the last century?

Data Set Sources
- Data set 6.14i A national probability sample of U.S. men in 1972. This study, known as OCGII, is a replication (redo) of the Blau-Duncan study in 6.14a. The data here

(continued)

CHAPTER 6   INTERGENERATIONAL MOBILITIES

> are taken from Alan C. Kerckhoff, Richard T. Campbell, and Idee Winfield-Laird. (1985). Social mobility in Great Britain and the United States. *American Journal of Sociology, 91*, 281–308.
> - Data set 6.14a: The classic Blau-Duncan mobility study—a national sample of U.S. men in 1962, known as OCGI. (Peter M. Blau and Otis D. Duncan. (1967). *The American occupational structure*. New York: John Wiley & Sons, Inc. Table J2.1, p. 496.)
> - Data set 6.14b: Male residents of Marion county, Indiana (Indianapolis), applying for marriage licenses in 1940. (Natalie Rogoff. (1953). *Recent trends in occupational mobility*. Glencoe, Ill.: Free Press, pp. 65, 76–79, 120–125.)
> - Data set 6.14c: Male household heads enumerated in the 1925 Iowa State Census. (Richard J. Jensen and Mark Friedberger. (1976). *Educational and social structure: An historical study of Iowa, 1870–1930*. Chicago: Newberry Library, Tables 4.11a, 4.12a, 4.13a.)
> - Data set 6.14d: Male marriage license applicants in Marion County, Indiana, in 1910 (see data set 6.14b).
> - Data set 6.14e: Adult males living in Boston, Massachusetts in 1880, 1910, and 1930, whose fathers could be located in earlier Boston and Census records. (Stephan Thernstrom. (1973). *The other Bostonians: Poverty and progress in the American metropolis, 1800–1970*. Cambridge: Harvard University Press, Table 5.3, p. 89.)

3. *Nations.* If America is *the land of opportunity*, it would seem that other nations are lands of lesser opportunity and this should be demonstrable by comparing American inter-generational occupation data with tables for other lands.
   a. What exactly do we mean by *opportunity*? Specifically, if country *A* has more opportunities than country *B*, how would their mobility tables differ?

Data sets 6.14f and 6.14h have father-son mobility tables (White-collar, Blue-collar, Farm) for Poland and England in 1972. Data set 6.14i has comparable figures for the United States in the same year. Use these sets to test your definition of opportunity.

b. Does educational attainment play the same linking role in different societies? Why might it? Why might it not? The English data do not include educational attainment, but the Polish survey (data set 6.14f) has schooling in five categories, and data set 6.14g contains U.S. results (GSS males, 1972–77) with the same categories (0–8, 9–11, 12, 13–15, 16–20). To compare the linking power of schooling in the two nations, run father-son d's in each country, before and after introducing Education as a control.
c. Is America *the* land of opportunity?
d. Can you come up with a sociological proposition that purports to explain the differences and similarities among the three nations?

Data Set Sources
- Data set 6.14f: National probability (0.5 percent) sample of "economically active" Polish men carried out by the Central Statistical Office. Figures are reconstructed from a table in John W. Meyer, Nancy Brandon Tuma, and Krzystof Zagorski. (1979). Education and occupational mobility: a comparison of Polish and American men. *American Journal of Sociology, 84,* 978–986. Original N's (total = 36,505) are divided by ten to simplify the computer displays.
- Data set 6.14h: Area probability sample of English and Welsh men, known as the *Oxford Mobility Survey.* Figures here are taken from Alan C. Kerckhoff, Richard T. Campbell, and Idee Winfield-Laird. (1985). Social mobility in Great Britain and the United States. *American Journal of Sociology, 91,* 281–308. (The table in their article is limited to civilians, twenty-five and older.)
- Data set 6.14i: National area probability sample of U.S. civilian, noninstitutionalized males carried out by the U.S. Census. This study, known as OCGII (Occupational Changes in a Generation), is a replication (redo) of the classic Blau-Duncan 1962 study. (The table is taken from the same article as data set 6.14h.) Set 6.14a is also drawn from this study.

CHAPTER 6 INTERGENERATIONAL MOBILITIES

Task 6-14: Parents, Children, and Subjective Class

Parental SES certainly plays an objective role in determining adult SES. That's the main point of this section. But does it influence our subjective SES? In deciding where we are on the vertical scale, does where we started from make any difference? Several possibilities come to mind:

- *Yes:* Family SES plays a strong role in adult thinking. Our current class self-placement tends to reflect the families from which we came, whether or not we have "done well."
- *Yes, but:* People from higher-status parental families are more likely to think they are high status, but this is explained by the objective influence of parental SES. Parental status influences our current placement only to the extent that it influences our current, objective SES.
- *No:* Class placement is vague and whimsical. It has little to do with current SES, much less parental SES.
- *No, indeed!:* America is obsessed with achievement and mobility. So we tend to judge ourselves by how far we have come, not by where we are. If so, at any particular level of current SES, the higher the parental SES the less the mobility and the less high our achievement.

1. Which hypothesis seems right to you?
2. Test your hunch with data set 6.13. It includes self-rating on social class (see discussion of data set X.3 in Appendix B for details), parental education (Either parent completed high school vs. Neither), the typological variable Dad (see discussion of data set X.60 in Appendix B for details), and birth cohort (1883–1923, 1924–1943, and 1944–1964).
3. It is often said that the younger generation pays less attention to *family background*. If so, you might find your results vary by birth cohort. Do they?

THE MOBILITY SYSTEM

Logically we should have a section on intergenerational income mobility, but the data are simply not available—we have a hard enough time getting good data on current finances, much less "your father's annual income when you were sixteen years old." Nevertheless, we know a lot about the three-variable system of parental SES–Education–Occupation, as illustrated on the opening page of this chapter. We have seen the degree of similarity in SES for parents and children, how education serves to link and sunder the generations, and how these patterns do and do not vary by sex, time, and nation. The system is not only a scientific model of continuity and discontinuity in SES, it can help us think carefully about the American dream—whether it is myth, reality, or something in between.

Task 6-15: Thinking about the System

1. Do you believe the current system, as revealed in our data, is basically "fair" or "unfair"?
2. What aspects of it seem fair and unfair?
3. Suppose you wished to make the system fairer. Draw an arrow diagram of a better system. Is your proposal a practical possibility?

SUMMARY

We have now looked at intergenerational mobility in:

- City Size
- Region
- Religion
- Education
- Occupation

Task 6-16: Summarizing the Results

1. Make a telephone pole graph in which the vertical axis is the percentage Stable and the poles are City Size (Task 6-1), Region (Figure 6-1), Religion (Task 6-5.1), Education (Task 6-9.4), and Occupation (Task 6-11.5).
2. For each of these, find the net shift in categories (for City Size in Task 6-1 the net shift for Metburb is +17, the net shift for

CHAPTER 6 INTERGENERATIONAL MOBILITIES

COUNTRY is −18). Present the shifts as telephone pole graphs on a single page.

3. What seem to be the most striking stabilities, instabilibies, and trends for American adults in the last quarter of the twentieth century?

———

7
Trends in Inequality

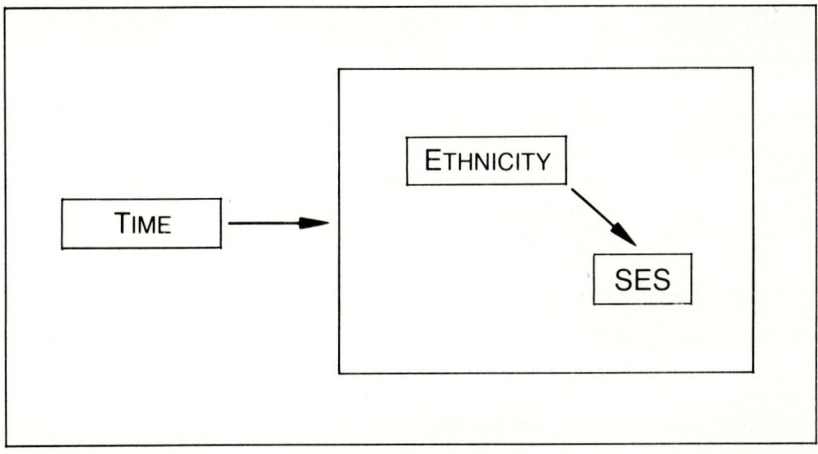

CHAPTER 7 TRENDS IN INEQUALITY

INTRODUCTION

Americans hold complicated attitudes toward inequality (SES differences). On the one hand, we are untroubled by the sheer existence of vertical differences. Not even the most extreme reformers suggest that we should all have identical incomes, job prestige, or schooling. We favor *equality of opportunity* (whatever that means), not *equality of results*.

But, what do Americans mean by equality of opportunity? A 1984 GSS battery of SES attitudes begins to sketch the outlines of an answer. Table 7-1 shows the results.

TABLE 7-1
Attitudes Toward Inequality

Item	Percent	(N)
"America has an open society. What one achieves in life no longer depends on one's family background, but on abilities one has and the education one acquires." **(Strongly agree, Somewhat agree)**	84	(1,448)
"Differences in social standing between people are acceptable because they basically reflect what people made out of the opportunities they had." **(Strongly agree, Somewhat agree)**	72	(1,446)
"Does everyone in this country have an opportunity to obtain an education corresponding to their abilities and talents?" **(Yes)**	70	(1,461)
"In the United States there are still great differences between social levels, and what one can achieve in life depends mainly on one's family background." **(Somewhat disagree, Strongly disagree)**	56	(1,448)

SOURCE: GSS 1984

Task 7-1: Ideology and Mobility

Give some consideration to the answers in Table 7-1. Do you think these opinions are consistent with the "hard facts" in Chapter

Six, or are Americans unrealistic about how our system actually works?

ETHNICITY AND SES

The belief that current levels of individual inequality are justified raises nasty questions when we come to group differences. It is one thing to believe that superior individuals rise to the top, another to believe that superior groups do. Confronted with ethnic differences in SES, we tend to either minimize them, or assume they are fading because they were based on factors that no longer apply (the language problems of immigrants or the degradation of slavery for example). But before we develop our rationalizations, we should know the empirical facts. In this chapter we will take a hard look at contemporary ethnic differences in SES and their apparent trends.

Task 7-2: Ethnicity and SES Today

1. Please review Tasks 4-2 and 6-4.
2. A somewhat comforting explanation of ethnic differences in SES draws on the mobility processes treated in Chapter Six. The argument goes something like this:

   When groups start at the same SES levels as children, their adult achievements are similar. But in the past, certain groups (Blacks, White Southerners, Catholics) "started from behind" because of slavery, rural poverty, recent immigration, and so on. But these handicaps have evaporated, so ethnic differences in SES are no longer a problem.

   Use data set 7.8 to probe these ideas. Look at ethnic differences in SES before and after standardizing the data to give each ethnic group the same parental characteristics (Parsed and Dad). Do family backgrounds account for any or all ethnic differences in SES?
3. Similar arguments have been made for educational attainment. If, as responses in Table 7-1 suggest, educational opportunities are equally available and if, as Chapters Three

and Six suggest, education is the key to adult SES, then perhaps the ethnic differences in adult SES are due to group differences in educational aspiration per se. We don't have direct data on aspirations (studies usually show Blacks have higher educational aspirations than do Whites) but data set 7.1 can tell us whether differences in schooling explain ethnic differences in jobs and incomes. (If they don't, then ethnic differences in educational aspiration can hardly explain ethnic differences in HSR and income.)
   a. Do contemporary ethnic groups differ in educational attainment? In HSR scores? In income?
   b. Use Whatif to give each ethnic group the same levels of schooling. What, if anything, happens to differences in occupational prestige and income when education is adjusted?
4. All in all, are the data on ethnicity and SES consistent or inconsistent with the *American Ideology*?

TRENDS

It is important to view these issues from a change perspective—not just because trend studies are trendy, but because of the life-cycle character of SES. If adult SES levels are relatively permanent and heavily influenced by schooling (Chapter Three), and if educational attainment has changed enormously in this century (Chapter Five), then it is quite possible that the Big Change has affected ethnic differences. Task 7-3 shows you how to test these notions against the data.

Task 7-3: Cohorts and Ethnic Inequality

Data set 7.6 allows you to explore cohort differences in the SES levels of the ethnic groups. It contains the seven cohort groups from Table 5-1, the eight ethnic types, and the SES index. If you look at ethnicity by SES in each birth cohort you can perhaps spot long-term trends in equality and inequality (if you are willing to assume these differences are mostly due to year-of-birth rather than life-cycle).

If you simply graph SES percentages over Time (see Table 5-1 for mean birth years of each cohort) the differences will be hard to see because there are too many curves. I suggest the following:

1. For each group, find the percentage difference between it and all the rest, with Cohort as a control. For example, the *d*'s for White Northern Protestant and SES in Cohort *2* are +12.5 for high, +6.2 for middle, and −18.7 for low SES. (Just to see if we are communicating, start by seeing whether you get these same numbers.)

    Plot the high and low SES *d*'s for each group against Time. Reverse the sign for low SES. (Why? The +12.5 for White Northern Protestants says that in the 1909 cohort they are 12.5 points above the others on high SES; the −18.7 says they are 18.7 points below the others on low. Being below on low indicates an SES advantage. So if you reverse the signs for the low *d*'s, both of your curves will be asking the same question, and the higher they are on the page, the better that group is doing in relation to everyone else.)

    Hint: Punching out forty-nine *d*'s (*d*'s for each of seven groups in each of seven cohorts) is not an enormous amount of fun. Perhaps your class can arrange a division of labor and pool the results.

    Note: In Cohorts *1* and *2* you will have fewer than twenty-five Northern Blacks (Task 6-2 tells why). Leave them out or mark them in a special way.

2. You now have seven graphs, each with a pair of curves for some ethnic group (ignoring Othwite, which is a mishmash) against Time. Those above zero indicate relatively high SES; those below zero indicate below average SES; any that cross the zero line one way or another indicate shifting relative status.

    - Which, if any, groups are consistently high SES?
    - Which, if any, groups are consistently low SES?
    - Which, if any, groups improve their relative status over the years?
    - Which, if any, groups lose in relative status over the years?
    - Do the curves tend to converge, stay parallel, or diverge over the years?

CHAPTER 7 TRENDS IN INEQUALITY

Task 7-4: Recent Changes(?)

Task 7-3 clearly revealed some changes. The SES gaps among American ethnic groups have not remained constant since the turn of the century. But society, at any given time, contains a mix of people from diverse cohorts and the cohort composition shifts steadily and inexorably (see Chapter Eight). So, while it is obvious from Task 7-3 that our macro-structure has changed, it is not obvious that it is changing rapidly today. If, however, we look at the GSS using Year as a variable, we can see how fast things have been moving since 1972.

Data sets 7.16a, 7.16b, and 7.16c include Ethtype, two time periods (1972–75 vs. 1982–85), and the three SES variables (Education in 7.16a, HSR in 7.16b, and Income in 7.16c). We can use them to look at the change in overall SES levels from the early 1970s to the early 1980s, the differential rates of change for the various ethnic groups, and the shifts in the SES gaps among the ethnic groups.

With two Times, it is convenient to measure change by a percentage difference. If, at Time1, X percent do something, and at Time2, Y percent do it, the difference in the two percentages, $Y - X$, describes the change. Since this "trick" will be used in Chapters Eight and Nine, let's nail it down with a non-imaginary example. Table 7-2 gives political party identification for 1972–74 and 1982–84 (data set X.11d).

TABLE 7-2

Change in Party Identification, (GSS 1972–74 vs. 1982–84)

Time	Democrats	Party Independents	Republications	Total	(N)
1982–84	53.7%	12.0%	34.2%	99.9%	(4,393)
1972–74	58.6	10.0	31.4	100.0	(4,263)
d	−4.9	+2.0	+2.8		

SOURCE: GSS 1972 to 1984

Table 7-2 tells us that over the decade the Democratic percentage slipped from 58.6 to 53.7 ($d = 4.9$) while Independents gained 2.0 points (12.0 − 10.0 = 2.0) and Republicans gained 2.8 points (34.2 − 31.4 = 2.8).

TRENDS

Remember, the *d* for a table in which Time is the independent variable is a convenient measure of change.

1. In the period from the early 1970s to the early 1980s how much change was there in national educational levels (data set 7.16a), occupational prestige (data set 7.16b) and (relative) income (data set 7.16c)?

2. If you introduce Ethnicity as a control for your change *d*'s and ask CHIP for the subtables, you can see the change for each of your groups. If a subgroup's *d*'s are larger (or smaller) than the overall rate, that group is changing faster (or slower) than the general population. If the 1970s and 1980s were a period of increasing equality, the convergence should show up in more favorable changes for lower ranking groups. Did this happen? In particular, did Black Americans tend to catch up with Whites?

3. You should have seen different rates of change in different ethnic groups. Were there any important changes in the *gaps* among the groups? To find out, make rickety-ladder graphs in which the two poles are different Times and the vertical scales are the proportions in high and low SES categories.

Task 7-5: Prognostication

From what you learned in Tasks 7-2 and 7-3 what do you predict about ethnic inequality (ethnicity and SES) in the next decade and in the next few decades?

Task 7-6: Digging into it

The simple curves and ladders in Tasks 7-3 and 7-4 summarize an extremely complex system of six variables (race, region, religion, education, occupational prestige, and income) changing in complex ways (parent-child mobility and stability, age-cohort processes).

You may wish to dig into these issues in more detail. To help you, the CHIP diskette contains fifteen data sets designed to allow you to examine fine-grain relations with appropriate controls. I will not give any particular assignment here, but if you wish to pursue these issues in more detail, Table 7-3 gives you a catalogue of the data.

TABLE 7-3

Detailed Data on Ethnicity, SES, and Time

Data Set	Cohort	Ethtype	Race	Parsed	Dad	Reg16	Relig16	EDUC	HSR	Income	SES
7.1		8						3	3	3	
7.2			2			3	3	3	3	3	
7.3			2			5		3	3	3	
7.4			2				6	3	3	3	
7.5						3	5	3	3	3	
7.6	7	8									3
7.7	3	8						3	3		
7.8		8		2	4						3
7.9		8		2	4			3			
7.10	3	8		2				3			
7.11	3	8		2	2			2	2		
7.12	3	3			4						
7.13	3	8			4				2		
7.14		8			4			3	2		
7.15	7	8						3			

SOURCE: All data sets are from the cumulative GSS 1972 to 1984.

Notes: a. Numbers in the table are the numbers of categories for that variable.
b. Data sets 7.8, 7.10, 7.12, 7.13, and 7.14 exclude persons 18–24 years of age.
c. Explanations of the variables can be found as follows:
  Cohort (Chapter Five)
  Ethtype, Race, Reg16, Relig16 (Chapter Two)
  EDUC, HSR, Income, SES (Chapter Three)
  Parsed (Appendix B, data set X.61)
  Dad (Appendix B, data set X.60)

SUMMARY

Ideologues and informal observers often draw quite opposite conclusions about trends in inequality. *Optimists* argue that while the past may have seen unfortunate differences in the SES of major groups, these differences are gone or are rapidly disappearing.

SUMMARY

Pessimists take the opposite position—that these differences are persistent and in some cases widening. In this chapter I have tried to adopt the stance of a *realist*—examining cohort patterns and trend data from the early 1970s to the early 1980s.

It is up to you to decide whether the numbers support the optimists or pessimists, but I think you will agree that such changes as we have seen are far from sudden. In the next chapter we will dig more deeply into the actual process of change to gain insight into the factors determining the pace of social change.

8

Cohorts and Short-term Social Change: The Stouffer Hypothesis

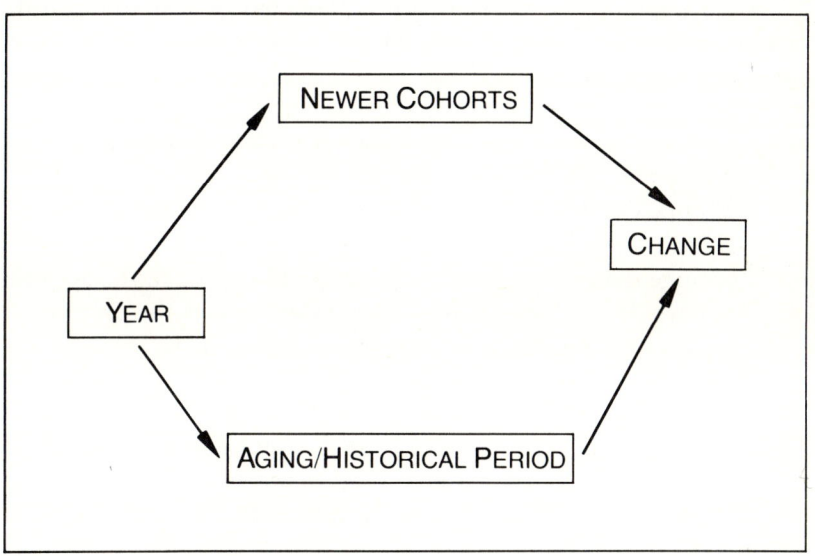

CHAPTER 8   COHORTS AND SHORT-TERM SOCIAL CHANGE

COUNTING YOUR CHANGE

One's image of society tends to be static—not unlike the checkerboard pattern of a countryside you see from an airplane. But it is probably better to think of society as a busy airport—always full of people, but with hundreds of them arriving and departing every minute, so the essentially constant population size conceals the high rate of turnover.

This image captures the essence of the *cohort approach to social change*. In Chapters Five, Six, and Seven we saw how American birth cohorts differed on a variety of variables. In this chapter we will see how these differences produce changes (and stabilities) in the macro-system. Just as Chapter Six showed how standard, tabular techniques can be applied to the special case of mobility, this chapter begins by explaining how tabular techniques may be used to analyze change due to *cohort replacement*.

The idea is to take a certain amount of change (a six-point shift in some attitude from Time1 to Time2 for example) and break it down into three parts:

- Change due to births, that is, the *Arrival* of distinctive newcomers. Call it A for arrivals.
- Change due to deaths, that is, the *Departure* of distinctive old timers. Call it D for departures.
- Change due to net shift in the scores of people in the system at both Times (see Chapter Six). Since Year is the unit of time for GSS data, we'll call this component Y.

Changes A and D together give the total effect of cohort replacement, the contribution to change coming from turnover in membership. Change Y is often called *aging* or *period* (the sheer effect of becoming x years older or the effect of a particular historical period on everybody within it; the permanent effects of living through "the Great Depression" for example).

So far we have merely defined letters, but three equations may help keep the letters straight:

*C*ohort change = *A*rrivals + *D*epartures
*T*otal change = *C*ohort + *Y*ear
$T = A + D + Y$

COUNTING YOUR CHANGE

If we know these four numbers we can tell (1) how big the change has been; (2) how much of the change came from cohort replacement, how much from net shifts among the "permanent" members of the group; and (3) how much of the cohort replacement effect is coming from the entrance of a new generation, how much from the Grim Reaper.

Let me show you how you can use CHIP to get these four numbers.

T = Total Change

Task 7-4 introduced a simple measure of Total Change (T) from Year*1* to Year*2*. Simply Cross Tab, with Year as the independent variable and the variable which might be changing dependent. Table 7-2 gave the example of political party identification; Table 8-1 shows changes in Dad (see also Task 5-2).

TABLE 8-1
Changes in Dad 1972–74 vs. 1982–84

	Nodad	Farm	HSR 9–37	HSR 38–82
d	+0.89	−6.32	+3.49	+1.95

SOURCE: data set X.60d

Table 8-1 shows us that the percentage of U.S. adults reporting:

- Nodad (not living with father at Age 16) increased 0.89 points.
- Farmer fathers declined 6.32 points.
- HSR 9–37 (lower occupational prestige) fathers increased 3.49 points.
- HSR 38–82 (higher occupational prestige) fathers increased 1.95 points.

> *Note:* of the four *d*'s only those for farmer and HSR 9–37 are statistically significant, that is, *d/sigma d* is 2.0 or larger. In this chapter we will take the *d*'s at face value without worrying about statistical inference. Your teacher may or may not allow you to do the same.

CHAPTER 8 COHORTS AND SHORT-TERM SOCIAL CHANGE

The proportion of American adults from farm backgrounds declined from the early 1970s to the early 1980s, the percentage *orphans* showed virtually no change, and the percentages in both non-farm HSR levels went up a bit. This is just about what we would expect from Chapter Five.

When the dependent variable has more than two categories (Dad for example) we can analyze each of them, and it is quite possible that we will get rather different answers, if the social forces influencing one category are different from the forces influencing others. (Thus, we would not be surprised if the analysis of Nodad came out quite different from the analysis of Farmer). With two categories, however, life becomes much simpler because results for one of them will be mirror images of results for the other (if females are increasing, males must be decreasing). I will use single categories to develop the examples, but you are not obliged to do so in your analyses.

I will spotlight Farmer. Table 8-2 shows change data for it and three others.

TABLE 8-2
Total Changes in Four Variables, 1972–74 vs. 1982–84

Data set	Variable	Topic	Category	T
X.60d	Dad	Father's Occupation	Farm	−6.3
X.64d	News	Newspaper Reading	Daily	−13.6
X.23d	Cappun	Death Penalty	Favor it	+9.9
X.3d	Class	Subjective Class	Middle	+0.2

SOURCE: GSS 1972–74 and 1982–84

Table 8-2 tells us that between the early 1970s and the early 1980s (1) the percentage reading a newspaper daily dropped 13.6 points, (2) the percentage favoring the death penalty for murderers increased 9.9 points, and (3) the percentage describing themselves as middle class changed hardly at all, 0.2 percent.

These four *d*'s (Dad, News, Cappun, and Class) give us examples of Total Change. Next let's see what change processes produced them.

N = *the Contribution of Newcomers*

Every group has some sort of *birth rate*—the actual delivery of babies for a total society, a new freshman class at a college or university, the number of persons turning eighteen—for the population sampled in the General Social Survey. Popular writings about *baby boomers* and *yuppies* call our attention to the impacts newcomers can produce. Our task is to find a way to state this impact precisely. Let us begin by comparing the GSS in the early 1970s and the early 1980s. Table 8-3 shows the distribution by birth cohort (review Table 5-1 if necessary) for the two periods.

TABLE 8-3

Birth Cohorts 1972–74 vs. 1982–84

Cohort	Birth Years	Percentages	
		1972–74	1982–84
1	1883–1903	9.7%	3.4%
2	1904–1913	12.9	8.1
3	1914–1923	17.3	13.0
4	1924–1933	17.0	13.7
5	1934–1943	19.5	14.4
6	1944–1953	23.0	22.8
7	1954–1964	0.6	24.7
		Total 100.0%	100.0%
		N (2,985)	(2,973)

SOURCE: GSS: 1972–74 and 1982–84

Look at Cohort 7, Americans born 1954–64. They are virtually nil in 1972–74 (0.6 percent of the total) but make up 24.7 percent of the population in 1982–84. Thus, when comparing the early 1970s and the early 1980s these young adults are newcomers. They contribute (essentially) nothing to the 1972–74 results, but make up a quarter of the population ten years later.

Do these newcomers contribute to the change in Farmer Fathers displayed in Table 8-2? If so, how? Table 8-4 shows how.

The bottom row (Total) shows that, overall, in 1972–74, 22.4 percent of American adults came from Farm backgrounds, while in 1982–84 the figure had dropped to 16.1 percent. The difference, 22.4 − 16.1 = − 6.3, is the total change shown in the top row of Table 8-2.

The cells inside Table 8-4 present the same figures for Cohort 7, the Newcomers, and Cohorts *1–6*, the non-newcomers. Look at the change in the top row, − 3.2. It is smaller than the total value of − 6.3. So total change is larger than change among the non-newcomers. Why? Look at the percentage for the newcomers.

Among them only 6.3 have farmer fathers. If they "hadn't been born," the 1982–84 percentage would be 19.2 and the total change would have been -3.2 not -6.3. Thus, newcomers contribute 3.1 points (6.3 vs. 3.2) to the total change.

TABLE 8-4

Newcomers and Change in Farmer Fathers

Birth Cohort	Percent Farmer Father				Change
	1972–74	(N)	1982–84	(N)	
1–6	22.4%	(4,315)	19.2%	(3,268)	−3.2
7		(25)	6.3	(1,068)	
Total	22.4%	(4,340)	16.1%	(4,336)	−6.3

SOURCE: GSS 1972–74 and 1982–84

Table 8-4 shows exactly how newcomers can contribute to change, but you can get these numbers more simply, as follows:

> **Change due to Newcomers**
> 1. Find the bivariate percentage difference for Year and the dependent variable. Call it I.
> 2. Then Omit the newcomers, using the Modify menu.
> 3. Repeat step (1). Call the new d: II.
> 4. Subtract II from I.
> $$I - II = N$$

Table 8-5 shows the N effects for the four variables in Table 8-2.

TABLE 8-5

Contribution of Newcomer Cohorts to Changes in Table 8-2

Difference	Dad = Farm	News = Daily	Cappun = Favor	Class = Middle
I = Total	−6.3	−13.6	+9.9	+0.2
II = After Omitting Cohort 7	−3.2	−7.4	+9.3	+3.4
I − II	−3.1	−6.2	+0.6	−3.2

SOURCE: GSS 1972–74 and 1982–84

The four variables tell the following stories. Between the early 1970s and the early 1980s, newcomers to the U.S. adult population:

- Accentuated the decline in persons from farm backgrounds by 3.1 points (as explained above).
- Accentuated the decline in daily newspaper reading by 6.2 points.
- Had little effect (+0.6 points) on the increased favorability to capital punishment.
- Had a negative effect (−3.2 points) on middle-class identification.

The last two examples merit comment. Why didn't the newcomers contribute to the shift toward capital punishment? Of mathematical necessity, it is because their 1982–84 attitudes were virtually the same as those in Cohorts *1* through *6*. Hence, an important principle; for newcomers to make an appreciable difference, two things must happen: there must be more than a handful of them, and they must differ from the non-newcomers on their Year2 scores.

The results for class-identification are mildly curious. The newcomers lower middle-classness by 3.2 points, but the overall change is zero (0.2). So something must be producing positive shifts to offset the entrance of the self-deprecating newcomers. The point here is that the components in change do not have to operate in the same direction. The total change can be a balance of positive and negative shifts.

Y = *Years (net shift within cohorts)*

People not only come and go, they also change. As they grow older, or the economic climate shifts, or political dramas unfold, or for whatever reason, members of a particular cohort may change their attitudes and behaviors. If changes in one direction outnumber changes in another, we can see this net shift within cohorts in our tables. This net shift within cohorts gives us the amount of change due to the passing Years and not due to Arrivals and Departures. Tables 8-6 (Farmer Father) and 8-7 (Daily Newspaper Reader) illustrate.

For each (non-newcomer) cohort we see their percentages for the dependent variable in 1972–74 and 1982–84. The difference between them is the shift. Look at Cohort *1* in the top row of Table 8-6. In 1972–74, 44.7 percent reported farmer fathers; ten years

CHAPTER 8   COHORTS AND SHORT-TERM SOCIAL CHANGE

later 42.4 percent gave that answer. Thus, Cohort 7 showed a net shift of −2.3 for Farmer Father. The right-hand column of Table 8-6 shows the six net shifts. They are all small and not in the same direction. That is, there was hardly any net shift within cohorts in Farmer Father. (If you ponder it for a moment, you will probably conclude this is to be expected. Among adults, reports of their early childhood situations should not change over time, save for sampling fluctuations.)

TABLE 8-6
Cohort, Percentage Farmer Father, and Decade

Cohort	1972–74	(N)	1982–84	(N)	Difference	
1	44.7%	(423)	42.4%	(144)	−2.3	
2	34.9	(558)	33.6	(351)	−1.3	
3	29.5	(757)	26.0	(558)	−3.5	Weighted Average =
4	20.0	(739)	21.8	(595)	+1.8	partial $d = -0.4$
5	15.7	(839)	14.5	(629)	−1.3	
6	8.1	(999)	8.4	(991)	+0.3	
1–6	22.4%	(4,315)	19.2%	(3,268)	−3.2	

SOURCE: GSS 1972–74 and 1982–84

But look at Table 8-7. In each cohort but one, there is a negative shift of five to ten points. Within cohorts there was a decline in daily newspaper reading, unlike the stability in Table 8-6.

Table 8-7
Cohort, Percentage Daily Newspaper Reader, and Decade

Cohort	1972–74	(N)	1982–84	(N)	Difference	
1	74.0%	(173)	69.2%	(107)	−4.8	
2	75.2	(210)	67.0	(261)	−8.2	
3	76.5	(281)	69.9	(402)	−6.6	Weighted Average =
4	80.2	(283)	70.5	(421)	−9.7	partial $d = -5.9$
5	68.1	(301)	59.4	(438)	−8.7	
6	46.8	(325)	49.1	(682)	+2.4	
1–6	69.0%	(1,573)	61.5%	(2,311)	−7.4	

SOURCE: GSS 1972–74 and 1982–84

It seems that, quite aside from the reading habits of newcomers or departers, Americans were actually changing their media patterns during the 1970s.

Because of sampling variation and the smaller case bases when we break the data down by cohort, we can hardly expect to get exactly the same values for net shift in each cohort. CHIP smooths this out for us with partial percentage differences, which are simply weighted averages of the d's within control categories. (The weights depend mostly on the number of cases since larger n's make sample results more reliable.) To get these numbers, introduce Cohort as your control variable in the Cross Tab branch and choose the % Diff option. CHIP does the rest.

The weighted average (partial d) for Farmer Father is -0.4, that is, zilch. Within cohorts there was virtually no change in Farmer Father. The weighted average (partial d) for Daily Newspaper Reading is -5.9. Within cohorts there was a Year effect of -5.9 points on Daily Newspaper Reading.

> **Change due to Year**
> After Omitting Newcomers, find the percentage difference for Year and the dependent variable, controlling for Cohort. This is the Y component of Change.

Table 8-8 displays the Year effects for our examples.

TABLE 8-8
Year Effects for Examples

Variable	Category	Y
Dad	Farm	-0.4
News	Daily	-5.9
Cappun	Favor it	$+9.0$
Class	Middle	$+4.3$

SOURCE: GSS 1972–74 and 1982–84

While there was no change in Farmer Fathers, within cohorts, daily newspaper reading declined an average of 5.9 points, favorability to capital punishment increased an average of 9.0 points, and middle-class identification increased an average of 4.3 points.

CHAPTER 8   COHORTS AND SHORT-TERM SOCIAL CHANGE

We now see how to assess the effects of Arrivals and Years. There remains the contribution of Departures.

$$D = \text{Change due to Departures}$$

Just as newcomers can change the average if they are numerous and different, departures from a population can also contribute to change. Departures may be due to emmigration, graduation, retirement or whatever, but for the GSS population the process is one of biological mortality. Table 8-9 will give you a good idea of how the Grim Reaper culls the U.S. adult population.

TABLE 8-9
Depletion of Cohorts by Deaths

Original Age	Five Years Later	Proportion Still Alive Ten Years Later	Fifteen Years Later
20–25	.993	.987	.980
25–30	.993	.987	.977
30–35	.993	.984	.970
35–40	.991	.977	.955
40–45	.986	.964	.930
45–50	.978	.943	.893
50–55	.965	.914	.841
55–60	.947	.872	.770
60–65	.921	.813	.676
65–70	.883	.734	.556
70–75	.831	.629	—
75–80	.757	—	—

SOURCE: National Center for Health Statistics, *Monthly Vital Statistics Report*. Vol. 32, No. 4, Supplement, August 11, 1983, Table 2, p. 11.

Note: All races, both sexes, assuming 1980 mortality rates apply in each year.

The data in Table 8-9 come from national vital statistics. The cell entries are the proportions (probablities) surviving five, ten, and fifteen years for Americans of various ages. Since the CHIPLIB data span a decade, the middle column is the one we need. For ages twenty through fifty-five, departures are rare. Thus, for cohorts 3 through 6 about 90 percent of the Americans sampled in the early

1970s were available in the early 1980s. (Later GSS's don't include the same *individuals* but the GSS samplers were fishing in essentially the same pond both times—for these groups anyway.) For older Americans, a decade takes a toll. True, a majority of those ages seventy to seventy-five are alive a decade later, but the probability is a grim .629.

GSS does not conduct follow-up studies of its respondents, so we can not identify the individuals who departed. But the effects of mortality are clear when one looks at the distribution by birth cohort over time, as shown in Table 8-10.

TABLE 8-10

Cohort and Decade (Cohorts 1–6 only)

Decade	Cohort						Total	(N)
	6	5	4	3	2	1		
1982–84	30.3	19.2	18.2	17.1	10.7	4.4	99.9%	(3,268)
1972–74	23.2	19.4	17.1	17.5	12.9	9.8	99.9	(4,315)
Difference	+7.2	−0.2	+1.1	−0.5	−2.2	−5.4		

SOURCE: GSS 1972–74 and 1982–84

Between 1972 and 1974 the percentages from the older cohorts (*1*, *2*, and *3*) dropped 8.1 points. This can not be explained by newcomers, since Cohort 7 is excluded from the table. What has happened, of course, is that mortality has thinned out the ranks of older Americans and lowered the proportions of non-newcomers from the more senior birth cohorts.

If those who depart are systematically different from survivors, mortality will produce change, as a sort of mirror image of the effects of arrivals. But, since we can not spot individual departures, we get at the effect indirectly. It is very simple. To see how, let's return to Farmer Fathers in Table 8-6. We know (from the Year analysis) that when Cohort is controlled the change is −0.4, but the bottom of the table tells us that prior to control, the change among the non-newcomers is −3.2. The difference between 0.4 and 3.2 turns on whether we control Cohort. This difference (3.2 − 0.4 = 2.8) is the effect of departures.

Similarly, consider Table 8-7. Among non-newcomers overall, the change in daily newspaper reading is −7.4, but when Cohort is controlled, the change is −5.9. Hence, 1.5 points (7.4 − 5.9) can be attributed to departures (in statistical terms, the relationship between cohort and decade and the relationship between cohort and the dependent variable).

D = *The Effect of Departures*

After omitting newcomers, calculate Change d's before and after controlling for Cohort. The former minus the latter is the contribution of departures.

Counting Your Change: A Summary

By now life (and death) may seem rather complicated since I have spelled out the steps in cohort analysis in detail so you will see what is going on when you push the buttons. But when we put the pieces back together, it turns out you can get a surprisingly complete analysis with a surprisingly small number of steps, like so:

I. Find the d's for Year and the dependent variable.

II. Omit Newcomers and repeat.

III. Control for Cohort and repeat.

That's it, in terms of button pushing. From which, by definition or simple arithmetic:

$$I = T \text{ (Total change)}$$
$$III = Y \text{ (Change due to Year)}$$
$$I - II = N \text{ (Change due to Newcomers)}$$
$$II - III = D \text{ (Change due to Departures)}$$
$$N + D = \text{Change due to Cohort Replacement}$$

Table 8-11 illustrates these procedures with complete analyses of our four examples:

- Change in Farmer Father is (naturally) completely due to replacement of older, rural-raised cohorts by newer, urban ones. The effects of newcomers and departures are about equal (-3.1 and -2.8) giving a total cohort effect of -5.9, against a virtually zero year effect.
- Change in attitude to capital punishment shows a completely opposite process. The net shift across years is 9.0 points and both cohort effects ($N = +0.6, D = +0.3$) are trivially small.
- Change in daily newspaper reading shows both processes at work in the same direction. Cohort replacement contributes 7.7 points (more from newcomers, -6.2, than departures, -1.5) to the decline, while Year contributes -5.9, giving a total of -13.6.
- Change in class identification shows causal processes working in opposite directions and canceling each other. The newcomers lower middle-class identification 3.2 points (presumably because of their lower-prestige, entry-level jobs) but over time, net shift (moving up the ladder) raises middle-class identification 4.3 points, giving a standoff total of 0.2. The apparent stability in class identification from the 1970s to the 1980s conceals two definite but contradictory causal processes.

TABLE 8-11
Examples of Change Analysis

Results	Dad = Farm	News = Daily	Cappun = Favor	Class = Middle
I = Total	−6.3	−13.6	+9.9	+0.2
II = (Omit newcomers)	−3.2	−7.4	+9.3	+3.4
III = Year	−0.4	−5.9	+9.0	+4.3
N = (I − II)	−3.1	−6.2	+0.6	−3.2
D = (II − III)	−2.8	−1.5	+0.3	−0.9
Cohort = N + D	−5.9	−7.7	+0.9	−4.1
Cohort	−5.9	−7.7	+0.9	−4.1
Year	−0.4	−5.9	+9.0	+4.3
Total	−6.3	−13.6	+9.9	+0.2

SOURCE: GSS 1972 to 1984

CHAPTER 8   COHORTS AND SHORT-TERM SOCIAL CHANGE

Task 8-1: Practice at Change Analysis

1. Repeat my analysis for one of the four examples in Table 8-11, just to show yourself you can get these same numbers.

2. Now, try one on your own. I think you will find data set X.63d (legalization of marijuana), X.27d ("women's place"), X.26d (local courts), or X.35d (strength of religious faith) interesting.

3. Some theoretical issues:

   - Consider a society where most change in attitudes is through cohort replacement and one where most change in attitudes is through Year. What might be some of the sociological consequences for these societies?
   - Since, in every society, newcomers to the adult population are the offspring of non-newcomers, how does it happen that they often have distinctive attitudes and behaviors which can produce change?

HOW RACE GAPS CHANGE

Over the long haul there have been important shifts in the SES ranks of the various ethnic groups (Task 7-3) and even a mere decade reveals discernible shifts in the gaps among groups (Task 7-4). The changes from the early 1970s to the early 1980s are small enough to support the pessimists, but their directions are such as to support the optimists.

We will now use the tools explained in the previous section to see how the process works. The aim here is somewhat more than practice in methodology—the underlying issue is about the amount of *stickiness* in the American social system. To the extent that gap changes are due to cohort replacement, one may argue that they will be slow but relentless. To the extent that gap changes are due to year effects, one may argue that they can be swift but they might be reversible. For example, if you find that newcomer cohorts show less inequality and that year effects are nil, you might conclude that inequality will lessen in the future as newcomers increase their proportion but that the inequalities among the older cohorts will remain—like flies stuck in amber—for decades. Conversely, if you find that year effects dominate the data, you might argue that *doing more of what we have been doing* could produce more equality faster.

Task 8-2: The Race Gaps

1. From what you know already, for Black-White differences in SES, which model seems the better bet: (a) trends toward equality are mostly due to cohort replacement; (b) trends toward equality are mostly due to year effects; or (c) trends toward equality are too slight to show much in fine-grain analysis?

2. Data set 8.1 contains the variables Year, Cohort (Birthyr), Race, Education, HSR, and Income. You can use it to compare Whites and Blacks in terms of their SES changes from the early 1970s to the early 1980s.

   For a complete picture you should do six cohort-change analyses—one for each of the three SES variables among Blacks and the same among Whites. (CHIP experts can figure out slightly faster ways, but the straightforward approach is to Omit one race, carry out the three analyses, fetch data set 8.1 anew, Omit the other race, and carry out the three analyses again.) A little team work might be in order here.

3. From all of which—what is your forecast for trends in racial equality during the next decade? As a citizen (rather than social scientist) are you satisfied or dissatisfied with the prospects?

THE STOUFFER HYPOTHESIS

In 1954, the late Samuel A. Stouffer, a pioneer in national sociological surveys, was asked by the Ford Foundation to carry out an inquiry on threats to free speech. Why 1954? Why free speech? The words "Senator Joseph R. McCarthy" come immediately to mind. The high point of the senator's onslaught against "domestic communists" was in 1954 (field work for the survey was carried out during the famous Army–McCarthy hearings), and the Ford Foundation wanted to find out whether the general climate for free speech had turned chilly.

Stouffer surveyed a large U.S. adult cross-section (4,933 cases). As insurance against measurement bias he commissioned identical field jobs by Gallup and the NORC (their samples and interviewers produced virtually identical results). His book length report, *Communism, Conformity, and Civil Liberties* (Doubleday, 1955), is a classic, well worth your attention as a rare combination of readability, sound science, and enduring ideas. We will focus on his famous Chapter Four, "How Tolerant Is the New Generation?"

The Stouffer measure of tolerance is a scale combining fifteen attitude items. Each pairs a nonconformist ("a man who admits he is a communist," "somebody who is against all churches and religion," "a person who favored government ownership of all the railroads and all big industries,") with an issue about free expression ("[should he be] allowed to make a speech in your city," "[should] a book he wrote be taken out of your public library?," "Suppose he is teaching in a college or university. Should he be fired or not?") Data sets X.51 (free speech for communists) and X.52 (free speech for atheists) include GSS replications (exact repetitions) of Stouffer items.

The gist of Stouffer's argument will already be familiar to you. His key findings are that controlling for education, younger adults are more tolerant; and, controlling for age, better-educated adults are more tolerant. You may hardly be surprised (thirty years afterwards), but Stouffer notes that his was the first national study to demonstrate their independent effects (recall the discussion of social science's progress since the 1950s in Chapter One).

Stouffer interprets the age difference as an *Aging effect*, a tendency for people to become more conservative as they grow older (he thinks this is because health and financial problems make older people psychologically rigid and hints that future health and economic progress might mitigate this tendency). But he also draws our attention to the striking cohort differences in educational attainment (see Chapter Five). Balancing aging against education trends, he puts his money on schooling: "As the educational level of those entering the older generation goes up decade after decade, we should expect our oldsters to be increasingly tolerant" (Wiley, p. 94).

Thus, Stouffer thought that aging lowers tolerance, while education increases it. Since he predicted educational levels would increase sharply (and apparently assumed age distributions would not change much), he predicted a long-term trend toward tolerance.

Social science predictions based on hard data are rare and Stouffer was anything but flamboyant personally. Nevertheless, he ends his chapter with a strong statement:

> [T]his chapter seeks to weigh some of the underlying forces in American society making for or against a tendency toward

growth of tolerance. On balance, the direction in which these underlying forces have been going should be encouraging to those who are concerned with preserving the American heritage of freedom (Wiley, p. 108).

Stouffer in a nutshell: over the long haul, education-driven cohort replacement will outweigh age-driven intolerance, so America will become progressively more tolerant.

If true, this is a pretty powerful intellectual tool since education has broad and diverse effects so the Stouffer hypothesis should apply to many topics, and we understand the dynamics of education well enough that we can forecast national educational levels for the next decade or so (you could do so with Whatif given the data in Table 8-9 and reasonable assumptions about the number and schooling of future newcomers).

Task 8-3: Testing Stouffer's Predictions

1. Data sets X.51d and X.52d allow you to examine tolerance of communists and atheists from the early 1970s to the early 1980s, using Stouffer's original questions. In addition, GSS added a new issue, free speech for homosexuals, not salient in the 1950s (data set X.55d). Use a cohort-change analysis to test Stouffer's predictions for one or more of these items.

2. To the extent the Stouffer hypothesis is correct, we can "read the future" by looking at the attitudes of younger and/or better-educated Americans. Try your hand at this using the X.d data sets for 1982–84 on some topic of interest to you. Cross Tab Cohort against the dependent variable. Of course, you know nothing about future newcomers, but the data will help you forecast the effect of departures and might give some hints about newcomers.

Task 8-4: But Is It Really Tolerance?

In the early 1970s, when the GSS repeated some of Stouffer's items, the data seemed to vindicate his predictions. Six Stouffer items which had shown an average of 25.2 percent tolerant in 1954, averaged 55.4 percent in GSS 72–73, an increase of 30.2 points over two decades. But in 1982, this conclusion was challenged by a team of political scientists (John L. Sullivan, James Pierson, and George E. Marcus, (1982) *Political tolerance and American democracy*, Chicago: University of Chicago Press). Sullivan and his colleagues developed complex methodological and theoretical arguments, but the burden of their argument is simple: almost by definition, you can only tolerate something you dislike. (Remember Voltaire's, "I disapprove of what you say, but I will defend to the death your right to say it." He didn't write, "I heartily endorse what you say and will defend...") Noting that *domestic* communism had almost disappeared as a threat in the 1970s the Sullivan group argued that Americans had not become more tolerant, merely less threatened by communists.

Stouffer himself was well aware of this issue. He wrote:

> This chapter disavows a flat prediction that the next generation will be more tolerant than the present one. If the Communist threat should become greater, pressures against tolerance might increase; if the threat should become less, pressures against tolerance might decrease," (Wiley, p. 108).

In sum, Sullivan and Stouffer (and Pierson and Marcus) agree that a proper analysis of trends in tolerance requires a three-variable analysis of the sort shown in Figure 8-1 below.

FIGURE 8-1

Trends in Tolerance

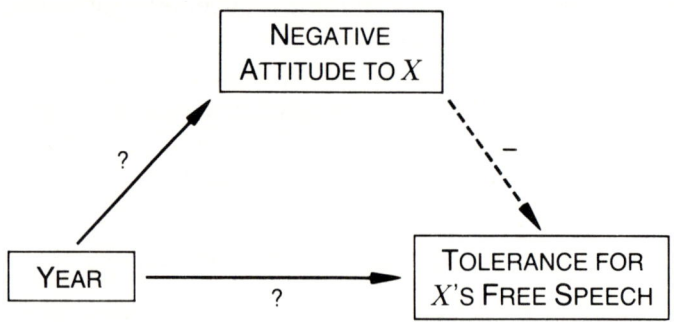

Data sets X.51 (communists), X.52 (atheists) and X.55 (homosexuals) were designed with this model in mind. Each includes an attitude-to-x item along with the tolerance-of-x item.

SUMMARY

1. Cross Tab Year against Tolerance. Find the partial d controlling for the attitude-to-x item. Compare the bivariate (T) change and the change with attitude controlled. Do the results lead you to modify your conclusions about the Stouffer hypotheses?

2. Cynics raise similar questions about Stouffer's famous findings on education and tolerance. They argue that the better-educated aren't *really* more tolerant; rather, they argue, Stouffer happened to pick x's (communists, atheists, socialists) less repugnant to better-educated Americans. To probe these ideas, the GSS added two new free speech questions where the x's are "toward the right politically," racists (data set X.53) and militarists (data set X.54). Each of these also includes an attitude-to-x item.
    Test whether schooling really promotes tolerance by:
    a. Cross Tabbing Education against Free Speech for the five Stouffer free speech items (the d for 13–20 vs. 0–11 is a handy summary).
    b. Cross Tabbing Education against the attitude-to-x items.
    c. Cross Tabbing Education against Free Speech with its attitude-to-x item controlled.

SUMMARY

This chapter presented a statistical "accounting scheme" for looking at the contributions of cohort replacement (departures and newcomers) and changes within cohorts (Year effects) to net shifts in variables. We first applied the scheme to trends in race gaps from the early 1970s to the early 1980s. Then we turned to a detailed scrutiny of the Stouffer hypothesis—that cohort replacement will make us increasingly tolerant of nonconformists.

Task 8-5: Predictions

From all of the above, dare you make any predictions about how American society will change in the next decade? If so, try to justify your claims by reference to specific findings.

9

The Changing American Family

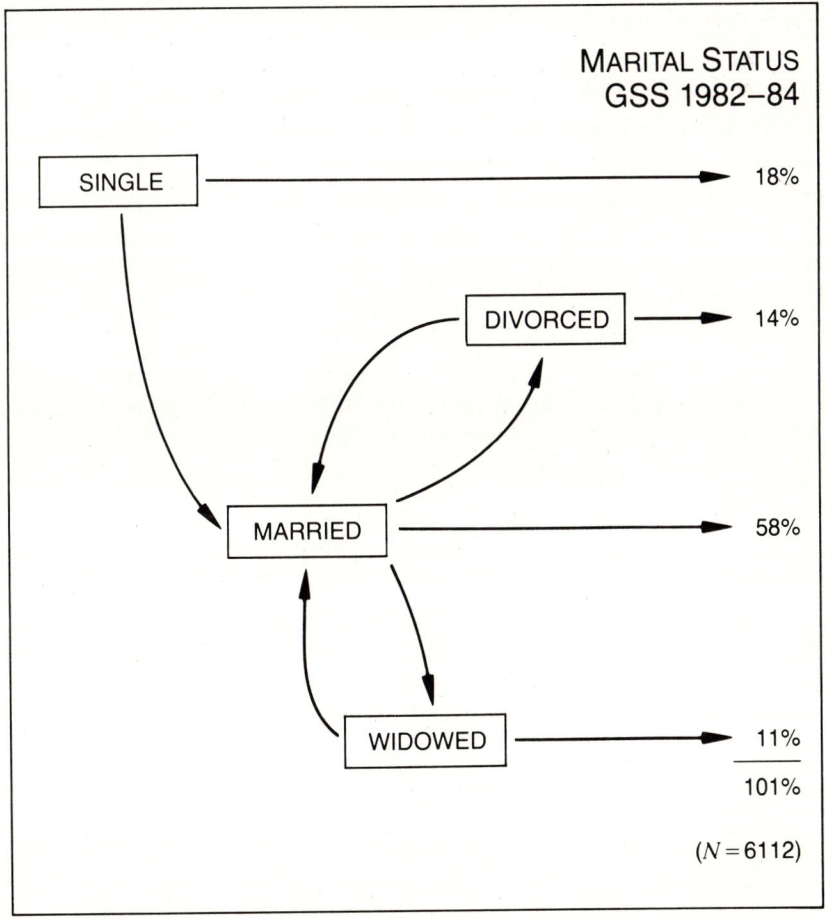

CHAPTER 9   THE CHANGING AMERICAN FAMILY

SOME BACKGROUND

A family, like life, is an extremely complicated phenomenon made from deceptively simple parts. Two *genders* (male and female), four *marital statuses* (never married, married, divorced/separated, and widowed), and three *descent possibilities* (ancestor of/descendent of/neither) just about cover it.

Part of the complexity arises because everything is defined *relationally* (*relatively*, you might say). You are the son/daughter of *your* particular parents, the brother or sister of *your* parents' direct descendents, the cousin of the direct descendents of the direct descendents of *your* parents' parents, and so on. Some of the most sophisticated mathematical modeling in social science has gone into analyzing such networks of marriage and descent, and much remains to be done.

Another complication arises because we move through family roles on the escalator of age. Single people, parents of young children, and widows can be of any age (among adults), but in point of fact certain roles are highly concentrated in certain ages and most of us move through a number of family roles during our lives.

On top of that, the American family has been changing rapidly. Journalists, politicians, clergymen, and your relatives have all been struck by the rapid change in American family life in the last few decades. While the tasks in this book have made us suspicious of such "pop sociology," this time the commentators are right. The American family is changing rapidly. But, as academic sociologists, we can go at it a bit more systematically, ground our conclusions in hard data, and be a little less moralistic—though some of our data sets will have morals begging to be drawn.

Actually, we have learned a lot about family trends already. Chapter Five reviewed the Big Change in families during the last one-hundred years. Chapter Six told us how families do and do not pass on SES characteristics from generation to generation and how mobility/inheritance has changed. Here in Chapter Nine we will concentrate on short-term, recent changes in family structure.

We will study trends in:

- Marital status.
- Fertility and fertility differences.
- Labor force participation of wives and mothers.

MARITAL STATUS

Sociologists have long cherished the notion of life cycle or stages of life, and some sociology classes have actually been forced to endure hammy renderings of Jacques' "All the world's a stage" speech from Shakespeare's *As You Like It*. Recently, there has been a subtle shift: instead of viewing life as a strict sequence of family roles through which we all move, sociologists are coming to view family careers as destinations connected by well-beaten paths, often running both ways. The diagram on the first page of this chapter illustrates: the arrows are not causal effects of variables, but possible shifts one might make. There is just one arrow from *single* (defined in the GSS as "never married") to *married*, but for married-widowed-divorced, the arrows run both ways because remarriage allows one to *go backward* in *normal* sequence. In fact, you may know a few people for whom married-unmarried-remarried seem to be an endless merry-go-round ride.

Cross-sectional (one-time) surveys which ask about current marital status do not catch this process. Thus, the percentages in the title page illustration (from GSS 1984) tell us that in the early 1980s a majority of U.S. adults (58 percent) were currently married, 18 percent were single, 14 percent were divorced (or legally separated) and 11 percent were widowed. These numbers make an important point: being married is only barely the majority situation among contemporary adults. But marital status per se hides a lot of important personal history.

The GSS helps us add some history with an item on divorce: *"If currently married or widowed:* Have you ever been divorced or legally separated?" Since GSS does not ascertain whether respondents ever remarried after widowhood, we can not reconstruct the scheme in our diagram. However, Table 9-1 presents a *Life-Course Typology* that offers an improvement over just plain marital status.

Table 9-1 defines six categories: (A) single, never married; (B) now married, never divorced; (C) now married, previously divorced; (D) now divorced; (E) now widowed, once divorced and hence presumably remarried prior to widowhood; (F) widowed, never divorced. (Because *divorced* still has an element of stigma in some groups and because divorced persons sometimes think of themselves as *single again*, it is probable that some D's are hidden among the A's. Therefore, *single* persons who reported they had one or more children, 1.5 percent of the total sample, were assigned to group D.)

As laid out in Table 9-1, these figures are not terribly informative, although we do see that less than half, 48.5 percent of the GSS 1982–84 respondents fall in the "normal" pattern of married, never divorced. However, we get a better grasp when we present them in graphic form, as in Figure 9-1.

TABLE 9-1

Life-Course Typology

Current Marital Status	Children Ever Born	Ever Divorced?	Category	Label	GSS 1982–84
Single	0		A	Single	16.0%
Married		No	B	Never Split	48.5
Married		Yes	C	Remarried	10.2
Single	1+		D	Still Split	1.5
Separated, Divorced			D	Still Split	12.9
Widowed		Yes	E	Remarried, Widowed	2.0
Widowed		No	F	Widowed	8.8
					99.9%
					(N = 5,963)

SOURCE: GSS 1982–84

Figure 9-1 presents the A through F percentages in a chart that helps one see the dynamics in the numbers. The bottom of the chart defines eight simple calculations that "tell the story." For the U.S. adult population in the early 1980s, 84 percent have been married. Of those ever married:

- 42 percent have experienced a break in a marriage.
- 32 percent have been divorced.
- 30 percent are currently ex-married:
  - 17 percent are currently divorced.
  - 13 percent are currently widowed.

Of those ever divorced, 46 percent have remarried.

MARITAL STATUS

FIGURE 9-1
Life Course

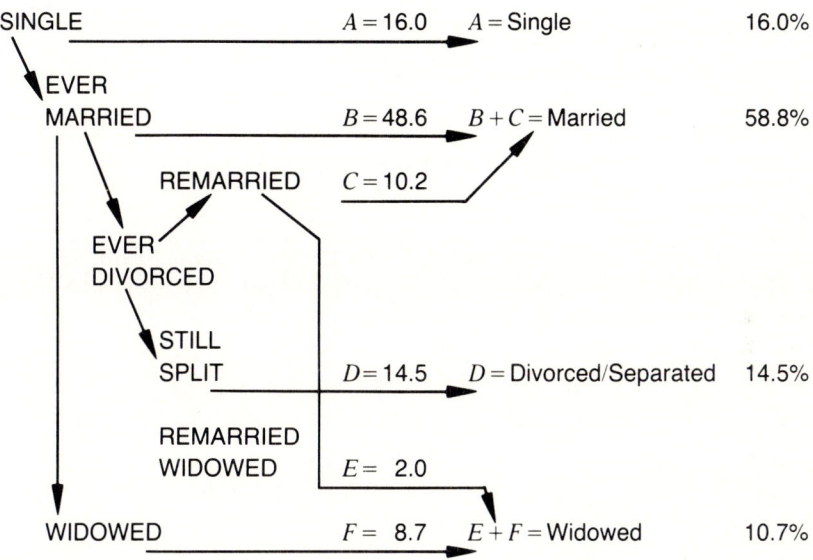

EVER MARRIED $= 1 - A = G$ 84.0%

EVER DIVORCED $= C + D + E = H$ 26.7%

IF EVER MARRIED
   EVER BROKEN $= 1 - (B/G)$ $= 42.1\%$
   EVER DIVORCED $= H/G$ $= 31.8\%$
   NOW WIDOWED $= (E + F)/G$ $= 12.7\%$
   NOW DIVORCED $= D/G$ $= 17.3\%$
   NOW BROKEN $= (D + E + F)/G$ $= 30.0\%$

IF EVER DIVORCED
   REMARRIED $= (C + E)/H$ $= 45.7\%$

These figures begin to convey the two-way flow or *loopy* character of modern marriage. Americans are quite likely to marry (84 percent have been married), quite likely to end their marriages (42 percent have experienced a divorce and/or are widowed), and quite likely to remarry (46 percent of the divorced and an unknown percentage of the widowed have remarried).

We now turn to the following questions: Are these figures changing? What groups show which marriage patterns? Is marital status becoming a social problem?

Task 9-1: Trends in Marital Status

Data set 9.1 contains the variable Decade (1972–74 vs. 1982–84) and the life-course typology so you can compare the marital-status distributions for the early 1980s and early 1970s.

1. Figure 9-2 is a blank version of Figure 9-1. You or your instructor should make several photocopies to use as work sheets. Jot down the 1972–74 results next to those for 1982–84 (you can take them from Figure 9-1) in the flow chart and in the calculations at the bottom of the page.

2. Summarize the trends you see in a sentence or two.

Task 9-2: Social Differences in Marital Status

Marital status gives a good opportunity to test the main propositions of this book—that ethnicity, SES, and time make a difference. Is the *Black family* really different? Are Catholic marriage patterns shaped by church doctrine? Do upper and lower SES groups have different family patterns? We shall see.

1. *Getting Married.* In Task 9-1 we saw a four-point decline in singles from the early 1970s to the early 1980s. This hardly seems like a social revolution, but one must bear in mind that the adult population in 1972 was heavily married to begin

FIGURE 9-2
Life Course

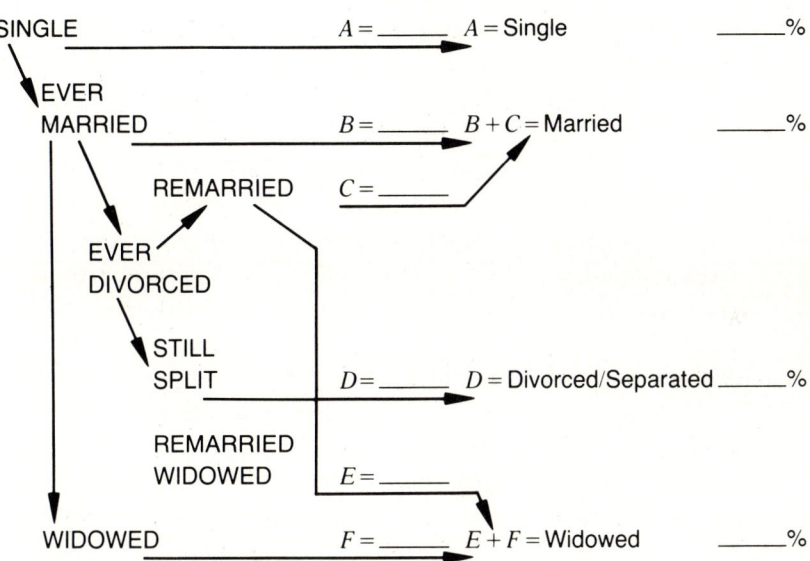

DATA SET _____
GROUP _____

EVER MARRIED = $1 - A = G$ _____%

EVER DIVORCED = $C + D + E = H$ _____%

IF EVER MARRIED
EVER BROKEN	$= 1 - (B/G)$	= _____%
EVER DIVORCED	$= H/G$	= _____%
NOW WIDOWED	$= (E + F)/G$	= _____%
NOW DIVORCED	$= D/G$	= _____%
NOW BROKEN	$= (D + E + F)/G$	= _____%

IF EVER DIVORCED
REMARRIED	$= (C + E)/H$	= _____%

with. When we introduce a third variable, Age, sharper patterns begin to emerge.

  a. Please find the percentage Never Married (category A of Life Course) by Age and Decade in data set 9.2. Graph your results with Age as the horizontal x axis (use 25, 35, 45, and so on for your x values) and the percentage Never Married as the vertical y axis. Draw one curve for 1972–74 and one for 1982–84. What does your graph suggest about trends in marriage?

  Just because someone isn't married, it doesn't mean he or she will never marry, though the shape of your curves is suggestive. Do you think your results mainly reflect a trend toward *postponing* marriage?, or *eschewing* marriage?

  b. Do macro-variables influence *marriage-ability*? Look at the proportions Ever Married (100 – % A) for the eight ethnic groups (data set 9.3), three educational levels (data set 9.4), and both sexes (data set 9.4). You will get clearer results if you limit your data to persons ages 18 to 29.

  Social reactionaries have argued that higher education for women lowers their chances of getting married. You can explore this notion with data set 9.4. Find the percentage Ever Married by Sex and Education within two Age groups, 18–29 and 30+. Display your results as two fishnet graphs, one for each Age. Do the data support or refute the reactionaries? What happens if you rethink the problem as the effect of marriage on schooling for the two sexes?

2. *Widowhood.* Widowhood, of all the marital statuses, is the least influenced by social structure. Getting married and getting divorced, after all, are voluntary decisions, while the law is quite cross with people who decide to become widows or widowers on their own. But, of course, there are social differences due to age and sex. You should become familiar with them as they are almost certain to affect your life sooner or later. This also gives us a good excuse to look at changes in the age distribution.

  a. Plot the percentage Widowed (Combine Life Course categories E and F) by Age with separate curves for men and women. Use data set 9.1 for the younger ages and data set 9.8 for the older ages. List some social consequences of the pattern you see.

b. Depending on rounding and the exact data set you use, you will find a two-to-three point increase in the percentage Currently Widowed between 1972–74 and 1982–84. This is about the smallest of the changes in Task 9-1, but it is statistically reliable. Your curves from (a) and the widely touted *aging of America* suggest an obvious explanation—the increase in the widowed is probably due to the increase in the percentage elderly.

Explore this hypothesis by looking at the trends in age distribution in data sets 9.8 and 9.2, and the change in percentage Widowed (data set 9.8) before and after standardizing on Age.

I expect you will be a bit disappointed in the amount of Aging you found. Are the *geriatric Cassandras* wrong? What aspects of the GSS sample design should be borne in mind here? (*Hint:* the problem is not GSS's limitation to households. According to the *Statistical Abstract,* in 1983 less than half of one percent of persons sixty-five and older were *not* living in households.)

3. *Divorce:*
   a. Task 9-1 showed that the trend toward divorce is not just a fantasy of hysterical social commentators. In point of fact, the probability of dissolution for American marriages these days is quite formidable. Again, you will get a better perspective by taking age into consideration. Plot the percentage Ever Divorced among the Ever Married (percentage $C + D + E$, after Omitting A, in Life Course) by Age in data set 9.2, with a separate curve for each decade. "Who" has the highest percentage in the graph? Do you think the two curves have odd shapes? Why might that be?
   b. Are some groups divorce prone? Black marriages are said to be less stable, but lots of beliefs about Black Americans are not borne out by the data; The Roman Catholic Church forbids divorce; Southerners are supposed to be extremely conservative on family matters; lower SES groups are notoriously unstable, higher SES groups may be so sophisticated they don't take their marriage vows seriously. Look at the Ever Divorced proportions by Ethnicity and Education in data set 9.7. Make a fishnet graph to summarize what you find, perhaps Combining some ethnic

groups. (In looking at SES and marital status I suggest you stick with education since both HSR and income may well be *effects* of marital status and not just causes.)

4. *Remarriage*. Remarriage trends have not received the publicity given divorce trends, but Task 9-1 showed a sharp shift away from remarriage of divorced persons (GSS data, you will remember, do not treat remarriage of the widowed). Remarriage rates are an important social indicator (a high divorce rate and a high remarriage rate have different implications than a high divorce rate and a low remarriage rate) and we shall soon see their import for social policy. Who remarries and who remains sundered? For the Life Course typology, $C + E/C + D + E$, gives the answer. Use data set 9.7 to compare remarriage rates among ethnic groups, sexes, and educational levels. Make fishnet graphs for each pair of variables to find especially high and low rates.

5. Given all of this are there any macro-structural factors that operate consistently to promote marriage? What are the marital characteristics of men, women, Blacks, Catholics, White Protestant groups, and high and low educational levels? Do any of these patterns seem especially *healthy* or *unhealthy* to you?

Task 9-3: Marital Status as a Social Problem

Divines and grandmothers believe the American family is in deep trouble, while defenders of the current scene stress the freedom and self-realization allegedly accompanying new marital status patterns. As sociologists, we are not about to pronounce on morality per se, but in the last decade social scientists have turned up some troubling patterns in the data. These patterns have generated two slogans, *the feminization of poverty* and *the breakdown of the Black family*. We shall dig into each, trying to maximize the contribution of data and minimize the contributions of ideology and rhetoric.

1. Data set 9.5 contains two indices of trouble, low income (Income) and low morale (Happy). The income measure is our familiar *Below Average;* the morale measure is the response

"Not Too Happy" to the standard happiness item (see X.7 in CHIPLIB). For each life-course category, find the percent Below Average, the percent Not Too and the percent giving one *or* the other response. How would you interpret the results to your grandmother?

Now look at the same percentages among men and among women. (Combine the two categories of Widowed to give more reliable results.) Is the impact of life-course Change the same for men and women? (*Suggestion:* display the data in two graphs, one for Happiness and one for Income, with a point for each life-course category. Use women's percents as the horizontal x axis, men's as the vertical y axis. Draw a straight line through points where men's and women's percentages are identical.)

2. "Your grandmother's" hypothesis is that the structural shifts in the American family are all pretty much undesirable. To see if she is right, divide life-course categories into *benign* and *problematic* on the basis of (1) above. Then Cross Tab Decade against combined Life Course (data set 9.6 will do nicely).

   The feminization-of-poverty hypothesis targets things a bit more by claiming that the trend toward problematic family situations is stronger for women than for men; the breakdown-of-the-Black-family hypothesis claims the trend is sharper for Blacks than for Whites. You can test them both simultaneously by looking at the 1972–74 to 1982–84 trend in *problematic family structures* for White men, White women, Black men, and Black women (data set 9.6).

3. All in all, do the data suggest the American family is "in trouble" or that the hue and cry is greatly exaggerated?

FERTILITY

Task 5-2.2 showed the Big Picture for American fertility trends. When you plotted number of siblings against birth cohort you saw a steady and substantial decline in large families from 1900 to 1950 followed by a blip for the famous baby boom (roughly 1950 to 1960). As usual, however, the overall picture conceals a number of social differences.

CHAPTER 9 THE CHANGING AMERICAN FAMILY

Task 9-4: "Traditional" Fertility Differences

1. Again using siblings as a marker of prior fertility patterns, let us see whether SES and ethnicity made much difference. Data set 5.1 allows you to plot Sibs for two SES variables: parental education (Pared) and father's occupation (Dad). Plot curves for the two educational levels and three paternal categories (Farm, HSR 9–37, and HSR 38–82) showing Sib size by Birth Cohort.
   a. What are the differences?
   b. Do the curves seem to converge over time?

2. Data set 9.9 allows you to ask the same two questions for the eight categories of the ethnic typology. You will find that eight curves tell you more than you wish to know; after inspecting the raw data, use Combine to group your ethnic categories.

Task 9-5: "Future" Fertility Differences

Past fertility patterns, as shown in Task 9-4, are pretty clear and surprisingly persistent. What is unclear is what to expect in the future. Demographers are quite shy in giving us forecasts, if only because they have been stung too often in the past (they didn't see the baby boom coming for example). Perhaps the most sophisticated prediction is that fertility will be increasingly volatile. Modern contraceptive technology (*the pill* was authorized for sale in June of 1960) means couples not only have the option of not having children, they have the option of not contracepting and having children. Thus, in any birth cohort, fertility can turn around on a dime at any time until its women reach their forties.

About the best we can do is to compare the attitudes and opinions of potential parents (the youngest cohorts) with those of their predecessors.

1. Use CHIPLIB data set X.2d to find cohort differences in fertility norms and trends within cohorts for the 1970s vs. the 1980s. From this, what is your forecast of future fertility?

2. Will the classic social differences in fertility disappear? One clue is to compare the fertility norms of various SES and

ethnic groups among the youngest adults. Data set 9.10 gives Ideal Number of Children for GSS respondents 18 to 29 years of age in 1982–84, the future parents of the late 1980s and early 1990s. Do the traditional SES, Education, and ethnic (Ethtype) differences persist or have they evaporated by now?

WOMEN'S EMPLOYMENT

We end this chapter (and the book) with perhaps the most publicized of all recent social trends—increased labor force participation among women. Doubtless, you were aware of the trend before you opened this book, but as has been the case before, scrutiny of objective data can add to your understanding.

To begin with, the question is not whether women have ceased being idle. Women have had long, busy days forever and ever, farm wives in particular. The difference is in work for pay, outside the home. And the question is not really one of all women vs. all men. In cohorts born since 1900, three-quarters or more of single women ages twenty-five to fifty-four were in the labor force, working or seeking work (Kreps and Clark, 1975, Figure 3.3, p. 35). Our question has to do with wives and mothers.

Task 9-6: Trends in Maternal Employment

Task 5-2.2 revealed a spectacular increase in the proportion of mothers who worked after marriage. Please review your data from that exercise. But data set 5.1 didn't tell us *when* she worked during her marriage. In particular, we are curious about the employment of mothers of small children. Since families are becoming smaller and first children are being postponed, it is logically possible that the increase is limited to periods before and after there are young children in the home. Data set 9.11 allows you to explore this question. It includes birth cohort and a three-way categorization of mother's employment: Never = mother never worked for pay after marriage; Not16 = mother worked, but not "around the time you were sixteen"; While16 = mother worked around the time the respondent was sixteen. (Ideally, the item should focus on the respondent's earlier ages too, but the GSS item on that is ambiguous—it doesn't sort out work *before* respondent was born from

CHAPTER 9 THE CHANGING AMERICAN FAMILY

work *while* respondent was under six.) Assuming While16 is a reasonable index of *working mother,* while Not16 taps *working wife,* graph these trends against birth cohort.

Task 9-7: Who Goes (Went) to Work?

Data set 9.12 is limited to married women ages eighteen to sixty-four. It shows half of them (51.4 percent) in the labor force during the GSS years. The recent trend variable, Decade (1982–84 vs. 1972–74), allows you to see whether married women's employment actually increased recently or whether the media are belatedly catching up with a trend that has already crested.

1. Cross Tab Decade and Labforce to see the change.

2. Data set 9.12 allows you to look at labor force participation of married women by race, education, and the presence of children in the household (the variable Athome sorts women by the age of the youngest child in the household: <6 = youngest child is under 6; 6–12 = youngest child is 6–12; 13–17 = youngest child is 13–17, Nokids = no one under 18 in the household).
   Are any of these variables related to married women's employment? What combinations of social characteristics produce the highest and lowest labor force participation?

3. Cross Tab Decade and Labforce, with one or more of the other variables as controls. Do your results suggest the trend to wives' employment was "across the board" or concentrated in certain subgroups?

Task 9-8: The Psychic Costs and Benefits

The trend toward wives' and mothers' employment may be the single most visible social change of the 1980s, though we know it to be far from sudden. Nevertheless, not everyone endorses the trend. (See CHIPLIB data set X.5 for opinion data), and as late as 1985, GSS respondents split about fifty-fifty on the item, "A preschool child is likely to suffer if his or her mother works." GSS data are not really useful for treating the issue of impact on children, though analysts who have looked at the variable Mawork haven't spotted any negative consequences. But we can use the GSS to look at impacts on the adults in the family.

1. Are working wives and mothers happier (perhaps because they feel more independent) or less happy (perhaps because they feel torn between home and job demands)? Data set 9.13 enables you to look at five predictors of self-reported happiness (see data set X.7 for details): race, education, children in the household (Athome), income, and labor force participation for married women in the GSS. Which variables seem to predict happiness? How does labor force participation stack up as a predictor? Are there any subgroups where labor force participation makes a bigger or smaller difference?

2. Sociological theory gives us a more subtle hypothesis: since some men may have more of their egos invested in their jobs, their wives' employment boosts their self-esteem when the wives' jobs are lower in status, but threaten them when their wives' jobs are higher in status. Data set 9.14 allows you to explore the proposition. The data are limited to married men and women in couples where the husband works full time. The variables are: Sex, Hisjob (HSR scores for the husband), Herjob (HSR scores for the wife plus NOTFTW for wives who do not have full-time jobs), Income, and Hapmar (marital happiness; see data set X.70).
   a. Do any of the variables in data set 9.14 appear to influence marital happiness?
   b. Use the Merge command to combine Hisjob and Herjob into an index of relative prestige for the couple. Is your index related to marital happiness, overall, among men and/or among women?

3. But do women really *want* to work? The decade between the early 1970s and early 1980s was economically volatile, to say the least. Whether the overall economy had stagnated or merely slowed its long-term growth is debatable, but there are definite storm warnings (see, for example, trends in Income in Task 8-2). Consequently, commentators on the left have argued

that the trend towards wives' employment is not women's *liberation* but a desperate attempt to make ends meet in a pinched economy.

The GSS item Richwork—"If you were to get enough money to live as comfortably as you would like for the rest of your life, would you continue to work (Work) or would you stop working? (Quit)"—is presented in data set 9.15 along with Decade, Sex, Age, EDUC, Marital (Married Vs. All Other), and Athome (<6 vs. All Other, see Task 9-7) for respondents Ages eighteen to sixty-four currently in the labor force. Presumably, persons forced into the labor force by economic pressure alone are more likely to say Quit.

Use data set 9.15 to explore the hypothesis that women, and/or wives, and/or mothers of young children are reluctant workers by comparison with men. Did the tougher economy of the early 1980s produce more reluctant workers overall or only in certain groups?

4. All in all, what have you learned about the consequences of the trends in wives' employment?

SUMMARY

Compared with other components of social structure (ethnic distributions or the occupational mix for example) the American family is changing at a very rapid rate. Marital status, fertility, women's labor force participation—all show sharp changes even over the short span of a decade.

All in all, the Big Change of Chapter Five, the shift from a rural, unsophisticated society to an urban, highly educated one, seems ended. If the farm population has not "hit bottom," it certainly hasn't far to go; if educational attainment is to increase further, we have not seen any signs of it doing so as of the early 1980s.

But this does not mean American society is frozen or fixed. The changes in family structure demonstrated in this final chapter are as sharp and dramatic as the trends making the Big Change. But we lack a neat formula (*modernization* for example) with which to wrap them up. Is the family "coming apart at the seams," or is it becoming "streamlined" to adapt to modern conditions?

SUMMARY

Inevitably, family matters have an evaluative tone not entirely consistent with sober, objective social science. I am not arguing you should be indifferent to values: the issues of marriage, children, and work will confront you sooner than you think; and running a few percentage tables will not tell you what to do. But data analysis in such a highly charged area is not without benefits. Whether you choose to swim with the tide or against it, you should, nevertheless, find some value in knowing where it seems to be flowing.

A

Suggested Readings

I will not attempt a comprehensive reading list of the sort that would summarize all of the research on the topics covered in *Social Differences*. This would require hundreds of titles. Nevertheless, I have found that students get more out of this text when they do some supplementary reading—other authors' words help you see the meaning in the numbers you generate with CHIP. I have tried to find books that are data based but do not require statistical training by the reader or that provide "qualitative" background and hypotheses to enrich your interpretations of the numbers. Where applicable, I have indicated the chapters in *Social Differences* where the reading is more relevant.

Alba, R. D. (1985). *Italian Americans: Into the twilight of ethnicity.* Englewood Cliffs, NJ: Prentice-Hall, Inc.
Combines an anthropological account of traditional Southern Italian culture with a sociological account of contemporary Italo-Americans using GSS data. Gives more detail on one of the most important subgroups among White Northern Catholics.

Blau, P. M. and Duncan, O. D. (1967). *The American occupational structure.* New York: John Wiley & Sons, Inc.
As explained in Chapter Three, a landmark in sociology. It is more statistically advanced than others in this list, but you can follow the argument and get the main conclusions without statistical training. Chewy, but worth the effort.

APPENDIX A   SUGGESTED READINGS

Bureau of the Census. *Statistical abstract of the United States.*
An annual compendium of statistical data on the United States, along with some international comparisons. An extraordinary source of information on SES and family matters, less so for ethnicity since it is government policy to not collect data on religious preferences.

Caplow, T. (1982). *Middletown families: Fifty years of change and continuity.* Minneapolis: University of Minnesota Press.
In 1924 and 1935, Robert and Helen Lynd carried out classic community studies of Muncie, Indiana. From 1976 to 1978, Caplow and a team of sociologists did it all over again. Their readable report will show you how the variables in *Social differences* (save for ethnicity—since Muncie is ethnically homogeneous) operate in real people's lives.

Cherlin, A. J. (1981). *Marriage, divorce, remarriage.* Cambridge: Harvard University Press.
A brief, readable summary of the trends studied in Chapter Nine.

Duncan, G. J. (1984). *Years of poverty, years of plenty: The changing economic fortunes of American workers and families.* Ann Arbor: Institute for Social Research, University of Michigan.
Summarizes the findings of the *Panel study of income dynamics*, a survey that does for family finances what GSS does for attitudes. Detailed and occasionally surprising findings on poverty, single parents, race differences, and so on. Highly germane for Chapters Three, Seven and Nine. Strongly recommended.

Farley, R. (1984). *Blacks and whites: Narrowing the gap?* Cambridge: Harvard University Press.
Summarizes the research literature on trends in race differences in SES. Treats the issues raised in Chapters Three and Seven.

Greeley, A. M. (1977). *The American Catholic: A social portrait.* New York: Basic Books.
A detailed sociological analysis à la Chapters Two and Four, with heavy use of GSS data.

Hamilton, R. F., and Wright, J. D. (1986). *The state of the masses.* New York: Aldine Publishing Company.

APPENDIX A   SUGGESTED READINGS

Reassesses a number of literary-political interpretations of American life in the cold light of data (much taken from the GSS). Sardonic and informative, with special relevance for Chapters Three and Nine. Strongly recommended.

Herberg, W. (1960). *Protestant, Catholic, Jew.* Garden City, New York: Anchor Books; University of Chicago Press, 1983.
Not data-based social science, but a fascinating historical account of the relations between ethnicity and religion in the United States. You do not have to accept Herberg's thesis (*the triple melting pot*) to get a great deal out of the book. Relevant for Chapter Two; discussed in Chapter Six.

Hofstadter, R. (1973). *America at 1750: A social portrait.* New York: Vintage Books.
Not, of course, based on survey data, but, in effect, how *Social differences* might have come out if it had been written shortly before the American Revolution.

Hyman, H., and Wright, C. R. (1979). *Education's lasting influence on values.* Chicago: University of Chicago Press.
Hyman and Wright reanalyze data from thirty-eight national surveys to document the impact of educational attainment on attitudes and opinions. Relevant for Chapters Four and Eight.

Jones, M. A. (1960). *American immigration.* Chicago: University of Chicago Press.
The standard professional historian's account of immigration from 1600 to 1959. More important than the Civil War battles and tariff laws you studied in U.S. History. Chapter Two.

Kreps, J. and Clark, R. (1975). *Sex, age and work: The changing composition of the labor force.* Baltimore: The Johns Hopkins University Press.
A concise review of trend data on women's labor force participation. Chapter Nine.

Lingeman, R. (1980). *Small town America: A narrative history 1620–the present.* New York: G.P. Putnam's Sons.
A journalist's readable, but documented account of *the Big Change*. Chapter Five.

APPENDIX A SUGGESTED READINGS

Lucas, J. (1985). *Common ground: A turbulent decade in the lives of three American families.* New York: Alfred A. Knopf, Inc.
Case studies of three Boston families during the school desegregation conflicts of the 1960s and 1970s. Three hand-picked cases do not provide much proof for the author's (fairly pessimistic) generalizations, but the vivid details illustrate how ethnicity and SES can shape American lives.

McNall, S. G., and McNall, S. A. (1983). *Plains families: Exploring sociology through social history.* New York: St. Martin's Press.
Life histories of ordinary Midwestern families from the Homestead Act to World War II. (Interspersed with not terribly inspiring discussions of sociological theories and concepts.) Relevant for Chapter Five and a good picture of some key Northern White Protestant groups.

Nie, N. H., Verba, S., and Petrocik, J. (1976). *The changing American voter.* Cambridge: Harvard University Press.
How SES, ethnicity, party affiliations, and issues did and did not influence voting from the 1930s to the early 1970s. Chapters Four and Eight.

Reed, J. S. (1975). *The enduring south: Subcultural persistence in mass society.* Chapel Hill: The University of North Carolina Press.
It is difficult to find good sociological analyses of White Southerners as the topic elicits sentimentalism or vitriol. Reed's three books are actually collections of articles, but they are objective, data based, and readable.

Reed, J. S. (1982). *One south: An ethnic approach to regional culture.* Baton Rouge: Louisiana State University Press.

Reed, J. S. (1983). *Southerners: The social psychology of sectionalism.* Chapel Hill: The University of North Carolina Press.

Rose, S. J. (1986). *The American profile poster: Who owns what, who makes how much, who works where, and who lives with whom.* New York: Pantheon Books.

APPENDIX A   SUGGESTED READINGS

An imaginative and unique attempt to display the main properties of SES (Chapter Three) in a single poster. Strongly recommended.

Schuman, H., Steeh, C., and Bobo, L. (1985). *Racial attitudes in America: Trends and interpretations.* Cambridge: Harvard University Press.
What the polls (including the GSS) have told us about shifts in White attitudes on racial matters from the 1940s to the early 1980s.

Singlemann, J. (1978). *From agriculture to services: The transformation of industrial employment.* Beverly Hills, CA: Sage Publications.
The Big Change of Chapter Five with comparative data for seven countries.

Sowell, T. (1981). *Ethnic America: A history.* New York: Basic Books, Inc.
Chapter length chronicles on the Irish, Germans, Jews, Italians, Chinese, Japanese, Blacks, Puerto Ricans, and Mexicans. Chapters Two and Seven.

Stouffer, S. A. (1955). *Communism, conformity, and civil liberties: A cross-section of the nation speaks its mind.* New York: Doubleday and Company; John Wiley & Sons, Inc., Science Editions, 1966.
The oldest, but far from the least valuable, reference in this list. Discussed at length in Chapter Eight.

Thernstrom, S. (1973). *The other Bostonians: Poverty and Progress in the American metropolis, 1880–1970.* Cambridge: Harvard University Press.
Ethnicity, SES and occupational mobility reconstructed from historical data. Some of its data turn up in Chapter Six.

Treiman, D. J. (1977). *Occupational prestige in comparative perspective.* New York: Academic Press.
An encyclopedic review of occupational prestige studies (HSR for example) with emphasis on the remarkable similarity in prestige ratings among diverse nations. An important book.

Wilson, W. J. (1978). *The declining significance of race: Blacks and changing American institutions.* Chicago: University of Chicago Press.

Controversial (in the good sense of stimulating controversy) argument on the changing contributions of SES and ethnicity to Black–White differences.

B

The CHIPLIB Data Set Library

CHIPLIB DATA SETS

The CHIP diskette contains the CHIP statistical program and a collection of data sets about U.S. society keyed to the chapters of *Social Differences* (see Appendix C). In addition, a second diskette, CHIPLIB, contains a library of 280 data sets with information on seventy dependent variables from the NORC General Social Survey.

The library was designed so you can apply the theories and models from *Social Differences* to a broad range of sociological topics—or use it as an *electric almanac* to look up basic sociological facts and relationships.

Each of the seventy dependent variables (Political Party Identification for example) appears in four tables—**a, b, c,** and **d.**

In addition to the dependent variables, each **a** table includes:
- Age: 18–44 vs. 45–89+
- Sex
- Ethtype: an eight-category ethnic typology based on Race, Region at Age 16, and Religion at Age 16 (see Chapter Two for details):

    WNCath = White, Northern, Roman Catholic
    WNProt = White, Northern, non-Fundamentalist Protestant
    WSFund = White, Southern, Fundamentalist Protestant
    WNFund = White, Northern, Fundamentalist Protestant
    WSProt = White, Southern, non-Fundamentalist Protestant

SBlack = Black, Southern, any religion
NBlack = Black, Northern, any religion
Othwite = White, any other region or religion

- SES: a three-category index of socioeconomic status. The index combines respondent's educational attainment, occupational prestige, and family income (see Chapter Three for details).

In addition to the dependent variables, each **b** table includes:
- Age (18–44 vs. 45–89),
- EDYRS (years of school completed: 0–11, 12, 13–20),
- HSR, see Chapter Three for details, (Hodge-Segal-Rossi occupational scores 12–32, 33–46, 47–82),
- Income (relative family income as judged by the respondent—below average, average, above average. GSS mnemonic = FINRELA).

In addition to the dependent variables, each **c** table includes:
- Race,
- Reg16 (region at Age 16; four Census regions plus foreign-born),
- Relig 16 (religion at Age 16, in six groups—Fundamentalist Protestant, Other Protestant, Catholic, Jewish, Other, and None; as explained in Chapter Two).

In addition to the dependent variables, each **d** table includes:
- XYear (Years 1972–74 vs. 1982–84),
- Birthyr (Birth Cohort. The categories are numbered from one to seven: 1 = 1883–1903; 2 = 1904–1913; 3 = 1914–1923; 4 = 1924–1933; 5 = 1934–1943; 6 = 1944–1953; 7 = 1954–1964),
- EDYRS (years of school completed: 0–11, 12, 13–20).

When plotting cohort data on a graph, you may use the mean years of birth within the seven cohorts: 1898, 1909, 1919, 1928, 1939, 1949, and 1957 (see Table 5-1 for details).

All data are from the cumulative GSS 1972 to 1984. Unless otherwise specified (a few sets are limited to married persons, persons in the labor force, and so on) the sample represents the continental United States, English-speaking, non-institutional population, eighteen years of age and older.

The four data sets are related like this: The **a** table lets you find the major correlates of the dependent variable. If it appears that SES is important, the **b** table allows you to analyze its components. If it appears that ethnicity is important, the **c** table allows you to look at the independent contributions of race, region, and religion. The **d** table allows you to look at changes in the variable from the early 1970s to the early 1980s and the relative contributions of schooling, age and cohort.

Sets are numbered from one to seventy and all begin with letter X. Thus, the data set X.31c is the **c** (ethnic details) table for dependent variable thirty-one. The numbers, unlike letters, have no substantive meaning. To help you find data of interest, I have grouped the sets in clusters: Crime, Family (roles), Family (sex and reproduction), Family (structure), Free Speech, Leisure, Macrostructure, Morale, Politics, Race relations, Religiosity, Sociability, and Stratification. Below, you will find a detailed description of each set.

Accessing data sets
1. Insert your CHIP diskette in the a: drive and the CHIPLIB diskette in the b: drive.
2. Get to the Old/New menu and choose **(1) Old.** When the computer asks for the name of the file, type:
b:/lib/filename. Thus, if you wish the data set X.48c, you would type **b:/lib/X48c.** (The "b:" directs CHIP to the b: drive diskette, the "lib" tells it to look for the file in a part of the diskette called "lib" and X.48c is the name of the data set. The slashes serve as punctuation. You can use either a forward (/) or backward (\) slash.

Crime

X.23 = Capital Punishment (Cappun)
"Do you favor or oppose the death penalty for persons convicted of murder?" (Favor; Oppose; "don't know" excluded.)

X.26 = Courts' Severity (Courts)
"In general, do you think the courts in this area deal too harshly or not harshly enough with criminals?" (Other = about right, too harshly; Not = not harshly enough.)

X.30 = Gun Control (Gunlaw)
"Would you favor or oppose a law which would require a person to obtain a police permit before he or she could buy a gun?" (Favor; Oppose)

X.63 = Legalization of Marijuana (Grass)
"Do you think the use of marijuana should be made legal or not?" (Legal; Not.)

Family: Roles

X.5 = Wives Employment (Fework)
"Do you approve or disapprove of a married woman earning money in business or industry if she has a husband capable of supporting her?" (Approve; Disapprove.)

X.21 = Intergenerational Cohabitation (Aged)
"As you know, many older people share a home with their grown children. Do you think this is generally a good idea or a bad idea?" (Good = Good idea, depends; Bad = bad idea.)

X.27 = Women's Place (Fehome)
"Do you agree or disagree with this statement: Women should take care of running their homes and leave running the country up to men." (Agree; Disagree.)

X.28 = Woman for President (Fepres)
"If your party nominated a woman for president, would you vote for her if she were qualified for the job?" (Yes; No.)

X.1 = Permit Abortion (Abnomore)
"Please tell me whether or not you think it should be possible for a pregnant woman to obtain a legal abortion if . . . she is married and does not want any more children?" (Yes = should be possible; No = should not be possible.)

X.2 = Ideal Number of Children (Chldidel)
"What do you think is the ideal number of children for a family to have?" (0–2* = 0,1,2; 3 = 3; 4up = 4 or more.) *94 percent of these respondents said "two."

X.14 = Sex, Premarital (Premarsx)
"If a man and a woman have sex relations before marriage, do you think it is always wrong, almost always wrong, wrong only

sometimes, or not wrong at all? (Wrong = Always wrong; Middle = Almost always wrong, wrong only sometimes; OK = not wrong at all.)

X.20 = Permit Abortion (Abrape)

"Please tell me whether or not you think it should be possible for a pregnant woman to obtain a legal abortion if ... she became pregnant as a result of rape?" (Yes = should be possible; No = should not be possible.)

X.24 = Children Ever Born (Childs)

"How many children have you ever had? Please count all that were born alive at any time (including any you had from a previous marriage)?" (0 = None; 1 = 1; 2 = 2; 3 = 3; 4+ = 4 or more.)

X.31 = Sex, Homosexual (Homosex)

"What about sexual relations between two adults of the same sex—do you think it is always wrong, almost always wrong, wrong only sometimes, or not wrong at all?" (Always = always wrong; Other = all other.)

X.34 = Total Siblings (Sibs)

"How many brothers and sisters did you have? Please count those born alive but no longer living, as well as those alive now. Also include stepbrothers and stepsisters, and children adopted by your parents." (0–2; 3–5; 6+ = 6–31.)

X.40 = Sex, Extramarital (Xmarsex)

"What is your opinion about a married person having sexual relations with someone other than the marriage partner—is it always wrong, almost always wrong, wrong only sometimes, or not wrong at all?" (Always = Always wrong; Other = all other.)

Family: Structure

X.8 = Household Size (Hompop)

(1; 2; 3; 4UP = 4–16.)

X.16 = Marital Status Typology (Rehitch)

(Single = Single never married and zero children; Nevsplit = Currently married, no previous divorces; Split = Currently divorced or separated or Single with one or more children; Remarr = currently married, one or more previous divorces; Widow = Widowed.)

APPENDIX B   THE CHIPLIB DATA SET LIBRARY

X.32 = Mother's Employment (Mawork)
"Did your mother ever work for pay for as long as a year, after she was married?" (Yes; No.)

X.39 = Wives' Employment (Wifwork)
(Housewif = keeping house; Labfor = In Labor Force employed or seeking a job; Other = retired, student.) *Note:* data are limited to currently married females.

X.45 = Life-Cycle Typology (Cycle)
(Lone1 = single, zero children, household size equals one; Group1 = single, zero children, household size greater than one; Couples = married, zero children, household size equals two; Fullnest = married, one or more children, household includes one or more persons seventeen or younger; Mtnest = married, one or more children, household includes zero persons seventeen or younger; Singpar = widowed, separated or divorced, or single with one or more children, household includes one or more persons zero to seventeen and exactly one person eighteen or older; Group2 = widowed, separated, or divorced, household includes two or more persons eighteen or older; Lone2 = widowed, separated, or divorced, household size equals exactly one.) *Note:* In the **a** table, Cycle is collapsed (to meet cell maxima for CHIP) as follows: Lone1 and Group1 are excluded (the data are limited to Ever Married, see X.16 for data on single persons). Group2 and Lone2 are collapsed to Lonegp.

Note: See also X.60 (Dad) in Macro-structure group.

Free Speech

X.51 = Free Speech for Communists (Spkcom)
"Suppose a man who admits he is a Communist wanted to make a speech in your community. Should he be allowed to speak or not?" (Allow; Not.) This data set also includes variable X.25, Commun.

X.52 = Free Speech for Atheists (Spkath)
"If . . . somebody who is against all churches and religion . . . wanted to make a speech in your (city/town/community) against churches and religion, should he be allowed to speak or not?" (Allow; Not.) This data set also includes variable X.35, Strong.

X.53 = Free Speech for Racists (Spkrac)
"Consider a person who believes that Blacks are genetically inferior. If such a person wanted to make a speech in your community claiming that Blacks are inferior, should he be allowed to speak, or not?" (Allow; Not.) This data set also contains variable X.50, Racmar and Race is added to X.53b and X.53d.

X.54 = Free Speech for Militarists (Spkmil, Conarmy)
"Consider a person who advocates doing away with elections and letting the military run the country . . . If such a person wanted to make a speech in your community, should he be allowed to speak or not?" (Allow; Not.) The tables also include the item Conarmy—"As far as the people running . . . (the) military . . . are concerned, would you say you have a great deal of confidence, only some confidence, or hardly any confidence at all in them?" (Great Deal vs. Other.) Data set X.54d does not contain Year as the items were not asked 1972–74.

X.55 = Free Speech for Homosexuals (Spkhomo)
"What about a man who admits he is a homosexual? Suppose this admitted homosexual wanted to make a speech in your community. Should he be allowed to speak, or not?" (Allow; Not.) The data sets also include variable X.31, Homosex.

Leisure

X.18 = Bars and Taverns (Socbar)
"How often do you go to a bar or tavern?" (Other = "almost every day" through "about once a year"; Never.)

X.64 = Newspaper Reading (News)
"How often do you read a newspaper?" (Daily; All Other.)

X.66 = Alcohol Consumption (Booze, GSS
mnemonics = Drink, Drunk)
"Do you ever have occasion to use any alcoholic beverages such as liquor, wine, or beer, or are you a total abstainer?" If not an abstainer, "Do you sometimes drink more than you think you should?" (TTotal = total abstainer; Noprob = uses alcohol, "no" on second question; Problem = uses alcohol, "yes" on second question.)

APPENDIX B   THE CHIPLIB DATA SET LIBRARY

X.66d does not include Year as these items were not asked in 1972–1974.

X.67 = Smoking Pattern (Smoker, GSS mnemonics = Smoke, Quitsmk, Evsmoke)

"Do you smoke?" If yes, "Have you ever tried to give up smoking?" If no, "Have you ever smoked regularly?" (Never = Does not smoke, "no" to "ever?"; Quit1 = does not smoke, "yes" to "ever?"; Quit2 = smokes now, "yes" to "tried to give up?"; Smoker = smokes now, "no" to "tried to give up?") X.67d does not include Year because the items were not asked 1972–74.

X.69 = Television Watching (TVHours)

"On the average day, about how many hours do you personally watch television?" (0–1 = zero or one hours; 2 = two hours; 3 = three hours; 4 Up = 4–24 hours.) Table X.69d does not include Year because the item was not asked 1972–74.

Macro-Structure

X.60 = Father's Occupation (Dad).

(Nodad = not living with male head at Age 16; Farm = father was a farmer or farm worker; HSR 9–37 = father nonfarm; Hodge-Segal-Rossi prestige score 9 to 37; HSR 38–82 = father nonfarm, Hodge-Segal-Rossi score 38 to 82.)

X.61 = Parents' Schooling (Parsed)

(Both = mother and father both 12–20 years; Mom = mother 12–20, father 0–11; Dad = mother 0–11, father 12–20; Neither = father and mother both 0-11.)

X.62 = Nationality Identification (Ethnum).

Respondents were asked "From what countries or part of the world did your ancestors come?" (Just1 = respondent names one country; Picks1 = names more than one origin, but chooses one in answer to "which one of these countries do you feel closer to?"; Cantpick = names more than one country, can not choose a closest one; Nonames = can't name any countries.)

X.65 = Geographic Mobility (Mobile16).

"When you were 16 years old, were you living in this same city/town/county?" (Stayer = same city; Difcity = same state, different city; Difstate = different state.)

Morale

X.7 = Happiness (Happy)

"Taken all together, how would you say things are these days—would you say that you are happy, pretty happy, not too happy?" (Very; Pretty; Not Too.)

X.9 = Excitement. (Life)

"In general, do you find life exciting, pretty routine, or dull?" (Exciting; Other = routine, dull.)

X.19 = Trust (Trust)

"Generally speaking, would you say most people can be trusted or that you can't be too careful in dealing with people?" (Trust = most people can be trusted; Other = can't be too careful, depends.)

X.33 = Health (Health)

"Would you say your own health, in general, is excellent, good, fair, or poor?" (Excellent; Good; Fair; Poor.)

X.46 = Job Satisfaction (Satjob, Worker)

"On the whole, how satisfied are you with the work you do—would you say you are very satisfied, moderately satisfied, a little dissatisfied, or very dissatisfied?" (Very Sat = very satisfied; Other = all other). The data are limited to housewives and full-time workers and the set includes the variable Worker (Fulltime, Housewife).

X.70 = Marital Happiness (Hapmar)

"Taking things all together, how would you describe your marriage? Would you say that your marriage is very happy, pretty happy, or not too happy?" (Very = very happy; Other = pretty happy, not too happy.) Data are limited to currently married respondents.

Politics

X.11 = Political Party Identification (Partyid)

"Generally speaking, do you usually think of yourself as a Republican, Democrat, Independent, or what?" (Dem = Democrat; Indep = Independent; GOP = Republican.) Other party (2 percent of the total) is excluded.

X.12 = Political Ideology (Polviews)

"We hear a lot of talk these days about liberals and conservatives. I'm going to show you a seven-point scale on which the political views that people might have are arranged from extremely liberal—point one—to extremely conservative—point seven. Where would you place yourself on this scale?" (Liberal = 1, 2, 3; Middle = 4 = Moderate, Middle of the road; Conserv = 5, 6, 7.)

X.25 = Communism (Commun)

"Thinking about all the different kinds of governments in the world today, which of these statements comes closest to how you feel about Communism as a form of government?" (Worst = It's the worst kind of all; Other = It's bad but no worse than some others, it's all right for some countries, it's a good form of government.)

X.29 = Government Spending (Govspend)

An index. Respondents were asked to judge whether we are "spending too much money on it, too little money, or the right amount" for eleven areas. Those who answered "too much" for "improving and protecting the environment" *or* "improving and protecting the nation's health" *or* "improving the nation's education system" *or* "welfare" are labeled Other. Those who said "about right" or "too little" for *all* four are labeled Allok.

X.41 = Presidential Preference, 1968 (Choice68)

Preference in presidential election: Nixon; Humphrey; Wallace.

X.42 = Presidential Preference, 1972 (Choice72)

Preference in presidential election: Nixon; McGovern.

X.43 = Presidential Preference, 1976 (Choice76)

Preference in presidential election: Ford, Carter.

X.44 = Presidential Preference, 1980 (Choice80)

Preference in presidential election: Reagan, Carter.

Note: For X.41d, X.42d, X.43d, and X.44d, Year does not appear. See also Misc. 1 and Misc. 2 described in Appendix C.

Race Relations

X.15 = Attitude: Open Housing (Racopen)

"Suppose there is a community-wide vote (on) two possible

laws—(1) homeowners can decide for themselves whom to sell their houses to, even if they prefer not to sell to (Negroes/Blacks); (2) homeowners cannot refuse to sell to someone because of their Race or color. Which law would you vote for? (OKdiscrm = owner decides; Nodiscrm = can't discriminate.) *Note:* Tables X.15b and X.15d contain Race as an additional variable. In X.15d there are no Blacks in 1972–74 since the question was not asked of them then.

X.17 = Attitude: Integrated Schools (Schools)

Index based on answers to "Would you have any objection to sending your children to a school where . . . a few of the children . . . half of the children . . . more than half of the children are (Negroes/Blacks if respondent is White) . . . (White if respondent is Black)?" (Lthalf = objects to "few"; Hafonly = objects to more than half, does not object to few or half; Mostok = does not object to few, half or most.) *Note:* Table X.17b and X.17d contain Race as an additional variable. In X.17d there are no Blacks in 1972–74 since the question was not asked of them then.

X.47 = Neighborhood Integration (Raclive)

"Are there any (Negroes/Blacks if Respondent is White) . . . (Whites if Respondent is Black) living in this neighborhood now?" (Yes; No.) *Note:* Tables X.15b and X.15d contain Race as an additional variable. In X.47d there are no Blacks in 1972–74 since the question was not asked of them then.

X.48 = Church Integration (Racchurh)

"Do (Blacks/Negroes if Respondent is White) . . . (Whites if Respondent is Black) attend the church that you, yourself, attend most often or not?" (Yes; No.) Fifteen percent who attend no church are excluded. *Note:* Tables X.48b and X.48d contain Race as an additional variable. In X.48d Year is not included since the question was not asked in 1972–74.

X.49 = Sociable Integration (Rachome)

"During the last few years, has anyone in your family brought a friend who was (Negro/Black if Respondent is White) . . . (White if Respondent is Black) home for dinner?" (Yes; No). *Note:* Tables X.49b and X.49d contain Race as an additional variable. In X.49d there are no Blacks in 1972–74 since the question was not asked of them then.

X.50 = Racial Intermarriage (Racmar)
"Do you think there should be laws against marriages between (Negroes/Blacks) and Whites?" (Yes; No.) *Note:* Tables X.50b and X.50d contain Race as an additional variable.

Religiosity

X.13 = Belief in Immortality (Postlife)
"Do you believe there is a life after death?" (Yes; No.)

X.22 = Church Attendance (Attend)
"How often do you attend religious services?" (Yearly = never, less than once a year; Tween = several times a year, about once a month, two to three times a month; Weekly + = nearly every week, weekly, several times a week.)

X.35 = Strength of religious preference (Strong)
(Norelig = current religion "None"; Other = "somewhat strong" or "not very strong" in religious preference; Strong = religious preference is "strong.")

Social Interaction

X.10 = Organizational Memberships (Memnum)
Respondents are given a list of groups—"fraternal groups," "sports groups," "political clubs," and so on, and asked whether they are members. This variable gives the total memberships (None; 1–2; 3+ = 3 or more.)

X.36 = Neighboring (Socommun)
"How often do you spend a social evening with someone who lives in your neighborhood?" (High = Almost every day, once or twice a week; Med = several times a month, about once a month; Low = several times a year, about once a year, never.)

X.37 = Socializing With Friends (Socfrend)
"How often do you spend a social evening with friends who live outside the neighborhood?" (High = almost every day, once or twice a week; Med = several times a month, about once a month; Low = several times a year, about once a year, never.)

X.38 = Socializing With Relatives (Socrel)
"How often do you spend a social evening with relatives?" (High =

almost every day, once or twice a week; Med = several times a month, about once a month; Low = several times a year, about once a year, never.)

Stratification

X.3 = Social Class Self-Placement (Class)

"If you were asked to use one of four names for your social class, which would you say you belong in: the lower class, the working class, the middle class, or the upper class?" (Working = lower, working; Middle = middle, upper.) *Note:* In the raw data 5 percent say Lower; 47 percent say Working; 45 percent say Middle; 3 percent say Upper.

X.4 = Should Government Reduce Income Differences? (Eqwlth)

"Here is a card with a scale from one to seven. Think of a score of one as meaning that the government ought to reduce income differences between rich and poor, and a score of seven meaning that the government should not concern itself with reducing income differences. What score between one and seven comes closest to the way you feel?" (Reduce = 1, 2; Middle = 3, 4; Ignore = 5, 6, 7.)

X.6 = Hard Work and Getting Ahead (Getahead)

"Some people say that people get ahead by their own hard work; others say that lucky breaks or help from other people are more important. Which do you think is most important?" (Hrdwrk = hard work most important; Other = hard work and luck equally important, luck most important.)

Note: X.56, X.57, X.58, and X.59 are all responses to the question, "Would you please look at this card and tell me which one thing on this list (of five items) you would most prefer in a job? Which comes next, which is third most important? Which is fourth most important? Answers are grouped to give near fifty-fifty splits.

X.56 = "High Income" (Jobinc)
(1–2 = first, second; 3–5 = third or below.)

X.57 = "No Danger of Being Fired" (Jobsec)
(1–3 = first, second, third; 4–5 = fourth, fifth.)

X.58 = "Chances For Advancement" (Jobpromo)
(1–2 = first, second; 3–5 = third or below.)

APPENDIX B   THE CHIPLIB DATA SET LIBRARY

X.59 = "Work Important and Gives a Feeling of Accomplishment" (Jobmeans)
(Most = first; 2–5 = second or below.)

X.68 = Unemployment in the Last Five Years (Unemp5)
(No = respondent has not been unemployed and seeking work in the last five years; Yes = respondent has been unemployed in the last five years but was not the main earner in the household when unemployed; Yesmain = respondent has been unemployed during the last five years and was main earner when unemployed.) Table X.68d does not include Year because the item was not asked 1972–74.

GSS MNEMONIC, SET NUMBERS, AND CLUSTERS

Abnomore (1) Family: Sex
Abrape (20) Family: Sex
Aged (21) Family: Roles
Attend (22) Religiosity

Booze (66) Leisure

Cappun (23) Crime
Childs (24) Family: Sex
Chldidel (2) Family: Sex
Choice68 (41) Politics
Choice72 (42) Politics
Choice76 (43) Politics
Choice80 (44) Politics
Class (3) Stratification
Commun (25) Politics
Conarmy (54) Free Speech
Courts (26) Crime
Cycle (45) Family: Structure

Dad (60) Macro-Structure

Eqwlth (4) Stratification
Ethnum (62) Macro-Structure

Fehome (27) Family: Roles
Fepres (28) Family: Roles

Fework (5) Family: Roles

Getahead (6) Stratification
Govspend (29) Politics
Grass (63) Crime
Gunlaw (30) Crime

Hapmar (70) Morale
Happy (7) Morale
Health (33) Morale
Homosex (31) Family: Sex
Hompop (8) Family: Structure

Jobinc (56) Stratification
Jobmeans (59) Stratification
Jobpromo (58) Stratification
Jobsec (57) Stratification

Life (9) Morale

Mawork (32) Family: Structure
Memnum (10) Social Interaction
Mobile16 (65) Macro-structure

(continued)

News (64) Leisure

Parsed (61) Macro-structure
Party (11) Politics
Polviews (12) Politics
Postlife (13) Religiosity
Premarsex (14) Family: Sex

Racchurh (48) Race Relations
Rachome (49) Race Relations
Raclive (47) Race Relations
Racmar (50) Race Relations
Racopen (15) Race Relations
Rehitch (16) Family:
   Structure

Satjob (46) Morale
Schools (17) Race Relations
Sibs (34) Family: Sex
Smoker (67) Leisure
Socbar (18) Leisure

Socommun (36) Social
   Interaction
Socfrend (37) Social
   Interaction
Socrel (38) Social Interaction
Spkath (52) Free Speech
Spkcom (51) Free Speech
Spkhomo (55) Free Speech
Spkmil (54) Free Speech
Spkrac (53) Free Speech
Strong (35) Religiosity

Trust (19) Morale
TVHours (69) Leisure

Unemp5 (68) Stratification

Wifwork (39) Family:
   Structure

Xmarsex (40) Family: Sex

C
Other Data Sets

The CHIP diskette contains 88 data sets in addition to the CHIP statistical program. (Appendix B explains the 270 data sets on the other diskette, CHIPLIB). The CHIP sets are keyed to assignments in the text, but they contain a lot of valuable sociological information which is not exhausted by the assignments.

Each set is explained in the main text at the point it is used. You can find the explanations easily since the set names comprise two numbers: first the chapter, and second, the approximate place in the chapter. For example, data set 7.4 is explained in Chapter Seven and you know it is discussed early since only three data sets have smaller numbers after the period.

In this appendix we present a skeletal description of these data sets: the descriptor which is printed by the computer, the names of the variables, and the names of the category labels for each variable. (Professor Karen Frederick of St. Anselm College kindly collated the information.)

The samples in these sets are mostly U.S. adult cross sections from the cumulative NORC General Social Surveys 1972 to 1984. Since not every GSS item appears every year, see the GSS codebook for information on exact timing during the 1972 to 1984 period. Exceptions (data limited to full-time workers for example) are indicated by an asterisk next to the set number and explained in a note.

LABEL, VARIABLES, AND CATEGORIES

2.1 The Tribal Trio

        Race   respondent's (R's) race: White/Black

APPENDIX C   OTHER DATA SETS

  Regin16 region at age 16: Foreign/NEast/Central/
        South/West
  Relig16 R's religious preference at 16: Funprot/
        Othprot/Cath/Jewish/Other/None

2.2 Immigration and Ethnicity

  Famorig family origin: German/Britin/SEEurp/Irelnd/
        UNEurp/Scndia/NWEurp/Noforn
  Grnborn grandparents' place of birth: none/1–3/all 4
  Ethtype ethnic type: WNCath/WSFund/WNFund/
        WSProt/SBlack/NBlack/Othwite

3.1 Educational Attainment by Sex

  Sex   R's sex: male/female
  EDUC education level of R: 0–7/8/9–11/12/13–15/
        16/17–20

3.2 Education and Vocabulary Score

  EDUC education level of R: 0–7/8/9–11/12/13–15/
        16/17–20
  Wordsum vocabulary score: 0–4/5–7/8–10

3.3 Census and HSR by Sex

  Sex   R's sex: male/female
  Census occupation: prof/mgr/sales/cleric/crafts/
        opslab/service/farm
  HSR   occupational prestige score: 12–32/33–38/
        39–46/47–82

3.4* HSR and Job Market

  HSR   occupational prestige score: 12–32/33–38/
        39–46/47–82
  Joblose how likely is R to lose job in next year:
        likely/unlikely
  Jobfind how easily R could find a job: not easy/easy

  *Limited to persons currently employed full time.

3.5* HSR and Job Satisfaction

> HSR   occupational prestige score: 12–32/33–38/ 39–46/47–82
> Satjob   R's satisfaction with job: verysat/mod/dissat

*Limited to persons currently employed full time.

3.6* Authority and HSR Score

> Peons   number of people who work for you: none/ 1level/more
> Bosses   number of bosses you have: Slfemp/Noboss/ 1level/layers
> HSR   occupational prestige score: 12–32/33–38/ 39–46/47–82

*Limited to persons currently employed.

3.7 Education and Occupational Prestige

> EDUC   education level of R: 0–7/8/9–11/12/13–15/ 16/17–20
> HSR   occupational prestige score: 12–32/33–38/ 39–46/47–82

3.8* Income

> Faminc   family income: 0–7k/7–12k/12–20k/20–24k/ 25–35k/35k+
> Finrela   relative family income: below/avg/above

*GSS years 1982–83–84 only.

3.9* The SES Trinity

> EDUC   education level of R: 0–11/12/13–20
> HSR   occupational prestige score: 12–32/33–46/ 47–82
> Finrela   relative family income: below/avg/above

*Limited to persons currently employed full time, living in households with exactly one earner.

APPENDIX C   OTHER DATA SETS

3.10 SES Index and its Components

EDUC	education level of R: 0–11/12/13–20
HSR	occupational prestige score: 12–32/33–46/47–82
Finrela	relative family income: below/avg/above
SES	socioeconomic status: low/medium/high

3.11* Cohort-Sex-Education

Birthyr	R's year of birth: 1883–1903/04–13/14–23/24–33/34–43/44–53/54–64
Sex	R's sex: male/female
EDUC	education level of R: 0–11/12/13–20

*Limited to persons twenty-five and older.

3.12* Sex Difference in Earnings

Cohort	year of birth: 1893–1943/1944–64
Sex	R's sex: male/female
EDUC	education level of R: 0–11/12/13–20
HSR	occupational prestige score: 12–32/33–46/47–82
Earns	income: <12.5k/<22.5k/22.5k+

*Limited to persons currently employed full time.

3.12a* Gender and Earnings, 1982–84

Sex	R's sex: male/female
EDUC	education of R: 0–11/12/13–20
Census	census group of R's occupation: prof/mgr/clerical/sales/crafts/service/opslab/farm
Earns	R's earnings: <12.5k/<22.5k/22.5k up
HSR	occupational prestige score: 12–32/33–46/47–82

*Limited to persons currently employed full time.

3.13 Who Are the Poor?

Age	R's age: under 65/65–89

206

LABEL, VARIABLES, AND CATEGORIES

Race	R's race: White/Black
Sex	R's sex: male/female
EDUC	education level of R: 0–11/12–20
Region	region of United States R resides: North/South
Marital	R's marital status: other/ex-marr
City	R's residence, rural or urban: metcent/other/2500+
Income	total family income of R: below/other

Note: Chapter Four has no data sets of its own.

5.1 The Big Change

Birthyr	R's year of birth: 1 = 1898/2 = 1909/3 = '19/4 = '29/5 = '39/6 = '49/7 = '57
Parsed	how much education did parents have: neither/either
Dad	father's occupation: Nodad/Farmer/HSR 9–37/HSR 38–82
Sibs	number of R's brothers and sisters: 0–3/4+
Mawork	did R's mother work for a year after marriage: yes/no

5.2* Cohort-Education-HSR

Cohort	year of birth: 1898/1909/'19/'28/'39/'48/'56
EDUC	education level of R: 0–11/12/13–15/16–20
HSR	occupational prestige score: 12–32/33–46/47–82

*Limited to persons twenty-five and older.

5.3 Combination B–D

XYear	survey year: 1972–74/1982–84
Birthyr	R's year of birth: 1, 2, 3, 4, 5, 6, 7
EDYRS	R's years of education completed: 0–11/12/13–20
HSR	occupational prestige score: 12–32/33–46/47–82
Finrela	relative family income: below/avg/above

APPENDIX C OTHER DATA SETS

5.4 Jobtrends-HSR-Census

Birthyr	cohort: 1, 2, 3, 4, 5, 6, 7
DadCNSS	father's job: prof/mgr/clerical/sales/crafts/service/opslabor/farm
DadHSR	father's job prestige: 9–32/33–46/47–82

5.5 Census OCC Trends By Sex

Sex	R's sex: male/female
Birthyr	cohort: 1, 2, 3, 4, 5, 6, 7
Census	R's occupation: prof/mgr/clerical/sales/crafts/service/opslabor/farm

5.6 Cohort, Daded, and DadHSR (Nonfarm Dads)

Birthyr	cohort: 1, 2, 3, 4, 5, 6, 7
Daded	father's schooling: 0–11, 12, 13–20
DadHSR	father job prestige: 9–32, 33–46, 47–82

6.1* Rural—Urban Mobility

Age 16	residence: country/town/city/meturb/metro
Age 25+	residence: country/town/city/meturb/metro

*Limited to persons 25 and older.

6.1a* Rural—Urban Mobility II

Age 16	residence: country/town/city/meturb/metro
Age 25+	residence: country/town/city/meturb/metro

*Same data set as 6.1, but non-mobile cells have been given frequencies of zero.

6.2 Ethnic "Mobility"

Then	ethnic type, age 16: WNCath/WNprot/WSFund/WNfund/WSProt/SBlack/NBlack/Othwite
Now	current ethnic type: WNCath/WNprot/WSFund/WNfund/WSProt/SBlack/NBlack/Othwite

6.3 Regional Mobility

Race	respondent's race: White/Black
Cohort	year of birth: 1883–1923/24–43/44–64
Reg16	region at age 16: NEast/Central/South/West/Foreign
Regnow	region at present: NEast/Central/South/West

6.3a* Regional Mobility

Race	R's race: White/Black
Cohort	year of birth: 1883–1923/24–43/44–64
Reg16	region at age 16: NEast/Central/South/West/Foreign
Regnow	region at present: NEast/Central/South/West

*Same data as 6.3, but non-mobile cells have been given frequencies of zero.

6.4 Large Tab

ZCohort	year of birth: 1883–1923/24–43/44–64
Race	R's race: Other/Black
Reg16	region at age 16: North/South
Res16	type of place R was living at age 16: LT250k/meturb/metro
Region	Current region: North/South
XNORCSIZ	population size of place: LT250k/meturb/metro

6.5 Black Migration

ZCohort	year of birth: 1883–1923/24–43/44–64
Race	R's race: White/Black
Reg16	region at age 16: Other/South
EDUC	education level of R: 0–11/12–20
Region	Current region: North/South
HSR	occupational prestige score of R: 12–32/33–82
Income	total family income of R: below/other

APPENDIX C   OTHER DATA SETS

6.5a* Black Migration

    Cohort   year of birth: 1883–1923/24–43/44–64
    Migr   NWhite/NBlack/SNBlack/SSBlack/SWhite
    EDUC   education level of R: 0–11/12–20
    HSR   occupational prestige score of R: 12–32/
                      33–82
    Income   total family income of R: below/other

*This is the same data set as 6.5, but Race, Reg16 and Region have been collapsed into a single variable, Migr.

6.6* Religious "Mobility"

    Cohort   year of birth: 1883–1923/24–43/44–64
    EDUC   education level of R: 0–11/12–20
    Relig16   R's religious preference at age 16: Funprot/
                      Othprot/Cath/Jewish/None
    Relignow   R's religious preference now: Funprot/
                      Othprot/Cath/Jewish/None

*"Other" religions have been excluded from Relig16 and Relignow.

6.6a* Data in Set 6.6 with Stables Set To Zero

    Relig 16   R's religious preference at age 16: Funprot/
                      Othprot/Cath/Jewish/None
    Relignow   R's religious preference now: Funprot/
                      Othprot/Cath/Jewish/None

*Data are from set 6.6, but stable cells have been reset to zero frequencies and Cohort and Education do not appear.

6.7* Cohort, Sex, and Religion

    XCohort   year of birth: 1883–1934/35–64
    Sex   R's sex: male/female
    Self16   R's religion at age 16: Funprot/Othprot/Cath/
                      Jewish/None
    Spouse16   spouse's religion at age 16: Funprot/Othprot/
                      Cath/Jewish/None

LABEL, VARIABLES, AND CATEGORIES

    Relnow   religion at present: Funprot/Othprot/Cath/Jewish/None

*"Other" religions have been excluded from all three preferences.

6.8 Educational Mobility

    Cohort   year of birth: 1883–1923/24–43/44–64
    Sex   R's sex: male/female
    Momsed   education level of R's mother: 0–11/12/13–20
    Dadsed   education level of R's father: 0–11/12/13–20
    EDUC   education level of R: 0–11/12/13–20

6.9* Intergenerational Occupational Mobility

    Cohort   year of birth: 1883–1923/24–43/44–64
    Sex   R's sex: male/female
    Dadsjob   occupation of R's father: prof/mgr/clercl/sales/craft/servic/opslab/farm
    Ownjob   R's occupation: prof/mgr/clercl/sales/craft/servic/opslab/farm

*Limited to persons twenty-five and older.

6.9a* Intergenerational Occupational Mobility III

    Cohort   year of birth: 1883–1923/24–43/44–64
    Sex   R's sex: male/female
    Dadsjob   occupation of R's father: prof/mgr/clercl/sales/craft/servic/opslab/farm
    Ownjob   R's occupation: prof/mgr/clercl/sales/craft/servic/opslab/farm

*Limited to persons twenty-five and older. Data are from set 6.9, with stable cells reset to zero frequencies.

6.9b* Intergenerational Occupational Mobility II

    Cohort   year of birth: 1883–1923/24–43/44–64
    Sex   R's sex: male/female
    Dadsjob   occupation of R's father: hiwhite/lowhite/craft/loblue/farm

APPENDIX C OTHER DATA SETS

    Ownjob   R's occupation: hiwhite/lowhite/craft/loblue/farm

*Limited to persons twenty-five and older. Data are the same as in set 6.9 with Occupation collapsed into five categories.

6.10* Education and Occupational Mobility

    Cohort   year of birth: 1883–1923/24–43/44–64
    Dadsjob   occupation of R's father: hiwhite/lowhite/craft/loblue/farm
    EDUC   education level of R: 0–11/12/13–20
    Ownjob   R's occupation: hiwhite/lowhite/craft/loblue/farm

*Limited to persons twenty-five and older.

6.11 Predictors of Occupational Mobility

    XCohort   year of birth: 1883–1934/35–64
    Sex   R's sex: male/female
    Race   R's race: Other/Black
    Reg16   region at age 16: South/Other
    XParsed   parents' schooling: neither/either
    XPapres   father's HSR score: 9–46/47–89
    Sibs   number of R's brothers and sisters: 0–3/4–31
    EDUC   education level of R: 0–12/13–20
    YPres   R's HSR score: 12–46/47–82

6.12 From Shirt Sleeves to

    Sex   R's sex: male/female
    Grandad   grandfather's occupation: hiwhite/lowhite/hiblue/loblue/farm/d.k
    Father   father's occupation: hiwhite/lowhite/hiblue/loblue/farm/d.k
    Self   R's employment status: hiwhite/lowhite/hiblue/loblue/farm/d.k

6.13 Family Background and Class

    Cohort   year of birth: 1883–1923/24–43/44–64

Parsed	how much education did parents have: neither/either
Dad	father's occupation: nodad/farmer/HSR9–37/HSR38–82
SES	socioeconomic status: low/mid/high
Class	R's subjective social class: working/middle

Note: Sets 6.14a through 6.14i are all father-son occupational mobility tables. Except for 6.14g, none are GSS data. Instead they are taken from well-known articles and monographs.

6.14a* Blau-Duncan 1962

Dadsjob	occupation of R's father: hiwhite/lowhite/crafts/loblue/farm
Sonsjob	occupation of R: hiwhite/lowhite/crafts/loblue/farm

*The classic Blau-Duncan mobility data—a probability sample of U.S. men in 1962. (Peter M. Blau and Otis D. Duncan. (1967). *The American occupational structure.* New York: John Wiley & Sons, Inc., Table J2.1, p. 496.)

6.14b* Rogoff 1940 Data

Age	R's age 24–30/31+
Dadsjob	occupation of R's father: hiwhite/lowhite/crafts/loblue/farm
Sonsjob	occupation of R: hiwhite/lowhite/crafts/loblue/farm

*Male residents of Marion county, Indiana (Indianapolis), applying for marriage licenses in 1940. (Natalie Rogoff. (1953). *Recent trends in occupational mobility.* Glencoe, Ill.: Free Press, pp. 65, 76–79, 120–125.)

6.14c* Iowa Men 1925

Dadsjob	occupation of R's father: whicol/bluecol/farm
EDUC	education level of R: 12+/9–11/0–8
Sonsjob	occupation of R: whicol/bluecol/farm

*Male household heads enumerated in the 1925 Iowa state

census. (Richard J. Jensen and Mark Friedberger. (1976). *Education and social structure: An historical study of Iowa, 1870–1930*, Chicago: Newberry Library, Tables 4.11a, 4.12a, 4.13a.)

6.14d* Rogoff 1910 Data

Age	R's age: 24–30/31+
Dadsjob	occupation of R's father: hiwhite/lowhite/crafts/loblue/farm
Sonsjob	occupation of R: hiwhite/lowhite/crafts/loblue/farm

*Male marriage license applicants in Marion County, Indiana, in 1910. (See 6.14b).

6.14e* Nineteenth Century Boston

Years	survey year: 1840–59/1860–79/1870–89
Dadsjob	occupation of R's father: hiwhite/lowhite/crafts/loblue
Sonsjob	occupation of R: hiwhite/lowhite/crafts/loblue

*Adult males living in Boston, Mass., in 1880, 1910 and 1930, whose fathers could be located in earlier Boston and Census records. (Stephan Thernstrom. (1973). *The other Bostonians: Poverty and progress in the American metropolis, 1880–1970*. Cambridge: Harvard University Press, Table 5.3, p. 89.)

6.14f* Mobility in Poland

Dadsjob	occupation of R's father: white/blue/farm
EDUC	education level of R: 16–20/13–15/12/9–11/0–8
Sonsjob	occupation of R: white/blue/farm

*National probability (0.5 percent) sample of "economically active" Polish men carried out by the Central Statistical Office. Figures are reconstructed from a table in John W. Meyer, Nancy Brandon Tuma, and Krzystof Zagorski.

(1979). Education and occupational mobility: A comparison of Polish and American men. *American Journal of Sociology. 84:* 978–986. Original *N*'s (total = 36,505) are divided by ten to simplify the computer displays.

6.14g* United States–Poland II

    Dadsjob   occupation of R's father: white/blue/farm
    EDUC   education level of R: 16–20/13–15/12/9–11/0–8
    Sonsjob   occupation of R: white/blue/farm

*GSS males, 1972–77.

6.14h* Occupational Mobility, Britain

    Father   occupation of R's father: hiwhite/lowhite/hiblue/loblue/farm
    Son   Occupation of R: hiwhite/lowhite/hiblue/loblue/farm

*Area probability sample of English and Welsh men, known as the "Oxford Mobility Survey." Figures here are taken from Alan C. Kerckhoff, Richard T. Campbell, and Idee Winfield-Laird. (1985). Social mobility in Great Britain and the United States. *American Journal of Sociology 91*: 281–308. (The Table in their article is limited to civilians, twenty-five years of age and older.)

6.14i* OCGII, U.S. Mobility, 1972

    Dadsjob   occupation of R's father: hiwhite/lowhite/hiblue/loblue/farm
    Sonsjob   occupation of R: hiwhite/lowhite/hiblue/loblue/farm

*National area probability sample of U.S. civilian noninstitutionalized males carried out by the U.S. Census. This study, known as OCGII (Occupational Changes in a Generation) is a replication (redo) of the classic Blau-Duncan 1962 study. (The table is taken from the same article as 6.14h.)

APPENDIX C   OTHER DATA SETS

Note: data sets 7.1 through 7.15 are designed to allow you to look at various facets of the relationship between Ethnicity and SES. The table below describes the variables in each.

TABLE C-1
Detailed Data on Ethnicity, SES, and Time

Set	Cohort	Ethtype	Race	Pared	Dad	Reg16	Relig16	EDUC	HSR	Income	SES
7.1			8					3	3	3	
7.2			2			3	3	3	3	3	
7.3			2			5		3	3	3	
7.4			2				6	3	3	3	
7.5						3	5	3	3	3	
7.6		7	8								3
7.7		3	8					3	3		
7.8			8	2	4						3
7.9			8	2	4			3			
7.10		3	8	2				3			
7.11		3	8	2	2			2	2		
7.12		3	3		4						
7.13		3	8		4				2		
7.14			8		4			3	2		
7.15		7	8					3			

SOURCE: All data sets are from the cummulative GSS 1972 to 1984.

Notes: Numbers in the table are the numbers of categories for that variable.
Data sets 7.8, 7.10, 7.12, 7.13, 7.14 exclude persons 18–24 years of age.
For explanations of the variables see
  Cohort (Chapter 5)
  Ethtype, Race, Reg16, Relig16 (Chapter Two)
  EDUC, HSR, Income, SES (Chapter Three)
  Pared (Appendix B, data set X.61)
  Dad (Appendix B, data set X.60)

7.16a Ethnicity and Education, 1973–1983

Decade	survey year: 1982–85/1972–75
Ethtype	ethnic type: WNCath/WNProt/WSFund/WNFund/WSProt/SBlack/NBlack/Othwite
EDUC	R's educational attainment: 0–11/12/13–20

7.16b Ethtype and HSR, 1973–1983

Decade	survey year: 1982–85/1972–75

Ethtype	ethnic type: WNCath/WNProt/WSFund/WNFund/WSProt/SBlack/NBlack/Othwite
HSR	R's occupational prestige: 12–32/33–46/47–82

7.16c Ethtype and Income, 1973–1983

Decade	survey year: 1982–85/1972–75
Ethtype	ethnic type: WNCath/WNProt/WSFund/WNFund/WSProt/SBlack/NBlack/Othwite
Income	relative family income: below/average/above

8.1 Race and SES Trends

Year	survey year: 1972–74/1982–84
Birthyr	respondent's year of birth: 1/2/3/4/5/6/7
Race	respondent's race: White/Black
EDUC	education level of R: 0–11/12–20
HSR	occupational prestige score: 12–32/33–82
Income	total family income of R: below/other

9.1 Life Course Trends by Race and Sex

Decade	survey year: 1972–74/1982–84
Age	R's age: 18–29/30–39/40–59/60+
Race	R's race: White/Black
Sex	R's sex: male/female
Course	R's life course category: (a) nevmar/(b) nevsplt/(c) remarr/(d) split/(e) widevr/(f) widnev

9.2* Family Structure, 1972–74 vs. 1982–84

Decade	survey year: 1972–74/1982–84
Age	R's age: 20–29/30–39/40–49/50–59/60–69/70–79
Course	R's life course category: (a) nevmar/(b) nevsplt/(c) remarr/(d) split/(e) widevr/(f) widnev

*Limited to ages 20–79.

APPENDIX C   OTHER DATA SETS

9.3 Ethnicity and Life Course

Decade	survey year: 1972–74/1982–84
Age	R's age: 18–29/30–39/40–59/60+
Ethtype	R's ethnic type: WNCath/WNProt/WSFund/WNFund/WSProt/SBlack/NBlack/Othwite
Course	R's life course category: (a) nevmar/(b) nevsplt/(c) remarr/(d) split/(e) widevr/(f) widnev

9.4 Education and Life Course

Decade	survey year: 1972–74/1982–84
Age	R's age: 18–29/30–39/40–59/60+
Sex	R's sex: male/female
EDUC	R's schooling: 0–11/12/13–20
Course	R's life course category: (a) nevmar/(b) nevsplt/(c) remarr/(d) split/(e) widevr/(f) widnev

9.5 Life Course, Income, and Happiness

Decade	survey year: 1972–74/1982–84
Race	R's race: White/Black
Sex	R's sex: male/female
Course	R's life course category: (a) nevmar/(b) nevsplt/(c) remarr/(d) split/(e) widevr/(f) widnev
Income	total family income of R: below/other
Happy	R's happiness: other/ not too

9.6 Life Course Predictors and Trends

Decade	survey year: 1972–74/1982–84
Race	R's race: White/Black
Sex	R's sex: male/female
EDUC	R's schooling: 0–11/12/13–20
Course	R's life course category: (a) nevmar/(b) nevsplt/(c) remarr/(d) split/(e) widevr/(f) widnev

9.7* Ethtype, Sex, Education, and Life Course

    Ethtype   ethnic type: WNCath/WNProt/WSFund/
                        WNFund/WSProt/SBlack/NBlack/Othwite
    Sex   R's sex: male/female
    EDUC   R's schooling: 0–11/12/13–20
    Course   R's life course category: (a) nevmar/
                        (b) nevsplt/(c) remarr/(d) split/(e) widevr/
                        (f) widnev

    *Cumulative GSS 1972–1985.

9.8 Marital Trends Among the Elderly

    Decade   survey year: 1972–74/1982–84
    Age   R's age: 18–59/60–69/70–79/80+
    Sex   R's sex: male/female
    Course   R's life course category: (a) nevmar/
                        (b) nevsplt/(c) remarr/(d) split/(e) widevr/
                        (f) widnev

9.9 Ethnicity and Long-term Fertility Trends

    Cohort   R's birth year: 1 = 1898/2 = 1909/3 = '19/4 =
                        '28/5 = '39/6 = '49/7 = '57
    Ethtype   ethnic type: WNCath/WNProt/WSFund/
                        WNFund/WSProt/SBlack/NBlack/Othwite
    Sibs   Number of siblings: 0–3/4+

9.10* Education, Ethnicity, and Fertility Norms (1982–84)

    Ethtype   ethnic type: WNCath/WNProt/WSFund/
                        WNFund/WSProt/SBlack/NBlack/Othwite
    EDUC   R's schooling: 0–11/12/13–20
    Chldidel   R's ideal number of children: 0–2/3+

    *Limited to respondents ages 18–29.

9.11 Cohort and Mother's Employment

    Cohort   year of birth: 1 = 1898/2 = 1909/3 = '19/4 =
                        '28/5 = '39/6 = '49/7 = '57
    Momjob   Mother's employment: never/not16/while16

APPENDIX C OTHER DATA SETS

9.12* Working Wives and Mothers, 1982–84 vs. 1972–74

  Decade survey year: 1972–74/1982–84
  Race   R's race: White/Black
  EDUC R's schooling: 0–11/12/13–20
  Athome youngest child in household: <6yrs/6–12yrs/
       13–17yrs/nokids
  Labforce R in labor force: yes/housewife

 *Limited to married women 18–64 years old.

9.13* The Happiness of Married Women

  Race   R's race: White/Black
  EDUC R's schooling 0–11/12/13–20
  Athome youngest child in household: <6yrs/6–12yrs/
       13–17yrs/nokids
  Labforce R in labor force: yes/housewife
  Income relative family income: below/other
  Happy happiness self-report: very/other

 *Limited to married women.

9.14* Career Wives and Marital Happiness

  Sex   R's sex: male/female
  Hisjob husband's HSR score: 12–32/33–46/47–82
  Herjob wife's HSR score: 12–32/33–46/47–82/notftw
  Income relative family income: below/average/above
  Hapmar marital happiness self-report: very/other

 *Limited to married men and women; husband employed full time.

9.15* Work Motivation

  Decade survey year: 1972–74/1982–84
  Sex   R's sex: male/female
  Age   R's age: 18–34/35–49/50–64
  EDUC R's schooling: 0–11/12/13–20
  Marital R's marital status: married/other

Athome   youngest child in household: other/<6
Richwork   would work if wealthy?: work/quit

*Limited to persons 18–64 current in labor force.

Miscellaneous Data Sets

Politics

Although *Social Differences* has no special treatment of politics, I have included two data sets on party identification and liberal-conservative ideology, in addition to the sets described in Appendix B (X.11, X.12, X.25, X.29, X.41, X.42, X.43, X.44).

misc.1 SES and Political Status

Ethtype   ethnic type: WNCath/WNProt/WSFund/
             WNFund/WSProt/SBlack/NBlack/Othwite
SES   socioeconomic status: low/mid/high
*Polviews   R's political ideology: lib/mid/conserv
*Partyid   R's political party identification:
             Dem/Ind/GOP

misc.2 Party and Ideology

Year   year of survey: 1972/1976/1980
*Party   R's political affiliation: Dem/Ind/Rep
*Ideology   R's political ideology: lib/mid/conserv
Vote   GOP/Dem

*See data sets X.11 and X.12.

Note: HSR.1 and HSR.2 are not tables of statistical data but information on occupational prestige to accompany Task 3-4. See Chapter Three for an explanation.

D

What Whatif Actually Does

Throughout *Social Differences* we use the Whatif routine in CHIP to see the effects of an independent variable before and after adjusting the data to remove influences of other independent variables (for example, looking at sex differences in earnings after adjusting for education and occupation—Task 3-14).

The logic of the technique (known as *direct standardization*) is simple. The reasoning goes like this:

1. Perhaps X's are more likely to be Y's only or partly because they are more likely to be T's; and T's tend to be Y's. (Perhaps men (X) earn more (Y) than women because they are better educated (T); and better-educated workers (T) make more money (Y). (T stands for "test variable," a variable introduced to test an hypothesis about the relationship between X and Y.)

2. Let's adjust the data so X's are no longer more likely to be T's. Then
   a. If X's are still more likely to be Y's, it is not due to T.
   b. If X's are no longer more likely to be Y's, the original difference was due to T.

For a pictorial version of the argument see Figure 3-3 and the following discussion. (For a more detailed explanation, see J.A. Davis, (1984), Extending Rosenberg's technique for standardizing percentage tables, *Social Forces, 62*, 679–708.)

APPENDIX D WHAT WHATIF ACTUALLY DOES

While the verbal argument is straightforward, many users are not satisfied until they understand exactly what the computer does with the numbers. By working step by step through a simple but real example, I think I can show you what happens in the Whatif routine.

A THREE-VARIABLE EXAMPLE

This example comes from 1982–84 NORC surveys of U.S. adults' attitudes to military service, in particular how they feel about a peacetime draft. We found a definite sex difference: men are more favorable to a draft than are women. Why? Perhaps women are more pacifistic. Perhaps they are more protective of their sons. The actual explanation is much simpler. It turns out that men (X) are much more likely to be veterans (T), and veterans are much more favorable to a peacetime draft (Y). So, we suspected that veteran status might explain the sex difference in draft attitudes.

We used CHIP to ask "Whatif men and women no longer differed on veteran status? Would they still differ in attitudes to the draft?" We used Change to eliminate sex differences in veteran status and reexamined draft attitudes. In the standardized data the sex difference had virtually disappeared. Thus, the real reason men and women differ in attitudes to the draft is because they differ in military experience and military experience shapes attitudes to the draft.

Now, let's see how this works with the actual numbers. No math or computer knowledge is necessary, but it is important to understand the properties of cross-tabs and to remember the difference between the dependent variable and the independent variables that might influence it. To follow the reasoning you should carefully scrutinize tables D-1 through D-6 as they are discussed. Do not just glance at the tables; find the actual locations in the tables of the specific numbers mentioned in the text.

Table D-1 is a frequency table for the sex/veteran-status/draft-attitude data.

The cell entries are counts of cases in particular categories. For example, there are 356 male veterans who opposed the draft, 379 male veterans who favored the draft, 785 male nonveterans who opposed the draft, and so on. This is how CHIP stores the data sets.

A THREE-VARIABLE EXAMPLE

If, for example, you exit CHIP and ask your computer to "Type 3.2," data set 3.2 will be displayed. You will see it consists of variable and category labels plus a string of cell frequencies separated by commas.

TABLE D-1
Draft Attitudes

Sex	Military Service	Favor Draft?	
		No	Yes
Male	Veteran	356	379
	Nonvet	785	329
Female	Veteran	18	16
	Nonvet	1,734	677

SOURCE: GSS 1982–84

In Table D-2, Table D-1 has been percentaged across.

TABLE D-2
Draft Attitudes: Percentages

Sex	Military Service	Total N	No	Yes	Total Percentage
Male	Veteran	735	48.4%	51.6%	100.0%
	Nonvet	1,114	70.5	29.5	100.0
Female	Veteran	34	52.9	47.1	100.0
	Nonvet	2,411	71.9	28.1	100.0

SOURCE: GSS 1982–84

Percentages, as we have seen throughout *Social Differences*, are more informative than raw frequencies. (We learn that about half of male veterans favor a draft.) The point here, however, is technical: we can reconstruct the raw data from the row percentages converted to proportions, and the total N's in each row. Observe, for example, the top row of Table D-2. We can obtain the frequencies in the top row of Table D-1 by simple multiplication: $.484 \times 735 = 355.7$; $.516 \times 735 = 379.26$.

This simple principle may be used to alter the data two ways: either keep the row *N*'s and change the percentages, or change the row *N*'s and keep the percentages. Whatif talks to the data exactly this way. With the Change command, instead of altering cell frequencies directly (as in Edit), we reset row percentages and the computer automatically multiplies them by the appropriate row *N*'s to get adjusted cell frequencies. (You now see why the Whatiffed frequencies often have decimal values.)

That's the first point: **in a percentage table one can adjust the underlying cell frequencies by altering the row percentages and multiplying the new proportions by their row *N*'s or by altering row *N*'s while keeping the percentages.**

Now the second point. We begin with a truism: a complete Cross Tab has other tables embedded in it—somewhat like children's picture puzzles where faces and animals are hidden in trees and bushes.

Actually, you knew this all along. In a data set with, say, six variables, when you ask the Cross Tab branch to make a table with just two or three or four or five variables, CHIP begins with the complete Cross Tab of frequencies and combines ("collapses") categories of the variables *Not* in the table to give the smaller cross-tab. Thus, Table D-1 crosses three variables, sex, military service, and draft attitude, but you or CHIP could use it to get a sex–by–military service table, a sex–by–draft attitude table, or a military service–by–draft attitude table.

With this faces–in–the–foliage notion in mind, let us look at Table D-3.

Table D-3 shows the original cell frequencies in Table D-1 plus the "hidden" tables: sex–by–military service, sex–by–draft attitude, and military service–by–draft attitude.

Let's start with the table for the two independent variables, sex and military service. It is in a box below and to the left of the main table. Follow the arrow up from that table to the main table and you will see the same numbers repeated as row totals. That is, we will get exactly the same numbers if we read off the row totals in Table D-3 or if we ask CHIP to Cross Tab sex by military service and display frequencies.

The proposition is quite general: **in any percentage (across) table, the row *N*'s are identical to the cell frequencies in a complete Cross Tab of the independent variables.**

From which, the second point follows logically:

A THREE-VARIABLE EXAMPLE

Since the Cross Tab of the independent variables provides the row *N*'s and new *N*'s will change the cell frequencies (given fixed percentages), **if one changes (Whatifs) relations among the independent variables while keeping the dependent percentages fixed, the cell frequencies will change.**

TABLE D-3
Draft Attitudes — the Hidden Cross Tabs

Sex	Military Service	Total N	No	Yes
Male	Veteran	735	356	379
	Nonvet	1,114	785	329
	Total		1,141	708
Female	Veteran	34	18	16
	Nonvet	2,411	1,734	677
	Total		1,752	693

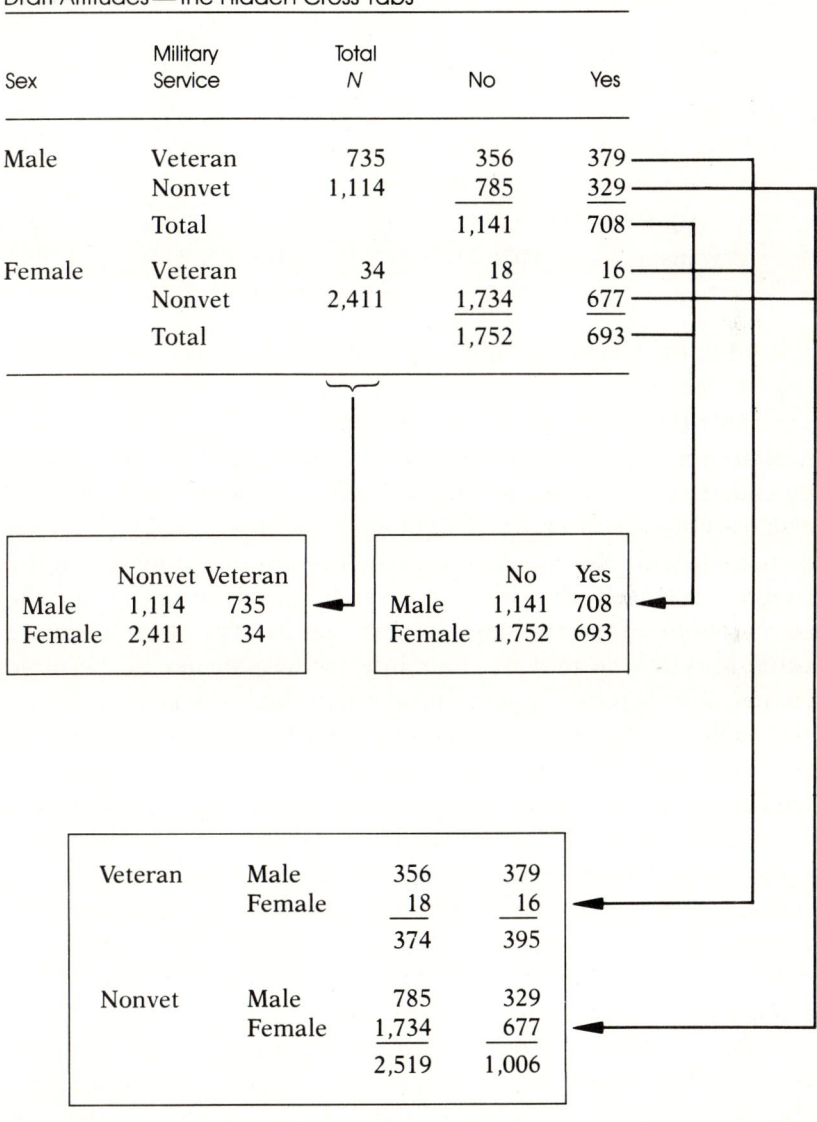

		Nonvet	Veteran
Male		1,114	735
Female		2,411	34

		No	Yes
Male		1,141	708
Female		1,752	693

Veteran	Male	356	379
	Female	18	16
		374	395
Nonvet	Male	785	329
	Female	1,734	677
		2,519	1,006

SOURCE: GSS 1982–84

Tables D-4 and D-5 illustrate.

TABLE D-4
Draft Attitudes: Change

Sex	Nonvet	Veteran	Total	% Veteran
		RAW		
Male	1,114	735	1,849	39.8%
Female	2,411	34	2,445	1.4
Total	3,525	769	4,294	17.9
		STANDARDIZED		
Male	1,518	331	1,849	17.9%
Female	2,007	438	2,445	17.9
Total	3,525	769	4,294	17.9

SOURCE: GSS 1982–84

Table D-4 shows Change in the independent variables, sex and military service. The top table gives the raw data. We see a marginal percentage of 17.9—17.9 percent of U.S. adults are veterans. And we also see a big sex difference. Only 1.4 percent of women are veterans compared with 39.8 percent of men. The bottom table shows the frequencies after the data are standardized, after telling the computer to adjust the data so that 17.9 percent of each sex are veterans. Observe that the four interior frequencies in the table change after standardization but the marginals do not.

Table D-5 shows the consequences for the complete Cross Tab.

Table D-5a shows the raw data; Table D-5b shows the standardized data after removing the sex difference in military service; and Table D-5c shows the difference between the two. The difference table shows the main results: the row totals shifted, each by 404 cases, producing fewer veterans among males and more veterans among females. Consequently, the eight cells all changed frequencies, with male veterans and female nonveterans shrinking while male nonveterans and female veterans increase.

Thus, Table D-5 illustrates the argument so far: changing the relationships among independent variables will alter the frequencies for the cells in the complete Cross-Tab even when the dependent percentages are unchanged.

A THREE-VARIABLE EXAMPLE

TABLE D-5
Draft Attitudes: the Complete Cross Tab

a. RAW DATA

Sex	Military Service	Total N	Favor Draft? No	Favor Draft? Yes	% Yes
Male	Veteran	735	356	379	51.6%
	Nonvet	1,114	785	329	29.5
Female	Veteran	34	18	16	47.1
	Nonvet	2,411	1,734	677	28.1

b. STANDARDIZED

Male	Veteran	331.1	160.4	170.7	51.6%
	Nonvet	1,517.9	1,069.6	448.3	29.5
Female	Veteran	437.9	231.8	206.1	47.1
	Nonvet	2,007.1	1,443.5	563.6	28.1

c. STANDARDIZED − RAW

Male	Veteran	− 403.9	− 195.6	− 208.3
	Nonvet	+ 403.9	+ 284.6	+ 119.3
			+ 89.0	− 89.0
Female	Veteran	+ 403.9	+ 213.8	+ 190.1
		− 403.9	− 290.5	− 113.4
			− 76.7	+ 76.7

Veteran	Male	− 195.6	− 208.3
	Female	+ 213.8	+ 190.1
		+ 18.2	− 18.2
Nonvet	Male	+ 284.6	+ 119.3
	Female	− 290.5	− 113.4
		− 5.9	+ 5.9

SOURCE: GSS 1982–84

Now, the final point—what happens to the other *embedded* tables? **Since adjusting independent variables can change all the cell frequencies involving the dependent variable, it can easily alter independent variable–dependent variable cross-tabs.** Table D-3 showed how the sex-by-draft attitude table and the military service-by-draft attitude tables can be produced by combining row results. Therefore, standardization is quite likely to change these tables since standardization changes the frequencies from which they are built. Table D-5c shows exactly what happens in our example.

For sex and draft attitude, standardization:

- Adds 89 cases to Male + No.
- Subtracts 89 cases from Male + Yes.
- Therefore lessens male favorability to the draft.
- Subtracts 76.7 cases from Female + No.
- Adds 76.7 cases to Female + Yes.
- Therefore increases female favorability to the draft.

Since standardization lessened male enthusiasm for the draft while increasing female enthusiasm, the sex difference in attitude must shift. Table D-6 shows how much.

TABLE D-6
Draft Attitudes: Shift by Sex

Sex	Favor Draft?		Total
	No	Yes	
	RAW		
Male	61.7%	38.3%	100.0%
Female	71.7	28.3	100.0
	$d = +10.3$		
	STANDARDIZED		
Male	66.5%	33.5%	100.0%
Female	68.5	31.5	100.0
	$d = +2.0$		

SOURCE: GSS 1982–84

In the raw data we see a difference of 10.3 points, while the standardized d is 2.0 points. Standardization virtually eliminated the difference (this, of course, is the point of the whole analysis).

A THREE-VARIABLE EXAMPLE

Mechanically, what happened is that standardization lowered the proportion of the heavily pro-draft veterans among men and added to the proportion of the heavily pro-draft veterans among women.

Table D-7 gives similar tables for military experience and draft attitude.

TABLE D-7
Draft Attitudes: Shift by Military Experience

Military Experience	Favor Draft? No	Yes	Total
RAW			
Veteran	48.6%	51.4%	100.0%
Nonveteran	71.5	28.5	100.0
	$d = +22.9$		
STANDARDIZED			
Veteran	51.0%	49.0%	100.0%
Nonveteran	71.3	28.7	100.0
	$d = +20.3$		

SOURCE: GSS 1982–84

Not much change here. The d is 22.9 for the raw figures and 20.3 for the standardized. Why? If you look at Table D-5 you will see that among veterans there isn't much sex difference in draft attitude, and among nonveterans, men and women differ little on attitude. Consequently, while standardization feminized the veterans, it didn't change their attitudes much and ditto among the nonvets. There is a point here: standardization is not a magic wand to wave and make correlations vanish. Whether they vanish or not depends on the numbers. In statistical language it depends heavily on whether the independent variables have strong *partial associations* with the dependent variable. Since military experience has a strong partial association with attitude, lowering the military experience differences between groups lowers attitude differences; since sex does not have a strong partial association with attitude, adjusting for it did not change the military experience–attitude d much. Similarly, the independent variables must be statistically related. If, for example, men and women had the same military experience distributions, standardizing would not change the row N's.

LARGER SYSTEMS

Standardization also applies to systems with four or more variables. Consider, for example, a table with variables A, B, C, D, and E. The Whatif branch "thinks of it" as a collection of percentage tables:

> A marginals
> A by B (A = rows; B = percents)
> A by B by C ($A \times B$ = rows; C = percents)
> A by B by C by D ($A \times B \times C$ = rows; D = percents)
> A by B by C by D by E ($A \times B \times C \times D$ = rows; E = percents)

Now, suppose we adjust the A marginals. What happens?

> The row totals change in $A \times B$ and hence
> the cell counts change in $A \times B$ and hence
> the row totals change in $A \times B \times C$ and hence
> the cell counts change in $A \times B \times C$ and hence
> the row totals change in $A \times B \times C \times D$ and hence
> the cell counts change in $A \times B \times C \times D$ and hence
> the row totals change in $A \times B \times C \times D \times E$ and hence
> the cell counts change in $A \times B \times C \times D \times E$ and hence . . .

Any table collapsed out of the data set may change.

Since these effects flow forward, causal order is important. Specifically:

- If one adjusts a variable in the middle of the sequence, *earlier* tables are not affected at all. For example, in the A–B–C–D–E table, if we were to only change D, the $A \times B \times C$ cross-tab would not change in the least.
- If one were to alter the order (the Reorder command) the effects of a standardization might be quite different.

Note: if you simply can not come up with a plausible order among two or three variables, in a larger table you can use the Merge command to make them into a single item.

SUMMARY

- When independent variables are statistically related, standardization (adjusting the data to eliminate their associations) alters the row N's in the percentage table for a dependent variable.
- When the dependent variable percentages are multiplied by the new row N's, the cell frequencies of the complete cross-tab change.
- Since the bivariate tables for independent and dependent variables are produced by collapsing the adjusted data, standardization may produce altered bivariate relationships with the dependent variable.
- Whether standardization will "make any difference" depends on the signs and size of (1) relations among the independent variables and (2) partial associations between independent and dependent variables.
- We have worked out a three-variable case in full detail, but systems with more variables operate the same way, with a ripple effect: Changing X_i alters row N's for X_j, which produces new cell values, which become new row N's for X_k, which produces new cell values, which become new row N's for X_l, ad infinitum.

INDEX

Achievement Process model, 42–44, 68 127–28, 129
Additive model, 14
Aging, 158–59
Aging effect, 158
American dream, the, 102, 131
Arrivals (births), 144, 146–51

Birth rate, 146–47
Blacks
  divorce and, 171
  marital status, 172, 173
  regional mobility of, 112–15
  religious mobility of, 118
Blau, Peter M., 42, 128
Blau-Duncan model, 42–44, 127–28, 129
Bogart, Ruth, 2

Campbell, Richard T., 128, 129
Causal model, 13–14
Causal order, 61–62, 155
Causal relationships, 13
Cell (non-total) percentages, 31
Census occupations, 47–50, 122
Change, social, 92–100, 102. *See also* Mobility
Change analysis, 154–56
CHIPendale program, 3
CHIP2 program, 3–4
  Cat Order command, 36
  Combine option, 45
  Command menu, 22, 30
  Cross Tab menu, 27
  Cross Tab option, 26, 103, 224
  Edit function, 106
  Enter-Enter-Enter command, 66–67, 104
  function keys, 21
  mobility tables, 105–10
  Modify menu, 36, 45, 106
  Percent menu, 27
  statistical options, 23, 29–30
  See also Whatif procedures
Cohort
  arrivals, 144, 146–55
  birth, 94–96
  defined, 16, 92–93
  ethnic inequality and, 136–41
  mortality, 144, 152–54
  status inflation and, 96
Cohort replacement, 144–61
Computer functions, 20
Conner, Chip, 2
Conservatism, 158
CPS (Current Population Survey), 6
Crossley poll, 5
Cross-sectional surveys, 165
Current Population Survey (CPS), 6

d (percentage difference), 28–31
Dash, 402–03
Departures (deaths), 144 152–54
Descent possibilities, 164
Direct standardization, 223. *See also* Whatif procedures
Divorce, 168, 171–72
Duncan, Otis D., 42, 128
Duncan SEI scale, 50

Education. *See* Schooling
Employment, women's, 175–78
Equality of opportunity, 134
Equality of results, 134
Ethnic differences, 37,134–41
Ethnic labels, 34–35
Ethnic mobility, 111–12
Ethnic typology (Ethtype), 35, 79–80
Ethnicity
  cohorts and, 156–57
  defined, 11–12
  divorce and, 171–72
  fertility norms and, 78–86
  gender and, 16
  immigration and, 36–37
  SES and, 13–15 77, 78–86, 135–41
Expected values, 104

Family, 164, 178–79. *See also* Fertility; Marital status; Women
Featherman, David L., 48
Fertility
  norms, 39, 78–86
  trends, 173–75
Fishnet graphs, 81–84

INDEX

Frequency tables, 27, 123
Friedberger, Mark, 128

Gallup poll, 4, 157
Gender (sex)
  ethnicity and, 16
  family and, 164
  occupational mobility and, 126
  SES and, 68–70
General Social Survey (GSS)
  methods, 7–9
  occupation questions, 47
  schooling distribution in, 44–45
  vocabulary test, 46
Graphics, 31–33
GSS. *See* General Social Survey

Hauser, Robert M., 48
Herberg, Will, 115
Heterogamy, 117
Hispanics, 35
Hodge, Robert W., 51
Hodge-Siegel-Rossi scale (HSR), 51–59, 61–65, 122
Homogamy, 113, 121
Hout, Michael, 105
HSR. *See* Hodge-Siegel-Rossi scale

Immigration, 35–37
Income
  disposable personal, 99–100
  gender and, 69–70
  occupation prestige and, 65
  perceived, 58–59
  in SES triad, 61–65
  trends, 98–100
Industrial revolution, 92
Inequality, 134, 136–37, 156
Inheritance
  educational, 120–25
  occupational, 124
  status, 118–19
Interactions, 84
Intermarriage, religious, 117

Jensen, Richard J., 128
Jews, 34, 35

Kahl, Joseph A., 42
Kemeny, John G., 2
Kerckhoff, Alan C., 128, 129

Macro-model, 13–14, 43–44
Macro-sociology, 2
Marcus, George E., 160
Marginals, 23, 61
Marital status, 165–73

Meyer, John W., 129
Migration. *See* Mobility, regional
Mobility
  downward, 104
  educational, 118–19
  ethnic, 111–12
  intergenerational, 102, 119
  intergenerational occupational, 122–23
  intragenerational, 102
  less-than-chance, 104
  occupational, 122–25
  racial, 111–12
  regional, 104–10, 112
  religious, 115–16
  social, 122
  upward, 104
Mobility patterns, 119, 122–23
Mobility system, 130–31
Mobility tables, 103–10
Modernization, 92
Modified-probability samples, 7
Mortality, 95–96, 152–54
Multi-stage area probability samples, 6

National Opinion Research Center (NORC), 6, 157
National Science Foundation, 9
Net shifts, 109–10, 155
Newcomers (births), 144, 146–51
Newspaper reading, daily, 150–51, 154, 155
NORC annual GSS codebook, 9
NORC General Social Survey. *See* General Social Survey
Normal-curve theory, 29

OCGII (Occupational Changes in a Generation), 127–28, 129
Occupation
  Census classification, 47–50
  GSS questions on, 46–47
  HSR scores, 51–58
  intergenerational, 122–27
  mobility, 122–27
  prestige, 56–57, 65
  in SES triad, 61–65
One-time surveys, 165

Percentage difference (d), 28–31
Percentage tables, 31
Percentages, 27–28
Piereson, James, 160
Poverty, 72, 172–73
Prestige, job, 56–57
Prestige score. *See* Hodge-Siegel-Rossi scale

INDEX

Quantitative sociology
  defined, 4–5
  history, 5–9
Quota sampling designs, 5–6

Race, 20. *See also* Ethnicity
Region, 24–25, 33–35
Religion, 24–25, 33–35
Religious mobility, 115–16
Remarriage, 168, 172
Rickety ladder graphs, 64
Rogoff, Natalie, 128
Roper poll, 5
Rossi, Peter H., 51

Samples, survey, 6, 7
Schooling
  completed, 44–45
  job prestige and, 57
  parental influence on, 120–21
  in SES triad, 61–65
  tolerance and, 158–59
  vocabulary and, 46
Secularization, 116
SES. *See* Socioeconomic status
SES index, 59–60
Siegal, Paul M., 51
Sigma d, 29–30
Social class, 12–13
Social mobility, 13
Socioeconomic status (SES)
  behavior and, 14
  divorce and, 171–72
  ethnic differences and, 135–41
  ethnicity and, 13–15, 77, 78–86
  fertility norms and, 78–86
  intergenerational, 102–32
  poverty and, 72–74
  triad, 61
  variables, 13, 42–43
SRC (Survey Research Center), 6
Stability-diagonal principle, 119–124
Standardization, 64–65, 70–72, 115, 232. *See also* Whatif procedures

Statistical Abstract, 171
Statistical inference, 3
Status inflation, 97
Stouffer, Samuel A., 6, 16, 157–61
Stouffer hypothesis, 156–61
Stratification, 12–15
Sullivan, John L., 160
Survey organizations, commercial, 6–7
Survey Research Center (SRC), 6

Telephone pole graph (tele-graph), 31–33
Thernstrom, Stephan, 128
Tolerance, 158–61
Treiman, Donald J., 51
Tribal principle, 11–12
Tribalism, 11–12, 20. *See also* Ethnicity
Triple melting pot, 115–16
Tuma, Nancy Brandon, 129

University of Chicago Department of Sociology, 5
Urbanization, 92
U.S. Census, 5

Variables, 7, 10–11
  change, 15–16
  cross-tab, 26
  dependent, 66
  ethnic, 26–37
  independent, 65
  SES, 13, 61–74
  single, 23, 61
  vertical, 42–67, 119
Vertical mobility, 118–19

Whatif procedures, 65–67, 223–33
Widowhood, 168, 170–71
Winfield-Laird, Idee, 128, 129
Women, 224–31
  working, 67, 175–78

Zagorski, Krzystof, 129